Democratic
Dictatorship

Contributions in American Studies
Series Editor: Robert H. Walker

Olmsted South: Old South Critic/New South Planner
Dana F. White and Victor A. Kramer, editors

In the Trough of the Sea: Selected American Sea-Deliverance
Narratives, 1610-1766
Donald P. Wharton, editor

Aaron Burr and the American Literary Imagination
Charles J. Nolan, Jr.

The Popular Mood of Pre-Civil War America
Lewis O. Saum

The Essays of Mark Van Doren
William Claire, editor

Touching Base: Professional Baseball and American Culture in the
Progressive Era
Steven A. Riess

Late Harvest: Essays and Addresses in American
Literature and Culture
Robert E. Spiller

Steppin' Out: New York Nightlife and the Transformation
of American Culture, 1890-1930
Lewis A. Erenberg

For Better or Worse: The American Influence in the World
Allen F. Davis, editor

The Silver Bullet: The Martini in American Civilization
Lowell Edmunds

Boosters and Businessmen: Popular Economic Thought and
Urban Growth in the Antebellum Middle West
Carl Abbott

Democratic Dictatorship

THE EMERGENT CONSTITUTION OF CONTROL

Arthur Selwyn Miller

CONTRIBUTIONS IN AMERICAN STUDIES, NUMBER 54

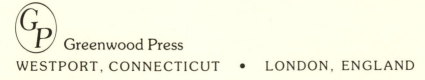

Greenwood Press

WESTPORT, CONNECTICUT • LONDON, ENGLAND

Library of Congress Cataloging in Publication Data

Miller, Arthur Selwyn, 1917-
    Democratic dictatorship.

    (Contributions in American studies ; no. 54 ISSN
0084-9227)
    Bibliography: p.
    Includes index.
    1. United States—Constitutional law. 2. Reason
of state. 3. Constitutional law. I. Title.
KF4550.M46   342.73   80-25424
ISBN 0-313-22836-1 (lib. bdg.)

Library of Congress Catalog Card Number: 80-25424
ISBN: 0-313-22836-1
ISSN: 0084-9227

First published in 1981

Greenwood Press
A division of Congressional Information Service, Inc.
88 Post Road West, Westport, Connecticut 06881

Printed in the United States of America

10 9 8 7 6 5 4 3 2 1

. . . for Dagmar

Contents

Preface

This volume is exploratory in nature: It suggests the emergence of a new American constitution that both exists with the former fundamental law and is superseding it. The words written in 1787, plus the amendments, are being updated by official decisions—presidential, congressional, judicial (and some of those in the private sector)—to adapt the ancient document to deal with present-day and future exigencies. The development has been labeled the *Constitution of Control*. The ancient constitutional words remain the same but their content is changing.

Because the emergence of the new Constitution, now in its early stage, must be seen in full politico-legal context to grasp all its implications, the outline of that fundamental law is preceded by discussion of some necessary background matters. The work is one of description rather than prescription. Problems in constitutional theory and practice are set forth, but no solutions are proffered. My purpose is far from spreading more gloom and doom—perhaps because, as with Cassandra, prophecies of disaster simply will not be believed. Rather, I want to pose some of the questions that must be asked and answered if the obvious "time of troubles" in which humankind finds itself is to be surmounted. Adequate answers will never be forthcoming unless the correct questions are asked. This long essay in the political economy of modern constitutionalism is an effort to do just that.

I make no pretense that this is anything more than a preliminary statement to an immensely complicated subject matter. No one volume can do more than probe a portion of the constitutional crisis that Americans (and others) now face. In a future work, which will be something like a sequel to this one, I hope to extend the discussion by setting forth ways and means of "getting there from here"—the "here" being today's climacteric of humankind and the "there" being the type of just society that is the ideal of American constitutionalism. I write as a constitutional lawyer; but since constitutional law is mainly juristic theories of politics and economics, this is no venture into "pure" legal analysis.

Each chapter has numerous notes, collected at the end of the volume. In the main, no additional text material is added in the notes. Citations are to appropriate references. If something is worth saying, then it should be said in the main text. I realize that runs against the usual type of writing about legal matters, but a decent respect for the tolerance of readers should lead all those who write nonfiction books to make their exposition readable. One way of making a book unreadable is to extend the argument in the notes.

If those who read this book consider some of the assertions to be controversial or even erroneous, that risk must be taken. My only hope is this work is taken seriously and that those who disagree do so on a reasoned plane.

To my knowledge, no one has yet undertaken to develop the constitutional law of the "crisis of crises"—the human climacteric. This book, therefore, is a pioneering effort. Those who have contributed most to my thinking about the Constitution of Control are listed in the notes and bibliography. Of those, two writers who lived almost five centuries apart—Niccolo Machiavelli and Hannah Arendt—have been most influential in the way that I perceive the political economy of American constitutionalism. I do not suggest that either one would, were they still alive, agree with my conclusions; but do say that anyone who wants to think seriously about the nature of American constitutionalism must come to terms with the challenges stated by Machiavelli and Arendt's insightful analyses.

Parts of the book have appeared, in slightly different form, in the *Ohio State Law Journal*, the *Minnesota Law Review*, and *Presidential Affairs Quarterly*. I wish to thank my friend and quondam colleague, Professor Robert H. Walker, for hard-headed and perceptive criticism, delivered, as always, with grace and humor. The book was completed in July 1980 and does not take into account anything that occurred since then.

Arthur S. Miller
July 1980

Prologue

Americans believe that they live under a written Constitution. That they do, but only in part—more in a metaphorical sense than as a description of reality. Another dimension exists: an unwritten Constitution far more important than the Document of 1787 and its amendments. This is the Constitution "in operation," which as Woodrow Wilson pointed out in 1885, "is manifestly a very different thing from the Constitution of the books."[1] Americans also believe that their government is one of limited powers, circumscribed by a written Constitution. But that, too, is only partially accurate. With new demands being laid upon government which well up from long-suppressed segments of society, both national and international, and come at precisely the time that those demands cannot be satisfied, its powers are increasing. Some type of authoritarianism, perhaps of totalitarianism, seems to be inevitable. Can it be staved off? By no means is that certain.

That is the thesis of this book. I do not expect it to be blindly accepted; for many, these are the best of times. Slowly and haltingly, with fits and often false starts, the ability of people to order their affairs with a degree of equity is apparently on the upswing. That appearance hides a gloomy reality; it is a false promise. It is not the dawn of a new age but, in all probability, the last burst of a declining era. The social ice age cometh: Liberal "democracy," as it was known, is dying. It may already be dead, with only a final shove needed to topple it. That, however, will not be known until the social conditions of America (and elsewhere) continue to eat away, as they inexorably will, at the underpinnings of the "democratic" order. The politics of scarcity have arrived; an economy of abundance is fast being transformed into one of shortages.

The Age of Frugality is upon us. Institutions useful in the Age of Abundance require reexamination and improvement.

Those statements tend to be truistic. They serve as background for this book—an essay mainly about crisis (emergency) government, but with a projection into the future. It was written to help counter increasing repressiveness in government, here and elsewhere, and to help stave off the creation of an authoritarian government in fact. But not in theory. Hence the title *Democratic Dictatorship*.

If that title seems to state a contradiction, it will later be seen as much less so. In essence, this volume inquires into the difference between the American Constitution as it appears in *formal* law and what it is in *operation*—the so-called "living Constitution." The organizing principle is "constitutional Machiavellianism," or, to put it more precisely, "constitutional reason of State," (often called raison d'état). It will become clear that raison d'état has always been an operative principle of American constitutionalism, even though it is not mentioned in the fundamental law and Supreme Court Justices and other governmental officials never talk about it as such. Only the disgraced Richard Nixon, in one of his postpresidential statements, has had the nerve to blurt out the nasty little secret of American constitutional law—that government has always been relative to circumstances.[2] No matter how many times the idealistic cliche of a "government of laws and not of men" is repeated, it still remains true that government will take such actions as are considered necessary to meet whatever crises may be thought at any time to be facing the nation. Sometimes the President acts alone; at other times, it is in concert with Congress and the courts.

What, then, is "reason of State"? Says Professor Carl Friedrich, it is "nothing but the doctrine that whatever is required to insure the survival of the state must be done by the individuals responsible for it, no matter how repugnant such an act may be to them in their private capacity as decent and moral men."[3] As such, it is the State's "first law of motion." But it is more. Friedrich speaks of "survival" of the State. We will see that principles similar to it have been invoked, often without regard to the actual problem of survival. Survival is the easiest question, raising relatively few problems. Only some insignificant anarchists dispute its necessity. Of far more complexity—and hence far more controversial—is the use of the doctrine in lesser and not so obvious situations.

An investigation such as this must of necessity concentrate on the "living" American Constitution—the one in actual operation that describes those who make the important societal decisions, as compared with how these decisions are supposedly made. This, in turn, involves analysis of the nature of the State that is the political entity called the United States of America. Suggested here, and developed later, is the view that the State is far more complex than it seems; it encompasses the dimensions of both public and private governments. Raison d'état at times includes raison de groupe. In an organized, highly bureaucratized society—which the United States is—there is no alternative to looking at the entire spectrum of important societal decisions; who makes them, how, in whose benefit, and with what effects.[5] They are made by officers in both American governments, public and private (the business corporation is by far the most important of the latter).

Why should one write about crises or emergencies in this of all nations? The answer is simple: emergencies, actual or asserted, small or large, have occurred far more often than most people realize. More importantly, they will probably take place with increasing frequency and intensity in the future. Americans—people generally—are, if not on the decline in the entire array of public policy matters, at least reaching a "steady state"—in economics and energy, population and nuclear proliferation, pollution and poverty, to name only a few categories. Emergencies have not been, and are not, aberrational. They are fast becoming the norm of human relations. We may not want to believe that, and indeed many will not, but it is a fact nonetheless.

What, finally, is an emergency? Webster's Dictionary tells us that it is an "unforeseen combination of circumstances or the resulting state that calls for immediate action."[6] This is not very satisfactory, save in part. The problem is semantical: the word is an abstraction, for which there is no ready and commonly accepted definition. Emergencies, two scholars have said, are "conditions of varying nature, intensity and duration, which are perceived to threaten life or well-being beyond tolerable limits."[7] Again, not very satisfactory. A better definition is needed. When tied to the concepts of raison d'état and raison de groupe, emergencies require a broader definition. *Emergencies, as the word is used in this book, are not only the conditions suggested above —those of an urgent nature—but also perceptions by political (and group) officers of actions necessary for the well-being of the entity (that means the well-being of the State, broadly defined.)* More than survival alone is at stake, although that, of course, is the irreducible minimum; also involved is improvement in, or enhancement of, the status of the entity (the State, the group). For example, the Vietnam conflict can be justified in constitutional theory by a notion of raison d'état; but no one could have believed in the 1960s, and surely no one believes today, that national survival was really at stake. Bribery of foreign officials by Lockheed Aircraft Company[8] is an example of raison de groupe. Surely the company's survival would not have been jeopardized by acting lawfully.

I do not particularly like to proceed on a verbal via dolorosa. Far from it; my preferences are to the contrary. But intellectually I can come to no other conclusion than that humankind is in the midst of an immense climacteric. We are not merely in a crisis, but something far deeper and much more significant. If that be pessimism so be it, for I believe that today to be an optimist one must be a pessimist. The danger to be avoided is of lapsing into cynicism.

One can believe, as I do, that the dark side of Homo sapiens is the most prevalent characteristic of the species, and still hope (and even believe) that at some time, and in some way, conditions can and will be bettered. It is far better to start from that position in analyzing "constitutional Machiavellianism," for then one will not be surprised when bad things are done by government officers (always, it seems, for an alleged greater good) and can be gratified when good things are done, as at times they are. Americans have always been an optimistic people. That mindset has not disappeared; but the American Dream has ended and this nation now faces, and will continue to face, all of the problems that others less favored have.

This is an essay in juristic theories of political economy. Constitutionalism involves the very stuff of politics and economics. Since it is an essay, rather than a heavily footnoted treatise, many of the statements are not documented. One can write a treatise about the emergency powers of government, and produce something of interest only to those who mole away in the nation's libraries, or one can write an essay of ideas—and hope that it will reach a larger audience. The latter is my goal, for I believe that the question of emergency powers cannot be suppresed and that it is high time we faced up to that fact.

The United States may be on a collision course with disaster.

Once called "the last, best hope of man," it is caught between two worlds—the past, an age of abundance when all seemed possible and much indeed was; and a future that looms, dark and foreboding, dead ahead. "There can be little doubt that humanity is on the verge of a profound social transformation, at the edge of a new social frontier."[9] Whether that frontier will be to the liking of Americans, many of whom still believe in the American Dream, is far from certain. In fact, it is not certain at all: Survival has become the problem, survival of the nation and of that system of rights and privileges that is called our constitutional order.

That is the underlying, basic premise of ths book. What will be the response of government to that new condition? That fundamental question and its answer make up the substance of the volume. My main theme may be simply stated: governmental powers are increasing to the extent that repression will become routine. We are, indeed, already well down the road toward a regimented society, one governed by a newly emergent Constitution of Control. The old Constitution of 1787 remains; but another layer is being added to the ancient parchment.

In all probability, neither the assumption or the theme will be accepted without question. Mr. Micawber, the character in Dickens, is far from dead; to many, even if a major problem exists, something is sure to show up to solve it. That is pathetic, but essentially an accurate description of how millions of

Americans think. There is, or was, a false promise that seems to be the dawn of a new age, but which actually is the last burst of a declining era. A social Ice Age seems to be coming.

A fifth horseman is joining the fabled Four Horsemen of the Apocalypse: Dictatorship is the consequence of Pestilence, War, Famine, and Death. When it comes, as it will, it will be in the name of democracy. Does the title of this book state a contradiction? Not necessarily. The basic thought is that government in the United States, despite a mountain of theory to the contrary, has always been relative to circumstances; it has always been as strong as conditions required. Those social conditions now are a series of crises that are rapidly coalescing into a super-crisis—a climacteric—a sea change in the environment in which human institutions, including government, operate. The meaning is clear: Americans are entering a period of permanent emergency or crisis government. What does—what will—this mean for time-honored constitutional mechanisms? That is the question this book examines and seeks to answer.

The first leg of the argument is that of "constitutional relativism"; but it will be taken one step further to show that "constitutional Machiavellianism" has always been followed in the United States. To speak of the "murderous Machiavel" will not rest easy with millions who consider this country to be special and different. Few, however, have ever taken the trouble to read the writings of Niccolò Machiavelli; or if they do, they have stopped with the Old Nick of *The Prince*. No one can know Machiavelli who has only read *The Prince*. That slim volume was written in a futile effort to cadge a job out of Lorenzo de' Medici, the "prince" of the city-state of Florence, where Machiavelli lived.

Indispensable to understanding the Florentine's message are *The Discourses*, in which he is shown to be a republican-statesman. "Those republics," he said, "which in time of danger cannot resort to dictatorship will generally be ruined when grave occasions occur."[10] "Grave occasions" now confront the United States—and, indeed, people throughout the world. In such a situation, he who neglects Machiavelli misses a principal thread in Western political thought. No one can write meaningfully about politics and constitutions without fully considering the Florentine, whose central message was reason of State. Machiavelli's theory, which forced people to consider the dark side of man, means that survival of the political order must be insured by fair means or foul. Anything can, and indeed must, be done to bring that about by those who hold positions of power, without regard to whether such acts are offensive to them in their private capacity.

In the rapidly emerging new world, government officers will be forced to draw upon reason of State more and more frequently. It will come to center stage, and stay there, when the terrible vulnerabilities confronting humankind become ever more evident. They include, but are not limited to, thermonuclear war, energy shortages, population pressure on diminishing resources, famine, social disorder, economic disruptions (such as inflation and unemployment), terrorism, and dependence on nonfuel minerals. "Industrial man now lives in a complex and largely synthetic ecological system, new in human experience and inadequately understood."[11]

The new world will not be an easy one. Social convulsions are sure to occur. That means that extraordinary demands will be placed upon constitutional institutions and, of more basic importance, upon the moral integrity and stamina of the people. If disaster is to be avoided, we must be aware of the problem—which means that not only the past and present must be analyzed but also the future must be forecast. Machiavelli viewed history neither as a movement toward progress, nor as an inevitable cycle of recurring forms, but as constant change and uncertainty. Nevertheless, although we may not be bound by history, we cannot escape it; as Justice Oliver Wendell Holmes once said, adherence to the past is not a duty but merely a necessity.[12]

Part I

THE CLIMACTERIC: HUMANKIND AT A TURNING POINT

Evidence is growing that the world is in the midst of an immense transformation. For some time — since, perhaps, the great discoveries of the sixteenth century — the environment in which humans live and act has been changing with accelerating speed. That this poses enormous challenges to the American constitutional order is obvious; the Constitution was written in a different age, one in which problems were manageable by simple exercises of human will. Whether that can or will continue is the crucial question. Part I develops the nature of the present crisis, and lays the groundwork for subsequent analysis. Many of the ideas suggested in this part will be discussed in detail in later chapters.

1

Introduction:
A Social Ice Age?

This essay is one in constitutional law and politics. It draws on insights and concepts from several disciplines to describe the present crisis, to indicate how past crises were met, and to project what will probably be done, as well as what should be done in the future. Man has learned to invent the technological future—as Whitehead said, the most important invention of the nineteenth century was the invention of the art of invention—but no consensus exists as to what it should be, or how human affairs should be ordered. A struggling antheap of humans on a small and obscure planet in a small and obscure part of the Milky Way, itself a small and obscure galaxy among untold millions of others, could order their own affairs with a measure of equity and decency, but will not. There is a flaw—fatal?—in the makeup of Homo sapiens.

Could we both see and act upon it, the planet Earth has indeed become a single unit, not much larger in technological fact than Thomas Jefferson's "ward system," those "elementary republics" where "the voice of the whole people would be fairly, fully, and peaceably expressed, discussed, and decided by the common reason" of all citizens.[1] A world of some 150 "nation-states" ever increasingly resembles the "city-state" of ancient Greece and the post-Roman era. The nation and the world are on the verge of revolution—indeed, they are already knee-deep in revolution—and the only questions remaining are how peaceful it will be and who will win) "No cause is left," asserts Hannah Arendt, "but the most ancient of all, the one, in fact, that from the beginning of our history has determined the very existence of politics, the cause of freedom versus tyranny."[2] We, however, still live in a situation where the strong do what they can, and the weak suffer what they must. For it is freedom for all, not the few, that is the ultimate issue. And it is true today, as it was in the past, that necessitous men cannot be free men. The drive for equality, evident worldwide, is only to be understood as an effort by the *demos* to obtain that level of material wealth without which freedom is illusory. The movement toward equality, coming when serious doubts exist that it can be fulfilled, is far from successful—both within the United States and throughout the world.

Can inequality change by political means alone? No doubt more is needed, but political (constitutional) change can be of help. People, however, believe more in technology than in politics. Technology is worshipped and there is a widespread faith that "technological fixes" will solve human problems. The magic of the ancient gods has been transferred in the modern age to white-coated technocrats toiling in laboratories. That technological fixes cannot by themselves rescue mankind in this time of continuing troubles should be obvious, but it is not, simply because belief in them is at least quasi-religious— irrational, that is, not verifiable. Political change must accompany technological change.

The effort to perfect man in his microscopic share of the universe is of relatively recent origin—within the past 300 years. During that time, the idea of progress was born, grew to fruition, and is now on the decline. No doubt the perfectability of man is a small goal, when viewed against the immensity of time and space. But that is all there is. Technological changes, unplanned though they were, have enabled a large measure of human betterment from the drab and dreary past, when most people not only lived lives of quiet desperation but also lives of penury, want, and even of starvation. Poverty, mean and soul- and belly-shriveling, has always been the lot of the mass of humans. It still is, even with all the wondrous advances of recent decades. There is no reason to venerate the past. Life, for most, as Hobbes said about people in a "state of nature," was "poor, nasty, brutish, and short"—but not "solitary."[3] Viewed historically and from the perspective of Americans and some others, today is a golden age of material plenty.

The technological bargain that permits apparent mastery of nature by one of nature's beings—the humanist ideal—may carry with it internal contradictions. There are seeds of destruction that could, in time, remove man and his institutions from the planet and return it to the animals and insects, as it was eons ago in prehistory when our ancestors first crawled out of the slime and began the long, violent path toward "civilization." Unless, that is, something is done to remove those inconsistencies and contradictions. It would be foolish, if not downright stupid, unthinkingly to believe with Mr. Micawber that that "something" will be identified and put into effect before catastrophe from one source or another swings its grim scythe of destruction. But the effort must be made. "Micawberism," however, characterizes many people—

Micawber being the Charles Dickens character who went about with the sublime belief that something would turn up to solve his problems.

The further truth, to repeat for emphasis, is: While we in the United States, together with the remainder of the world, stand poised on the edge of revolution—of a new constitutional order—technology will not by itself bring a social order of equity and decency for all. Technology, emphatically, is not an independent force; it is a servant, not the master. It can and will be used for good or ill (quite possibly in the most violent manner) by those who in fact rule the 4.3 billion people who throng the global village. Those rulers face not only a rising demand for equality but many ominous and intractable crises. No one can predict the future with confidence, with one important exception: There is no reason to relieve that whatever motivated people in the past will change in the future. If violence and aggression characterized previous human acitivity, as they did, no valid reason exists to think that altruism will replace selfishness. Surely we have learned enough about human actions, particularly when people are under stress, to realize that the likelihood of behavioral change in reactions to crises is remote at best. Since the dawn of time, man has been a predator, not only against his fellow humans, but also the rest of the natural world. With an increasing population pressing ever harder on dwindling resources, that predatory nature will become more evident. Some perceive a possible change—a religious revival that will alter human behavior patterns and institutions.[4] That, however, is most unlikely.

Modern man is not only technologically oriented; he is still, as Aristotle said, a political animal. So it behooves those who care—and only saints and fools do not—to try to determine both the nature of the problem and possible ways to try to resolve it. The way that society is ordered, which is what politics or constitutionalism are about, may help to bring technological fixes that will be at least a temporary expedient. In the final analysis, the struggle may be absurd; that humans can control their future may be, as Professor David Ehrenfeld has called it, the "arrogance of humanism."[5] Even so, the effort must be made, if for no other reason than, like Mallory's Mt. Everest, "it is there."

This essay carves a segment out of a much larger problem: By concentrating on crisis government, it depicts the means employed by the United States in the past to confront both revolutionary changes and natural disasters. It also illustrates the tribal struggles of the species, the inadequate present-day reaction to similar changes and struggles, and projects possible political (constitutional) consequences. Crisis government is here and can mean repressive, even authoritarian, government. The task is to avert that, while making government more efficient. The need, in sum, is to make governmental power that is necessary as tolerable and decent as possible.

In the brief time since Copernicus forever smashed the Ptolemaic (man-centered) universe around which the Judeo-Christian religions were built, one brutal fact has become utterly clear: Man as a species truly is all alone and afraid in a world he never made. Several other intellectual shocks since Copernicus have made that obvious even to the unthinking and uncaring: Darwin exploded the notion of special creation; Freud that man is a rational being; and Einstein (and other physicists) that there are absolute truths in the universe. A single, silver, luminous ball floats in an eternity of space, the bounds of which are neither known nor knowable; and on that ball, slightly squashed at each pole, live more than four billion people, some of whom still believe that they were created in His image. Rather they fervently want to believe, for without that belief in a larger cause, life itself becomes wholly meaningless to them. That organized religion has little or no relation to public behavior is obvious, even though there is a connection between religion and State—but as we will see, not between church and State.

Disdain for authority characterizes the age. As a result, modern democracies, we are enjoined by "neo-conservatives" to believe, have become ungovernable.[6] Possibly that is true: the *demos* want their share of material goods, a share that they have been led to believe by the gospel of economic growth will be theirs. Their ancestors may have lived and died in misery, but people today dare to hope and even to believe that they, too, may sup at the groaning table of opulence. Those hopes could be satisfied, at least in the short run (although the short run may be very short in fact), if only the will were present to harness known scientific and technological techniques for human betterment. The purpose here is not to argue that point, but to reveal the consequences of that attitude and what may happen unless there be very clear thinking about political and economic institutions. Political (read "constitutional") institutions constructed in ages past must be examined and perfected, if indeed they can be, in the light of the increasing evidence of socioeconomic crises. Both technology and economics are out of control, the received wisdom from the past is at best a flickering light to guide the present and no guide at all for the future, and political institutions will have to adapt to new conditions and new imperatives. Unknown at present is the form that adaptation will take. The basic values of constitutionalism—of liberal democracy—are at stake. For them to be preserved even partially, hard and continuing thought must be given to steps that should be taken to perfect the art of governance. We have only ourselves—and that is not much. We cannot call upon a god or gods. There is not much time. We are in for it, deeply and irretrievably. The pains of existence press ever harder on nerves already beginning to rub raw. We may not succeed, but we must make the attempt.

This volume has four parts. Part I is devoted to the socioeconomic context in which the United States government has operated in the past and the new environment in which it probably will operate in the future, both immediate and long-range. In the past, emergencies were aberrational, but we are now in the midst of the crisis of crises. The principle of coalescence of crises—technological, economic, political—is developed.

In part II, the problem of how government has dealt with crises in the past is developed. The myth of the Golden Age is discussed—that time in which, some believe, things were better, men were stronger, women were pure, and children did not smoke pot. A relative few, mainly in the Western world, are now riding the crest of material plenty, but face unparalleled challenges from elsewhere. The problem today for the political order is how best to deal with situations of continuing crises. It will be shown that a principle of constitutional Machiavellianism has always been a part of the living American Constitution —the one in operation as compared with the constitution of the books. Government in the United States, in sum, has always been relative to circumstances. For a political system to cope with crisis under a written Constitution that makes little provision for it (other than declared war, and even then the constitutional silences are more eloquent than the express language) means that two sets of moral principles exist in the fundamental law; and in fact two fundamental laws exist. Morality, or propriety, in public behavior has never been of one piece in the United States. Actions at times are taken by officials (in both public and private governments) which are morally improper by one set of standards but right by another—but all of them lawful under the Constitution. This basic constitutional dualism is seldom mentioned by the Supreme Court—the usual response is to deny it—and little discussed in the literature.

Part III sets out some of the constitutional implications of the principle of constitutional Machiavellianism. The demise of liberal democracy, as it has ostensibly operated, is posited. No principle of political uncertainty, comparable to Werner Heisenberg's uncertainty principle in physics, exists. There are only a very few ways in which humans can order their affairs. We must face this certainty: Probable authoritarian government, and possibly worse, unless major steps are taken without delay. The trend most evident today is toward an elective "benevolent" despotism, or, as Auguste Comte once put it, "popular dictatorship with freedom of expression." Personal liberties of the type that do not harm the State are the trade-off for greater overall social controls; examples are marijuana and permissiveness in sexuality. The most ominous of all developments is the creation of the State—sometime called "society" or "government"—as an anthropomorphic superperson with drives and interests of its own.

Part IV deals with the future. It shows that the American Dream has ended; no longer can Americans believe that they are special. They now must face all of the problems that other peoples have through time. This means that a new type of Constitution is emerging, without fanfare and without amendment of the ancient document. The new Constitution is labeled the Constitution of

Control, in order to describe the probable repressive nature of the future of American constitutionalism) The tyranny of technology, which will be used to control people rather than accord them more freedom, is discussed.

In a brief epilogue following part IV, it is suggested that Hobbes's Leviathan may have come and will remain permanently.

In the United States the theory of government and the practice of politics (and development of formal constitutional law) have always been out of phase with one another. The gap between pretense and reality in American "democracy" has always been large. That it will grow even larger is as sure a proposition as can be stated. (The State has always been exactly as strong as it needed to be in order to survive. If this means a "democratical despotism," then it will occur as crises pile on crises on this dying cinder called Earth.) John Adams remarked in 1775 that a "democratical despotism is a contradiction in terms,"[8] and Thomas Jefferson, dismayed by uncontrolled legislatures, wrote soon after the Revolution that "an elective despotism was not the government we fought for."[9] But that, unhappily, is precisely the direction we are headed, and fast, and precisely the means that have been used in the past when conditions so required (The need is clear: Heed the flags of danger already stiff in the breeze of impending constitutional catastrophe.)

The analysis that follows is one that focuses more on the "living" than the "formal" Constitution. Over a century ago, Walter Bagehot wrote in the preface to the second edition of his classic *The English Constitution*, about the hazards of such an inquiry in these words: "There is a great difficulty in the way of a writer who attempts to sketch a living Constitution— a Constitution that is in actual work and power. The difficulty is that the object is in constant change."[10] The task of this volume is to sketch some of the enduring realities of the living American Constitution, one that changes, if not daily, then certainly routinely.

2

Our Threatened and Threatening Planet

"Are we in a crisis or in a climacteric? It is important to have a view on this."[1] That it is a climacteric, not a mere crisis, is fast becoming one of the truisms of the day. This chapter outlines that new fact in history.

Constitutions and legal systems cannot be understood apart from the social context in which they operate—and purportedly control. History provides some understanding of the past. What, however, of the present and the future? The future may be a shore dimly seen, but forecasting is necessary. What are the main challenges now facing mankind, challenges that surely will become even more critical in the future? The threat comes from several coalescing crises—which increasingly make the environment a threatening medium in which people must live and order their affairs.

First, a brief mention of what the immediate, and probable distant, future will not be. Two complementary statements are possible. It will not be a calm and ordered existence. Not only in the trouble spots of the world, but also in those nations which have managed to sail rather steadily thus far, social turmoil is sure to either remain or come. That will continue for the foreseeable future. Second, a steady progression toward a better society or group of societies is increasingly unlikely. The idea of progress, born out of the Enlightenment, is now dead. Change we will have, of that one may be certain, but progress? No. The best one can hope for is a continuation of the uncertain past.

Perhaps that is really too much to expect. We should hope for the best; preparation must be for the worst. The doomsayers must be taken seriously. They are ignored at our peril. What chance there may be must be preceded by acknowledgment that mankind is now faced with a continuing time of troubles. To plod along, to muddle from crisis to crisis as man has done from time immemorial, will no longer suffice. Crises grow ever deeper. We are in for it, completely and irretrievably, and the sooner we realize it the better. It will do no good to ask, as some have, "What has posterity done for me?" because we are our own posterity. In a time, such as the present, of extra-ordinary rapid social change, most people alive today are the posterity of tomorrow. That is something wholly new. By preparing for the worst, we can then be gratified if things turn out for the better, but we will not be surprised, and may even be prepared, if disaster strikes—as strike it will if social trends now only too obvious continue or accelerate.

A cancer is eating away in the bowels of mankind. Call it what one will—a "climacteric," with Lord Ashby; "the crisis of crises," with Professor John Platt; "the twenty-ninth day," with Lester Brown[2]—or whatever—can there be any question that man has become an endangered species? Certainly not. The evidence is too massive, too clear to believe otherwise. One has only to extend present conditions to reach that conclusion. That is so even though some—Herman Kahn and colleagues at the Hudson Institution are examples —maintain the contrary. Kahn believes that there will be difficulties, but that by some means or other—mainly, it appears, through technological "fixes"— a "yes" should be given to Robert Heilbroner's painful question: "Can man survive?"[3] One can only hope that Kahn is the better prophet. The problem is not whether we can hunker down and try to let the storm blow over. That would be relatively easy. Rather, it is to recognize that the storm has become the norm; and that we should heed the Ashbys, the Browns (both Lester and Harrison), the Platts, the Pecceis, the Vaccas—the so-called "gloom and doom" people—if the continuing storm is to be weathered, even in a mini-mally satisfactory way.

That the dangers, as with other species either exterminated or nearly so during the past few centuries, come from man himself is more than merely ironic or grimly amusing. Those dangers make the problem of extrication from the human predicament devilishly difficult (possibly even impossible). That effort must, of necessity, be a bootstraps operation; we must do it our-selves, and soon. There is no Archimedes off to the side with the tools necessary to lift mankind from the swamp he is in and the quicksand he is approaching. No god or gods will save us. Only human effort, feeble though it is, can be used.

The problem now is to describe the context in which the constitutional sys-tem operates today and that in which it will probably have to operate in the future. A contextual analysis is necessary because all law, including the fundamental law of the Constitution, reflects life, particularly economics. That is no statement of crude economic determinism. It merely iterates what many have said—that law is only a memorandum and is only to be understood by knowing that it is closely connected with the State and other societal institutions.

What are the dangers—the crises—that confront the human race? None is particularly new. All are well known, so much so that some verge on being clichés. What is novel is that they come simultaneously; the problems are converging or coalescing to the point where man, as Lord Ashby maintains, faces not a crisis but a climacteric in his existence. (When speaking of "man" I refer to humans everywhere, not merely the few hundred millions who have the good fortune to be citizens of the United States or some other Western derived nations—for example, Australia and New Zealand.)

Two further preliminary observations are in order. One is the fact that should be obvious—that the problems set forth below interlock; they complement each other. This means that although each can be dealt with separately by public policy measures, unavoidably, what happens in one sector affects and influences the others. That is one of the reasons why dealing with them is so difficult, and possibly even impossible.

Second, it is another truism, although one that has not yet been adequately evaluated, that change has become a social constant; it is not only built into the social order, it is accelerating. Fluidity is the norm, both in social affairs and in law. As sociologist W. Lloyd Warner observed, "The processes of change are in themselves integral parts of the social system. . . . Each part has within it something coming into being and something ceasing to be. . . . Innovations themselves are constantly being reorganized and reevaluated in terms of the old . . . nothing is static . . . all is movement and change."[4] We are back to Heraclitus. The old—the past—is, however, not mere prologue to the present and future; it was something wholly different. The environment—the social context—has been altered so radically in the past 150 years that today bears little resemblence even to the nineteenth century. Whether the process of change will continue is not at all certain. The pace may be slowing; a "steady state" society may be emerging. One more massive social change— to a form of modern feudalism—may be the last such alteration in human behavior patterns.

Change, however, still characterizes American society, as does the "telescoping" of time. Intervals between important events tend to diminish. Before one can be adequately appreciated and assimilated, another appears. Electronic communications provide apt illustration. The telegraph was a major technological breakthrough, as was the telephone. Both came in the nineteenth century. Then came radio and television. Today, we are in the midst of a communications revolution. In the next ten years, tiny slivers of silicon barely larger than a pinhead will transform our lives; they will affect education, health, work and leisure—indeed, all of life. These micro-information processors may not be far behind the wheel in terms of industrial and commercial—and thus of human—significance.

The developments traced below result largely from the scientific-technological revolution—which is *the* important social fact of modern times. They began within the past 200 to 300 years, and until recently were confined to the Western world. Their spread planet-wide is a major reason for the climacteric mankind is now undergoing. Much of what is, or has been, taken for granted in the West—the rule of law, representative "democracy," the drives for individual freedom and for equality (inconsistent though they may be), the nation-state as the characteristic form of political order—was unknown before the American and French revolutions. Within the past 300 or so years—since, say, the Treaty of Westphalia in 1648—human existence has been more radically transformed since, at least, the agricultural revolution eons ago when man first began to till the soil and form communities. Much of that massive, unprecedented alteration has occurred during the past 100 years. As a consequence, mankind's way of life, as Herbert Rosinski put it, has become an unending process rather than a static existence.[5] The critical question now is whether the climacteric will return mankind to a form of static existence. Since 1648, and with an accelerating pace, the cultural structure has been transformed, human population has made an exponential increase, and the world has become one unit in fact (but not in theory).

An intellectually satisfactory reason for the immense alterations in the human environment has not yet been produced. The fact of fundamental change is clear enough; the "why" is unknown. Why the Industrial Revolution (the primitive beginning of the scientific-technological revolution)? Why the rapid rise in population after 1650? Why the capitalist revolution? Why Protestantism? Why the birth of freedom and of democracy in a small corner of the world? Why the nation-state? Why nationalism (a form of secular religion)? Why the drive for equality?

These questions, and others like them, are not answerable in any definitive sense. There is no simple, and at the same time adequate, explanation for any human phenomenon. Human affairs are far too complex for that. To take only one example, Professor John K. Galbraith states with insouciant certainty that the "imperatives of technology" made the giant business corporation necessary, but his explanation of the rise of corporate giantism is simplistic at best.[6] Says David Landes, speaking of the relationship of technology to economic growth: "If there is some general conclusion to be drawn from all this, it is the complexity of economic development. This is a process that, particularly when it takes the form of industrialization, affects all aspects of social life and is affected in turn by them."[7] No one knows the reasons for the burst of technological innovation that has so transformed the milieu in which humans live.

A generation ago, historian Walter Prescott Webb suggested that much that occurred in the Western world since 1500 can be traced to the "boom" of the "great frontier" brought about by the discovery of the Western hemisphere and the consequent flow of wealth (gold and silver) to Europe.[8] At least a smidgen of validity may be found in that idea, just as there may be some truth in Max Weber's hypothesis, proffered seventy-five years ago, that the rise of Protestantism was a principal factor in the development of capitalism.[9] (Both, however, are hypotheses, rather than proved conclusions.) But if one asks, what major event or events occurred in the past 500 years that may have influenced the change from existence to process in mankind's way of life, two happenings may be cited: First, the Copernican discoveries that forever shattered the Ptolemaic (man-centered) conception of the universe and released Western man from intellectual stagnation. Rather than a closed, finite universe, the perception was of an open system that knew no bounds. After centuries of being in relative somnolence, the mind of man was freed to explore theretofore unknown territories, terrestrial and intellectual. One of today's difficulties, however, is the stubborn refusal of many to give up ideas no longer tenable. To use the jargon, much that passes for thought today is still anthropocentric—man-centered. Second is Webb's "great frontier" (which is Frederick Jackson Turner's American frontier hypothesis[10] writ large); wealth poured into Europe; capitalism replaced mercantilism as an economic system. Terrestrially, Western man expanded; intellectual discoveries accompanied the physical. Not without significance is the fact that the American Revolution, James Watt's use of steam power, and Adam Smith's publication of The Wealth of Nations all took place in the same year—1776. The analogue of a private enterprise economic system (which Smith advocated) is representative "democracy" (neither can exist without the other). Contract replaced status as the core principle of the legal system. The modern notion of human freedom was born. Feudalism died, replaced by liberal "democracy"—or, more accurately, the facade of liberal "democracy."

No one has yet produced valid reasons for those developments. But without the great discoveries and the Copernican revolution, surely they would not have occurred. If that be so, are there counterparts now in existence, or reasonably foreseeable, that will serve in the same way? No new territories remain to be explored. Space colonization in anything more than a rudimentary fashion is a fatuous dream. Science and technology continue their rapid, uncharted voyages of discovery, but those discoveries are usually "micro" rather than "macro." People in white gowns in the laboratories are delving into the minute, as in the experiments on the human cell, or in data processing. All that remains for them to do—save, of course, for an occasional burst into outer space—is to penetrate the inner core of the cell. All the mountains have been climbed, all the oceans plumbed. Nothing physical remains, except in the laboratories under the microscope. The race of discovery has been run, or almost so; what is left is the finishing canter—the rearrangement of details within finite space. If the universe knows no bounds, surely the planet Earth does—as do all of Earth's creatures.

The basic problem is not whether the technological future can be invented. Of course it can, and will be. What is technologically possible will be done, sooner or later. Invention has become the mother of necessity, rather than the other way around. The problem is how, given that certainty, humans can so order their affairs that at least a modicum of decency in treatment and condition is available to all. That deals with the nature of man himself: Can ways be found to alter the nasty and brutish nature of man? No evidence now exists that this can be done. (Arthur Koestler once asserted that chemical alteration of human behavior might produce this result, a point to which we return.)[11] A valid answer to that fundamental question is indispensable if the species is ever to move from its present state of growing peril to a reasonably safe condition. Will technology produce the answer? Surely no one should be optimistic on that score: A fantasy of the technological fix exists, but it is just that—a fantasy.

Western man has for centuries exploited nature and nature's creatures (what is called the "Faustian ethic"), and now must confront the harsh fact that it is man himself who is the problem. Man is part of the seamless web of nature; his survival depends upon recognition of, and accommodation to, that irreducible condition of existence. If "the problem is us," as Pogo said, at the very least a radical change is required in man's possessive attitude to nature. Professor Lynn White, in a famous essay published in 1967, observed: "Despite Darwin, we are *not*, in our hearts, part of the natural process. We are superior to nature, contemptuous of it."[12] White suggested that this elitism is part of the Judeo-Christian tradition. That tradition must now be altered, and soon. No more hubristic view can be conceived; those the gods would destroy they first inflict with what the ancient Greeks called *hubris*—which can be defined as wanton insolence or arrogance resulting from excessive pride or from passion. "We had better respect and preserve the stability of our natural ecosystems and try to learn the secret of their stability, so that if we succeed we can apply the secret to our man-made institutions."[13] That neatly poses the problem, one made all the more acute because man now lives, and increasingly will live, in a synthetic ecosystem. Part of man's predicament are the tensions that emerge from conflicts between natural and synthetic eco-systems. Humans, with an arrogance that knows no bounds, think they can control nature and nature's creatures. The short answer to that is: Not bloody likely, as some British are wont to say. But the effort can, and will, be made.

So much for prologue. We turn now to the four *Ps* of man's predicament: people, peace, poverty, pollution.

None requires extensive discussion; all are among the commonplaces of the day. Do common threads unite them? Several factors may be suggested. Many, perhaps most, of the details that come under each are traceable to the explosion of science and technology in the past two to three hundred years.

That technological revolution has made it seem as if human problems could be solved if only people of good will put their minds to it. This is what "the idea of progress" ultimately means; it is an idea under severe stress at the present time. Science and technology have provided the bases for the *appearance* of the possibility of satisfaction of submerged demands for equality of conditions, as well as equality of opportunity, by the world's peoples. The demands come from the world over, not merely from within the United States; they have a definite, albeit immeasurable impact upon American public policies. For the first time in human history, people en masse dare to hope, and even to believe, that conditions of desperate destitution can be alleviated. Whether those hopes and beliefs are realizable is not the point. (They are not.) What is important—surpassingly so—is the credence paid to them by billions of people the planet over. The four categories of social action are closely intermeshed; each affects all, and each is now rapidly getting out of control. Each is, at least, a crisis in human history; taken together, they make up the climacteric—a sea change in man's relationship to the environment. And, taken together (as well as singly), they describe conditions that now necessitate, and will do so increasingly in the future, emergency responses from the State (from government). Social emergency is the norm and political action to counteract it is becoming routine. One need only to lift his eyes from the day-do-day trivia to see that. We may wish it to be otherwise, and being prisoners of our intellectual heritage, try to make those wishes reality. But it will not come about, absent major institutional change (and probably not then). The task now is not to prescribe what could or what should be done, but to describe the past and emergent future.

If what is said in the remainder of this chapter seems familiar, it must be repeated because few in positions of influence and power take it seriously. Nor do many Americans. That ostrich-like mentality is one of the many barriers that must be hurdled. Stanford University Professor Willis W. Harman has aptly noted: "Society tends to hide knowledge that is superficially threatening to the status quo, even though this knowledge may be badly needed to resolve its most fundamental problem."[14]

The prospects for peace provide a good starting point. They are not, at this writing, very bright. Possibly, nuclear warfare can be averted. Not that conventional warfare is more pleasant or less bloody. But it can be, and usually is, contained in time and space. The Korean peninsula is apt illustration. Only when American forces approached the Chinese border did China respond. Vietnam is another example. (Quite possibly it was the Spanish Civil War of the modern age, with sophisticated conventional weapons tested and tactics improved.) That adventure ended in ignoble defeat for proud Americans; but one would be foolish to assume that it will stop future engagements when considered necessary by the leaders of this nation. The *Mayaguez* incident, which was a "famous victory" for President Gerald Ford, shows what can—

what will—be done.[15] As this is written, evidence is mounting that some type of intervention by American forces may occur in Africa or the Middle East. If so, nuclear weapons probably will not be employed, unless the localized conflicts expand into warfare between the superpowers.

Violence on an organized national scale has not disappeared. Nor does it seem likely that it will. If anything, the probability of war remains high. "Brushfire" wars will continue. Little doubt exists that the United States will be involved, in one way or another, in many of these. The "balance of terror" may keep intercontinental nuclear warfare from erupting.

Aggression, always the norm in human behavior, has now intensified. Scientists now can guarantee the annihilation of the human race, and, indeed, of all life on the planet. Nuclear war would likely produce not one Rome but two (or more) Carthages. But that does not deter the madness of an arms race that knows few limits. In sum, as Harrison Brown tells us, "the possibility of all-out thermonuclear war is the most serious danger confronting industrial civilization today."[16] Add to that the equally terrifying prospect of the use of nerve gas—a weapon possibly even worse than nuclear bombs—and one can readily see dangers without parallel in human history. And nothing—or next to nothing—is being done about it. Even a new strategic arms limitation treaty (SALT) between the United States and the USSR will do little more than stabilize the destructive forces of the two countries at levels high enough to make mutual destruction almost a certainty. Neither nation displays any real desire to cut back its armed might.

Without peace, nothing is possible. With peace, or at least the absence of nuclear war, something might be done to extricate man from the present predicament—but only if something radical is done about the proliferating masses of humans. That is the "people" problem: there are far too many now, a condition that is rapidly worsening.

For a number of reasons, world population is exploding. The United Nations has projected that the present 4.3 billion people will not level off before it reaches from 10 to 16 billion. Whether this is ecologically possible, given present knowledge and policies, may be doubted. Stresses on the world's biological systems—forests, fisheries, grasslands, crop lands, and waters—have so overloaded them that they are at the breaking point in many parts of the world.

Central America provides a ready example of what is happening: Between 1950 and 1975 its population more than doubled—from 8.9 million to 18.5 million. In the next twenty-two years the population will redouble, to an approximate 39 million. The nations are Costa Rica, El Salvador, Guatemala, Honduras, Nicaragua, and Panama. Add Mexico: that country annually adds more people to its population than does the United States. By 2000 A.D., Mexico City will be the world's largest city (it is already the Calcutta of the

West); some observers predict as many as 30 million people living there. Mexico's present 67 million people will double in less than a quarter of a century.

The same dreary pattern may be seen worldwide. In forty-one years, under present estimates, the world's population will double. That means 8.6 billion people crowding Earth—by the year 2020. People alive today will still be alive then, living in an antheap civilization on an antheap planet.

The numbers alone are both unnerving and appalling—something new in human history. Never before have so many crowded the planet. No one knows the impact on the human psyche of the hordes of people that throng the earth. Literally no place is an island, separate from elsewhere. That creates social conditions that necessitate rethinking the premises of the American system of constitutionalism.

Other aspects of the "people" factor deserve mention. One is the fact of "structural" unemployment, now not even admitted; it is the label for science and technology making many people unemployable. They are not needed for the labor force. Not having the requisite skills, they are surplus to the system. They live, but do not contribute; they exist, but do not produce. Not that it is their fault; speaking generally, it is not. Fault, however, has nothing to do with the matter. Even were the unskilled suddenly to become skilled, there would be no room for them. A technological society does not require mass manpower. The fact of surplusage of people simply cannot be gainsaid. The "third industrial revolution" of silicon chips makes that conclusion a truism.[17] The economic system today has no place for most of them, and will have far less in the future. This, in itself, will be a source of social turmoil. How long will the unemployed and disadvantaged put up with crumbs left over from the groaning table of opulence that the more fortunate—the employed—have?

Add the rise of an "educated proletariat," and what does one see? By educated proletariat is meant that the United States has slipped without planning, and without fanfare, into a system of mass higher education. A college education, or at least a possibility of getting one, is now considered to be the birthright of all young Americans. Hence the explosion in colleges and universities, particularly at the community college level. It might be argued that education really is a means by which young people postpone entering the labor market, thus helping employment figures. Nonetheless, surely it is true that expectations are raised by matriculation and graduation. The question is what will occur when ever larger numbers of young people, each armed with some sort of higher degree, are denied entry into the labor market at their expectancy levels? Nothing is quite so dangerous as a situation when peoples' expectations are raised, and then dashed. This is occurring, certainly for blacks and Hispanics but for whites as well, and surely will continue as the machine replaces the human in the industrial sector. No one in government—or, indeed, outside of it—has confronted the problems brought by mass enforced leisure (enforced because of structural unemployment). A mammal that has had work as its raison d'être for untold millennia will not easily adapt to a social condition where many people's efforts are considered worthless, surplus to the system.

Another aspect of the "people" factor is the rise of bureaucracy. No longer is the individual the central part of the social system. The person as a person is important only as a member of a group or groups. He spends his life in groups and is meaningless and purposeless outside of them. (The occasional hermit merely proves the rule.) Economically, he has lost whatever sovereignty he once had as a consumer. Politically, only groups can command power in a highly organized, bureaucratized society. The individual confronts groups wherever he turns. With few exceptions he works in groups, socializes in groups, and does almost everything except die (and sometimes even then) as a group member.

Whatever may have been the original intention of those who wrote the Constitution, the United States is not composed of atomistic individuals operating as such. That is no new insight: as long ago as 1927 John Dewey maintained that "the human being whom we fasten upon as individual *par excellence* is moved and regulated by his association with others; what he does and what the consequences of his behavior are, what his experience consists of, cannot even be described, much less accounted for, in isolation."[18] It cannot be otherwise; the organizational revolution has made the United States a nation of organizations, of groups, of collective activity. True, American collectivism is at least nominally private, rather than public; but for the person confronting the collectivities of our time, the distinction does not matter.

That the movement toward bureaucracy, public and private (and a combination of both), will both continue and intensify cannot be seriously doubted. As population grows, technology continues its dizzy pace, cities expand, corporations grow larger, government becomes even larger, emergencies occur, the individual will ineluctably face a congeries of groups too powerful to battle. The nature of freedom will have changed: at the very most, it will be the freedom to join a group and then submit to its internal norms—if, indeed, the group will have the person, which by no means is certain. Today, the "autonomous" man does not exist as such; that will not change in the future.

A third aspect of the "people" factor is that more and more Americans (and others) have been led by subtle (and not so subtle) processes of conditioning to expect more and more—at precisely the time in history when they cannot get it. That dovetails with the expectations brought by mass higher education. The social and economic institutions of the nation are geared toward higher and higher levels of consumption. Continued economic growth is considered to be indispensable. The mass media, particularly television, daily exhort Americans to buy more, to consume more, to live the "good" material life. This has led some of them—many of them—to "want it all now," to settle for immediate gains without thought of, or heed to, the future. Hedonism and selfishness characterize the modern age. The taxpayers' revolt which began in the 1970s is probably merely the beginning of institutionalized selfishness. The result is easy to forecast: social turmoil.

A leisure society is possible (at least for a time) in the industrialized West, and even possible elsewhere—given the will and the resources. But man at leisure—permanent leisure—is purposeless; his life has no meaning. Homo sapiens is also Homo faber.[19] He works to live; and his work often is his life. It is not likely that drives and instincts built up over millions of years can, or will, change to permit mass leisure unless something replaces work.

Leisure is indeed possible, in the United States, at least for a time. The few, using new technologies, can produce for the many. But if so, then some new way of allocating resources other than work must be found. For untold millenia, people have been work-oriented, even work-dominated. One, however, has only to view those afflicted with "retirement syndrome" in the nation's Sun Belt to realize that, absent work, most people are adrift, even lost. The leisure society is possible, but it may be a curse—unless, and until, a new ethic is created.

Finally, the individual psyche has had to bear too many intellectual shocks in the past few centuries. Through most of human history, known and unknown, people could and did think in terms of a man-centered universe. The sun revolved around the earth; and man was at its center. This meant that people could, and did, think in terms of dominion over the earth and earth's creatures. But then came Copernicus, Darwin, Freud, Pavlov, Einstein, and Heisenberg. Small wonder that man now finds himself all alone and afraid in a world he never made.

Not surprisingly, under these conditions, strange and exotic religions have flourished. People look out into the emptiness of space and resort to assorted gurus and to the State for mental and psychological sustenance. A small struggling lot of humans, realizing either consciously or subconsciously that they are adrift on a tiny dying cinder in the immensity of space, does not have the moral fiber to sustain that brutal thought and looks elsewhere. One way to deal with that perilous situation will be developed later: through use of updated versions of Aldous Huxley's "soma" pills,[20] people are being kept quiescent. The modern version of soma, as we will show, is marijuana, pornography, gambling, permissiveness in general—in short, a person will be permitted to do anything he wishes so long as he does not jeopardize the stability of the social structure.

For most of their history, Americans lived in a relative paradise. An almost empty continent with untold natural resources, capital from Europe, cheap labor (also mainly from Europe), protected by two oceans and the British navy—all these and more, led Americans to believe that they were special, that the problems that beset others would not touch them. That America exists only in the myth, not in the harsh realities of the nineteenth and early twentieth centuries. There has always been a large gap between pretense and actuality, between myth and reality, in American history.

Nowhere is this better seen than in the third of our four Ps—that of poverty. Hard and grinding poverty was the lot of most Americans, of whatever color or national origin, in colonial America and after the revolution. As long ago as the 1840s Thoreau could observe that the mass of men lived lives of quiet desperation. The desperation in which men (and women) lived derived in large part from a continuing absence of minimum material goods. Whether in the cities, or on farms, life for many was on the ragged edge of starvation. Colonial America, historian Michael Kammen tells us, began as a "covenanted" society "in which most men were bound by clusters of formal obligation: oaths, covenants, bonds and indentures."[21] Most obvious was slavery; but indentured servants made up a considerable part of the labor force. Most men were necessitous and had to sell their time, either by indenture or by wages. When the Industrial Revolution came in the nineteenth century, cheap labor was needed—and it arrived, by the millions, from Europe and even from China. The point here is not to trace American labor history, but to assert what seems to be incontrovertible: the quiet desperation about which Thoreau spoke emanated from not being able to get adequate or sufficient food, clothing, or housing.

The myth is otherwise, of course; particularly so because a certain amount of social mobility from the working to the moneyed class did take, and still takes, place. Necessarily so, because of the need for talent that was not being produced in sufficient quality or quantity by the ruling elites. There were, and still are, tales worthy of Horatio Alger, but far fewer than most think. Most people did not in the past, cannot at present, and will not in the future be able to mount very high on the ladder of materialistic success.

Prior to the 1940s, that was better understood than it is now. For since World War II, American economic growth took giant leaps. But that has now stopped—or rather, is stopping. The evidence lies all around us, and need not be repeated here, save in briefest summary. An even larger economic pie suddenly is shrinking relative to the population and to the expectations of the people: Both are on a sharply rising curve.

What has been said in this section can be summarized. To repeat an earlier statement: Thomas Hobbes asserted that man in a state of nature lived a life that was poor, nasty, brutish, and short. Historically, in the United States, the majority of people were poor, their lives often were nasty and brutish, and until recent years their lives were short. A problem is that many people are poor today and their lives are long. Misery is the result—a relatively quiet misery, thus far, but one that may change to a noisy and demanding misery.

More people are affluent, however. People who still are riding the crest of the wave of economic expansion of the past thirty years create yet another problem. There is not enough of some things, which should be considered luxuries, to go around. What matters most among the affluent is their status, measured either by personal wealth or prestige. Economists put the matter in these terms: There is an unbridgeable gap between what Roy Harrod has called "democratic wealth" and Fred Hirsch has called a "material economy" and Harrod's "oligarchic wealth" (Hirsch's "positional economy").[22] The former are goods available to everyone and which increase without stress by industrial activity. It does not, for example, make any difference (other than the use of energy) if everyone has a television set. Each can enjoy it alone. But consider "oligarchic" or "positional" goods; these are limited in an absolute sense, as are land or great art, or are subject to congestion and crowding through extensive use. National parks in the United States fit the latter category exactly. Forty years ago, Yosemite and Yellowstone were, if not unspoiled, at least enjoyable. Now they are overcrowded, the Coney Islands of the mountains. That is a new type of poverty, one peculiar to the antheap civilization. It is impossible for more than a few really to enjoy some goods. Status, therefore, comes not only from position, but from being able to command a share of positional goods—a Picasso or a Rembrandt, a seat at the opera, or whatever. By definition, all cannot enjoy them. There are social as well as economic and physical limits to growth.

No amount of economic growth can cure this second kind of poverty. "So what?" may well be the response. So more people get to see Yosemite or Old Faithful gush up. What is wrong with that? Nothing—if one is willing to run in ever-increasing packs. For other oligarchic or positional goods there is no answer. Only one person, or a museum, can own the Mona Lisa or any other masterpiece. Small wonder, thus, that Elmyr de Hory made a fortune peddling fake Picassos, Modiglianis, and Van Goghs. With so much money around (in a relatively few hands), the way to get a masterpiece (and thus be cultured) was to buy a fake. Add to that the worst of all possible inventions— the automobile. When everyone gets one or more, the situation verges on the intolerable. Cities have been rendered almost unlivable by the internal combustion engine. The automobile should be considered a luxury, not, as in the Western world, a necessity.

The second type of poverty is so new that few recognize it as such. Much, much worse is the first kind: the grinding harshness of lives that do not know adequate food, housing or clothing. Enough exists in the United States to make it a serious problem. But it is far worse elsewhere—in Asia, in Africa, in South America, in Central America. There, famine could and will strike at any time. By the year 2000, says Robert McNamara of the World Bank, at least 600 million people will live in "absolute" poverty—from which there is no escape. His figure probably errs on the low side.[23]

Man has made a Faustian bargain with technology. He has sold his (material) soul for short-term benefits reaped from new technologies. Progress is considered to be technological advance. It is out of control. Says physicist Ralph Lapp: "No one—not even the most brilliant scientist alive today—really knows where science is taking us. We are aboard a train which is gathering speed, racing down a track on which there are an unknown number of switches leading to unknown destinations. No single scientist is in the engine cab and there may be demons at the switch. Most of society is in the caboose looking backwards."[24] The benefits of technology are obvious. Not so obvious, but nonetheless present, are the detriments—the unanticipated consequences of new developments. Pollution, endemic in modern America, will be pandemic in the future.

Pollution is the generic term for "second-order" consequences of new technologies. Examples are easily found. The noise of jet aircraft. The smoke from exhausts of internal combustion engines. The intrusions of the telephone. "Wonder" drugs that eventually create "super-bugs." Radiation. Pollution takes many forms. Living, as increasingly Western man does, in a largely synthetic environment, the second-order consequences of new technologies pose obvious dangers. The cost of complying with American air pollution and water quality legislation has been computed by the Brookings Institution to be $500 billion. That price tag can be met—given the will to do so. But hidden behind that figure is the hard fact that payment must be at the expense of other desires. There simply is not enough money to go around. Will Americans choose material plenty over environmental hazards? In all likelihood, they will—just as they appear to be willing to sacrifice safety standards (at best, badly regulated) to save a few dollars.

No need exists to dwell overly long on the pollution aspect of humankind's climacteric. The facts are too well known for extended discourse. One matter, however, deserves emphasis: the health hazards of new technologies. "Industrial society," says Dr. Harrison Brown, "now confronts Americans with a broad range of hazards which are new to the human experience." These environmental effects may, says Brown, "help to explain the fact that cancer deaths have been increasing more rapidly than can be accounted for simply on the basis of the aging of the population."[25] Newspapers often, and increasingly, report discoveries about newly found carcinogens, most of which come from long-used products (for example, asbestos).

The point is that hard choices will have to be made between some beneficial products and paying through health and other hazards for them. DDT, for example, is an extremely effective pest-killer, but its second-order consequences are enough to make its use dubious at best. With a decline in the use of DDT, malaria is again becoming a major health problem in many parts of the world.

The dilemma is obvious—and unresolved. Whether technicians in the world's laboratories will be able to eliminate undesirable, even dangerous, second-order consequences of new technologies is by no means certain. The probability is that they will not.

Dr. Willis W. Harman maintains that "there are numerous signs that we may be approaching a 'societal nervous breakdown': tradeoffs between inflation and unemployment and between energy and environment grow increasingly intolerable; indications of fundamental alienation change form but fail to abate; and above all, the erosion of past goals and values continues, coupled with a growing sense that no one knows where society is heading—or should head. Yet the implication of these signs—that the old order is becoming unworkable—is extraordinarily threatening and largely resisted."[26] There are reasons for that resistance, which Harman does not discuss, revolving around the fact that for the first time in human history it has become possible to invent the future. The result is the Ostrich Society, a perfectly understandable reaction to that fact, particularly when it is coupled with the consequences of following the pervasive American philosophy—pragmatism. Things have worked out all right in the past, if not for all then surely for most, and things are (or recently have been) getting even better. Small wonder that resistance to a societal nervous breakdown is so evident.

Not that such an attitude and response is adequate to the need. Far from it. Humankind is indeed in a predicament. Lord Ashby is correct; it is a climacteric, rather than a mere crisis, that is being experienced. Life will get no better —at least for the foreseeable future. Quite the contrary. The principle of coalescence of crises is at work. Each of the four Ps interlocks with the others, and thereby makes the problem immensely more difficult. People—most of them—are willfully or unthinkingly blind; they fail to acknowledge the predicament of mankind.

Emphatically, that is not a prediction of disaster. That forecast is not necessary, for disaster is already striking. The developments subsumed under the four Ps are rapidly converging. "The convergence point," says Dr. Harrison Brown, "is not so very far in the future, probably within the lifetime of most of us, certainly within the lifetimes of our children."[27] That means (to repeat) that "posterity" in the sense of people in the distant future is not those who will suffer: It is us, or most of us (those who live for the next quarter century or more), who will bear the brunt of that convergence of crises. We are indeed our own posterity—something as yet unrecognized and something new in human history.

That is the context in which the question of constitutional Machiavellianism should be seen. Social order is visibly disintegrating; institutions tortuously built during the past few centuries are toppling. We are in for it, and had better realize it now. The instinct for survival is still present, but it will propel us down the road toward authoritarianism, even totalitarianism. The time is short, the changes massive and imminent. Americans are in the midst of the first—and perhaps last—climacteric in their history. Hard and sustained thought must be given to ways to extricate not only the United States, but all of humankind from the predicament it now is in.

A paradox exists, however: at the very time that the foundations of Western society are being undermined, mainly by technological developments that seem to have a logic and special drive of their own, a higher degree of general affluence is apparent in the United States, coupled with the highest degree of personal freedoms in American history. Americans are now living in the last years of a Golden Age. The next chapter briefly outlines that paradox.

Part II

THE HISTORY:
THE SEAMY SIDE OF
DEMOCRACY

That American government has always been exactly as strong as it needed to be in differing circumstances is the theme of part II. The so-called "negative, nightwatchman State" existed mainly in the myth. It was only negative in the sense that the businessman for years was able, through use of a compliant judiciary, to stave off adverse regulation. When the values of those in actual power in the nation were threatened, neither the Constitution nor the legal system prevented prompt and at times harsh dealing with those threats. The organs of government were, in sum, at the disposal of the ruling class. That means that there was and is a seamy side to "democracy." Chapter 6 summarizes the reactions of government to actual or pretended emergencies. It is preceded by brief discussions of the Golden Age, the nature of the legal system, the idea of "reason of State," and the nature of the modern State.

3
The Myth of the Golden Age

The idea of a Golden Age is one of the most pervasive in human history. Each nation seems to have one. Even individuals, when they grow older, believe that things used to be better. The collective nostalgia so evident during the Bicentennial Year (1976) is a typical example. We need not delve into the psychological reasons for this, save to say that its very prevalence would seem to indicate that it serves some deep-seated purpose.

What, then is a Golden Age? A beginning may be made with Greek mythology. Hesiod wrote in the eighth century B.C., pining for a lost paradise. According to him, our age (the "Iron Age") would be the fifth in a series that has been declining since the first stage (the Golden Age). In the Golden Age, a superior race of people "lived like gods without sorrow of heart, remote and free from toil and grief; miserable age rested not on them, but with legs and arms never failing they made merry feasting beyond the reach of all evil. When they died, it was as though they were overcome with sleep, and they had all good things; for the fruitful earth bore them fruit abundantly without stint. They dwelt in ease and peace upon their lands with many good things, rich in flocks, and loved by the blessed gods."[1] Hesiod maintained that the Age ended when Pandora opened her box and allowed previously unknown evils to escape. Then came the Silver, Brass, and Heroic Ages, each one progressively more deteriorated than its predecessor, and finally the Iron Age. In the Iron Age, says Hesiod, men "never rest from labor and sorrow by day, and from perishing by night; and the gods shall lay sore trouble upon them." (Something Hesiod did not foresee—the Technological Age—has replaced the Iron Age.)

Any similarity between Hesiod's account of the Golden Age and the Garden of Eden myth of Christianity is by no means a mere coincidence. Our point, however, is not that. Rather it is twofold: (a) the mythology of a Golden Age in American history; and (b) with the coming of the Technological Age, we were briefly in a Golden Age. The myth always places that time, for Americans and others, in the past; my point is that it was in the 1945-1970 period. A corollary is that the ancients' (and even some contemporaries') views of human history are contrary to fact. Things were distinctly not better in the past than they are now.

This chapter develops the two matters suggested above; and suggests that for one brief moment in history some humans did dare to hope, and even at times to realize, the material plenty without which they cannot live "remote and free from toil and grief." That time was 1945-1970. The Technological Age made it possible. The Golden Age is still with us, but it is declining.

Americans do not look much beyond 1776—when a small group of men, with consummate daring, broke away from England and became a nation. Not much of one, for a war had to be fought, a war that found victory mainly because France aided the new nation (and also because England simply did not care much how the struggle went). But win they did; and after finding that congressional government under the Articles of Confederation was not sufficient to the need, convened a constitutional convention in 1787 supposedly to revise the Articles. Instead, the fifty-five men who attended that convention (of the eighty-four who were named to attend, twenty-nine did not come to Philadelphia) produced the Constitution—a radically different document from the Articles. (Only thirty-nine of the fifty-five signed the draft constitution—less than half of those who originally were supposed to attend.) Since then, the Founding Fathers are the principal but not the only saints in America's pantheon of heroes.

They are still considered to have had a special wisdom and superior prescience. Gladstone, the British prime minister, in a fit of effusiveness maintained: "But, as the British Constitution is the most subtle organism which has proceeded from the womb and the long gestation of progressive history, so the American Constitution is, so far as I can see, the most wonderful work ever struck off at a given time by the brain and purpose of man."[2] One need not believe such hyperbole—one may believe with Macaulay that, "Your Constitution, sir, is all sail and no anchor"[3]—but nonetheless it remains true that lawyers (and others) view the Document with mystical reverence. Small matter that most people, including lawyers and Supreme Court justices, cannot name more than a handful of the framers: they are still accorded a respect akin to that given the Deity.

These views, whether of the professoriate or the legal profession, deserve attention but not respect. At most, the intentions of the Founding Fathers—

note the capital Fs, not without significance—even when ascertainable, which in the usual case they are not, are but one of the criteria—and not the most important—of judgment for constitutional interpreters to consult. If ever there was a Golden Age in American constitutional history, so the assumption goes, it was the time circa 1787-1789 when men of ostensible superior wisdom produced in Philadelphia a Constitution much like Moses bringing down the Ten Commandments from Mt. Sinai. The fact that only a few of them are mentioned, or their names known today, does not diminish the point. The myth is still fervidly believed. There apparently is a hierarchy within America's Valhalla; only some of the Founding Fathers are in the first rank. Why that should be is not difficult to ascertain. Those framers whose views most closely coincide with the ruling elites of any succeeding generation are those who are revered. The others are quietly forgotten (an example of the human propensity to bury the inconvenient fact).

Reverence for those who wrote the Constitution is undeserved. For present-day Americans to invoke the words of the saints in our pantheon as unchanging verities bespeaks a collective mind of limited capacity, a mind unwilling to face the hard choices that must be made to adapt ancient constitutional words to modern problems. It is a mass intellectual cop-out. That belief is, at best, irrational—but who believes today that people, including professionals, are more than partially rational?

One example will suffice. Lawyers can seriously argue, and judges can as seriously appear to consider the arguments, that the principal and preferred way of interpreting the Constitution is to ascertain the intentions of the framers. Thus, Professor Abraham Sofaer of the Columbia University Law School:

Any study of the legality of conduct under a written constitution should begin with the document itself. Where the United States Constitution is unclear, its meaning *must* be sought in all the available sources; the ratification debates; the minutes of the Convention; the views of those who drafted or voted on the relevant provisions; and the background—intellectual, social, economic, and political—of the participants, of the ratifiers, of the society in which it all took place, and indeed of the British system from which the United States had only recently separated.[4] (Emphasis added.)

That is an impossible task, even if one were to assume that it is the proper objective of those who interpret the Constitution—which, emphatically, it is not. Others echo Sofaer's views. An example is Raoul Berger, who in a silly book published in 1977 maintained that ours is a "government by judiciary"[5] —mostly, it seems, because judges do not follow the intentions of members of the 39th Congress which drafted the fourteenth amendment. And Supreme Court justices at times refer to the views of specific individuals who lived generations ago in a far different society. Madison and Jefferson are favorites, even though the latter did not attend the Convention of 1787 (he was ambassador to France).

Lawyers are far from alone in that mindset. People generally seem to believe, or want to believe, that at some unnamed time in the past and usually in some unnamed place or places in the nation, things were better. But were they? Even a casual reading of the social history of the United States quickly reveals the contrary. During colonial days life was dreary and boring and dangerous. People hacked out a living from the wilderness. Grinding poverty and monotony characterized the time. Many workers were "indentured"—a form of wage slavery from which they often did not escape. Blacks were slaves and remained so until the Civil War when ostensible freedom was gained. The "reconstruction," however, failed; and it is not until modern times—and then seldom, taking the totality of those of African descent—that black Americans can be said to have achieved a decent measure of freedom.

But, ah, it might be said, how about the nineteenth century? The answer is the same—for most of the people. For the favored few—those with property or wealth of some type—there was material plenty, coupled with power and prestige. For the masses, many of them immigrants from even worse situations, the contrary was true. The Irish are illustrative, but far from unique: Says J. C. Furnas, ". . . penniless Irish were so rife in Philadelphia [in 1819] that the well-meaning urged Congress to rescue them with a special land grant in Illinois."[6] But the Irish stuck to "fetid" urban slums. In Ireland, "the symptoms of their despair had included individual and mass riot and hard drinking. In America, where as yet the miseries had lifted only partly and the habit of despair was still strong, they went on fighting and drinking. . . ."[7] As with the Irish, so, too, with Germans and Poles and other migrants from Europe. For them—the majority?—life was indeed poor and nasty, brutish and short. They worked long hours, when they could find work, and lived in slums. Part of the point is that as bad as things were in the United States, they were worse back home. But a Golden Age for them? Hardly. So, too, on the farms. Novelists such as Hamlin Garland graphically portrayed the bleak lives of those fated to spend their days wrestling with climate and soil in the Middle West. When Sinclair Lewis published *Main Street* in 1927, any notion of an idyllic life in small towns was forever smashed. For women, the mills in Massachusetts may not have been dark and Satanic, as they were in Manchester, but nonetheless the hours were long, the work boring, and the employer had the whip hand whenever discontent surfaced. An industrial proletariat and an agricultural peasantry existed in fact—but not in theory.

I do not suggest that conditions were worse in the United States; merely that by any criterion of modern times, things are far better today. Health. Longevity. Slums. Income, Material goods. Social mobility. Even crime. One has only to read Thucydides to learn that crime was the norm in ancient Greece; and one has only to travel through Europe to see walled cities to know that violence was the norm. So, too, in the United States: Freedom from crime, and its reasonable expectation, is a modern phenomenon.

The point is simple and should be underscored: *The Golden Age for Americans never existed in the past; if it exists at all, it is in the post-1945 period.* The nineteenth century did add one saint to America's Valhalla—Abraham Lincoln. He alone among the millions who lived then is revered today.

How, then, may we account for the change from yesteryear to today?

Several factors coalesced, in a set of circumstances unique in world history. An empty continent, with fabulous resources, millions of people emigrating from Europe and Asia to form a cheap manpower pool, protected by two oceans and the British navy, no external wars (save wars of conquest, as against Mexico)—all these and more, jelled when technology began its inexorable impact upon the nation. The railroads did more to unify the country than did all the political actions. Communications—the telegraph and then the telephone—added their contribution. It was, however, the application of the scientific method to production and the consequent mass production that spelled the coming of material plenty. Suddenly—by hindsight, at least—the economic pie became enormously larger.

This meant something that, if not unique, was certainly rare in human history: People theretofore among the poor and impoverished were able to get a larger part of that pie. The age of economic plenty was born in the early twentieth century and continues to the present day. (That it will come to an end, and soon, is a commonplace.) A Golden Age came into existence, one in which people dared to hope and often to realize that freedom from necessity that is basic to all other freedoms. That Age lasted from roughly 1945 to 1970—a year when, for the United States, things began to become unglued.

One has only to travel in many other parts of the world—in almost every other nation—to perceive the sheer comparative opulence that characterizes the United States. The age of plenty is indeed the age of material abundance; and while there are still many—far too many—below the poverty line, on a comparative basis (both with the past and with other nations) the United States has become a worldly paradise.

Technology made it possible—but the second-order consequences of that very technology are helping to bring it to an end. For one moment of historical time, people are able to hope for escape for themselves and their progeny from the grinding poverty that characterized the mass of men since the dawn of time. One brief interlude in the untold millenia that Homo sapiens has been on earth could be enough to build upon if people are wise enough to take full advantage of circumstances. Whether they will be that wise is an open question.

The material wealth that came with the application of technology to production not only created a much larger economic pie; it made it appear as if a massive redistribution of wealth took place. This is not so. There is a myth of the egalitarian revolution. People who should know better confuse the statement of *legal equality*, by the Supreme Court and other governmental organs, with the contrary facts of *social inequality*. The same small percentage of people control as much, or even more, of wealth as was true in, say, 1900 or 1930. No redistribution has occurred.[8] There was just more to go around. With the marked slowing of growth, which is already upon us, that "more" is becoming relatively less. As population rises, the economic pie is becoming proportionally smaller. The shares for the masses, if present distribution patterns continue, will unavoidably diminish. No other conclusion is possible. The Golden Age is coming to an end.

If economic growth is slowing, and if technology is making mass manpower obsolete, as it is (through the second and third Industrial Revolutions), that time when many Americans had, in Hesiod's words, "all good things" is now staggering to a halt. That, however, is not the only adverse consequence of the Age of Technology. A brief Golden Age of material plenty is one thing, now being cut short by several forces, including second-order consequences of those technologies. Other consequences include: what John Kenneth Galbraith called "the imperatives" of technology, which he thought led inexorably to the creation of giant business enterprises.[9] If that is so, then much of the bureaucratization of the nation may be traced, first, to those overmighty economic entities, and second, to the technology that made them possible. If today the individual feels all alone and afraid, buffeted by huge impersonal bureaucracies, public and private, then the benefits of technology have a high price tag on them. To that should be added the political fact that technology works toward the consolidation of power; or as Franz Neumann put it, "The higher the state of technological development, the greater the concentration of political power."[10] The price tag is becoming far too high. Private bureaucracies have their counterparts in government, whose public bureaucracies are often surrogate for the allegedly private groups.

The economic and political costs that have been, are being, and will be paid for the good things that come from technology, are being outweighed by the social costs that accompany those benefits. In addition to those listed is the decline in social mobility. It is far more difficult today for one to bootstrap his way to wealth and affluence (it never was as easy as the myth would have it). That means that a nation of social *class*, such as this country has always been, is becoming one of *caste*—not caste in the sense of legal barriers placed upon individuals; they have been and will continue to be lowered. But caste in the sense that members of the working class will find it increasingly difficult to achieve goals of economic (and psychic) security. The barriers will be there, but they will be social—the resultant of social conditions rather than of law. The social order is becoming rigidly stratified. That means that the United

States is reverting—has already reverted—to a new type of feudalism. The movement of modern industrialized societies is away from contract as the primary basis of economic allocation toward a condition of status—the precise opposite of Sir Henry Maine's famous aphorism uttered in the mid-nineteenth century.[11] Individualism is dying and status is becoming as impor-tant—or more so—then contract.

Not that the public statements of prominent Americans, or even the law as declared by any government organ, will either in fact or in theory recognize it. A refusal to perceive, however, does not mean that what was said heretofore is erroneous. Americans have always been a contradictory people; as Profes-sor Michael Kammen says, theirs is a "contrapuntal civilization."[12] Nowhere has this been better stated than by the late Professor Carl Becker, who in 1945 listed these dualisms in American civilization:

Whether it has been a matter of clearing the forest or exterminating the redskins, orga-nising a government or exploiting it for private advantage, building railroads for the public good or rigging the market in order to milk them for private profit, establishing free schools by law or placing illegal restraints on the freedom of teaching, conferring on Negroes their God-given constitutional rights or making sure they do not vote, applauding the value of temperance or perceiving the convenience of bootlegging— whatever the immediate task may be, the short cut, the ready-made device for dealing with it, is apt to seem to us good enough so long as it gets the business done. Through-out our history ruthlessness and humane dealing, respect for law and right and disregard of them, have run side by side: in almost equal degree we have exhibited the temper of conformity and revolt, the disposition to submit voluntarily to law and custom when they serve our purposes and to ignore them when they cease to do so.[13]

Ambivalence has indeed characterized the American past. This is, or should be, obvious in law and the legal system, including the Constitution. Chapter 6 will develop the contradictions of the responses to crisis or emergency situa-tions, actual or purported. First, however, some preliminary matters must be discussed.

4

The Nature of the American Constitution and Legal System

Americans are a nation of Constitution and law worshippers. As with religion and God, they have astonishingly little knowledge about either. Neither the specifics nor the generalities of constitutional law are generally known; and even though Americans probably are the most litigious people in the world's history, little is known about how the legal system actually operates. The Constitution (note the capital C, not without significance itself) and the law are revered, but not really understood. That is both significant and amusing, significant because it gives a special character to the American experience, amusing because the fervent but erroneous belief in the power of law simply does not jibe with reality. In this brief chapter, some basic aspects about the Constitution and the legal system are set forth. These are assumptions, rather than commonly accepted ideas, for by no means would they get unanimous consent in their validity. Even after about 3000 years of Western legal history, much disagreement exists about the nature and function of law. There is no such thing as a science of law, akin to the hard or natural sciences. As with politics, much of law is an art. In any event, the reader is entitled to know the assumptions underlying the ensuing discussion.

First, however, a word about what constitutions are not. Even though the United States has a written Constitution—the oldest in the world—the words written in 1787 (plus twenty-six amendments) are related to the present-day Constitution only in metaphorical ways. Those who drafted America's fundamental law established a framework of government and a set of limitations on government. That basic framework remains only in theory. The facts of American life differ. The words are the same, to be sure, but their content has changed. That is the nature of any fundamentalist text, legal or religious, with which people ostensibly govern themselves.

So, too, with law. It has only a spurious certainty. Law should be stable, but it cannot stand still. The great antinomies of rest and motion, of change and stability, permeate it and its application. Change is indeed the law of life —and the life of the law. We may not like that, but we must accept and live with it. In a technological age, repose is not our lot. Americans must always be playing "catch-up" with the alterations in life brought by science and technology. Discretion, rather than limitation, becomes the inevitable rule for public officials. We are emphatically a government of men, not of laws.

What, then, is a constitution? Rather, what is *the* American Constitution? Some 5000 words written in Philadelphia one hot summer almost two centuries ago and twenty-six times amended? Or a mere lawyers' document? Or the vehicle of the nation's life? Or the law of the land, as enunciated by the Supreme Court in more than 450 fat volumes of judicial reports? Or a body of custom and usage that has become a patina on the original meaning? Or "the most wonderful work ever struck off at a given time," by the mind of man, as Gladstone said? Or "all sail and no anchor," as Macauley put it? Or a sacred document, divinely inspired? Or "a monstrous fraud," as Lord Acton called it?[1] And, finally, does the United States have both a written and an unwritten Constitution?

The short answer to those questions—all of them—is yes. A longer answer requires, and will receive, development throughout this volume.

To understand the Constitution is a theme that forces lawyers to become political theorists. Very few are, perhaps because the Constitution is much more than a mere lawyers' instrument. Far from the plaything (or workthing) of the legal profession only, it is a document important to all Americans (indeed, people throughout the world) as much for its mystical symbolism as for its actual content. No one has a monopoly on its meaning or interpretation, certainly not lawyers—the drudges, some very rich, but drudges nonetheless—who assert clairvoyance as to its meaning. They are successful only because others often defer to them, particularly when they wear the black robes of judicial office—and thus exemplify a cult of the robe. Deference to judges, however, is more apparent than real; the judges do not have the power that many attribute to them. Judges, the priests of a secular society, have in the overall settlement of American public policies little more actual power than do members of the ministry.

Certain basic principles about American constitutionalism should be understood before the concept of democratic dictatorship can be discussed in detail. These principles are briefly discussed here in order to provide a framework for thinking about the Constitution of the United States of America. They include the following:

1. A difference usually exists between what the Constitution seems to command, and the ways that decisions actually are made in the political order. To understand the true operations of the constitutional order requires, therefore, knowledge about both the formal document (what is said in the fundamental law and its interpretations by the Supreme Court) and the living Constitution (the Constitution in action). Of the two constitutions, the latter is by far the more important. To understand it requires asking and answering these questions: *Who* makes *what* decisions, *how*, and with what *effects*? Focus, then, must be concentrated upon the decisions of basic significance to the American people—in the way they act and order their affairs. In other words, the constitutional order is not only the formal structure of government. That is only the appearance; the reality often differs. To understand the Constitution therefore involves both scrutiny of those who are clothed with formal authority to make decisions—that is, governmental officers at all levels—and those who have effective control over what those officers do, plus (this is important) officers of some of the private groups of the nation.

The "living" constitution about which Walter Bagehot (and others)[2] have spoken, has at least two dimensions. First is the manner in which the terms of the formal document have evolved since 1787, not through amendment but through judicial interpretation. The Supreme Court each year updates at least part of the fundamental law; but it, despite some beliefs to the contrary, is not the only branch of government with power to make decisions of constitutional dimension. Second, the living constitution encompasses the fact, little recognized in formal theory, that persons other than government officials (judges, presidents, the Congress) can, and do, make decisions that so significantly affect the lives of Americans (and others) that they also must be called constitutional. These are officers of the important social groups within the nation—corporations, unions, churches, farmers' organizations, universities, veterans' legions, and foundations. Officers of public and private government routinely interact; the two governments are only ostensibly separate.[3]

Who under the formal Constitution is authorized to make decisions of constitutional dimension? Since at least 1803,[4] lawyers are accustomed to say that it is the province and function of the judicial department to say what the law is. In part, that is correct: The Supreme Court has indeed had the major formal role in interpreting the Constitution, even though it was not expressly granted that power (the Justices reached out and grabbed it). The Justices act as a continuing constitutional convention, updating the fundamental law to meet the exigencies of succeeding generations of Americans. That means that the Court routinely makes law—legislates—despite the myth to the contrary, as Justice Byron White candidly admitted in 1966:

That the Court's holding today [in the case of *Miranda* v. *Arizona*] is neither compelled or even strongly suggested by the language of the Fifth Amendment, is at odds with

American and legal history, and involves a departure from a long line of precedent does not prove that the Court is wrong or unwise in its present reinterpretation of the Fifth Amendment. It does, however, underscore the obvious—that the Court has not discovered or found the law in making today's decision, nor has it derived it from some irrefutable sources; *what it has done is to make new law and new public policy in much the same way that it has in the course of interpreting other great clauses of the Constitution. That is what the Court historically has done. Indeed, it is what it must do and will continue to do until and unless there is some fundamental change in the constitutional distribution of government powers.*[5] (Emphasis added.)

That, as White says, is obvious, although there is a large body of opinion that asserts that judicial lawmaking is not constitutionally legitimate. It is far too late in our history to debate the point: judges do indeed make law— always have and always will. The willfully blind deny its legitimacy in the American system, asserting that courts are not "democratic" bodies. That position, however, usually hides a dislike of what courts do—the law they make—not that they are lawmaking. The one continually valid principle of evaluating what courts do is the adage, "It all depends upon whose ox is gored." If one likes results, he is content with judicial lawmaking—and vice versa.

Left unanswered by Justice White (and others) are the questions of how much law, when, in what circumstances, and to what extent does judicial lawmaking prevail over that of other officers of government. These questions are merely posed here, but one point requires emphasis at this time. Constitutional interpretation is *not* a judicial monopoly. Despite assertions by Chief Justices John Marshall (in 1803) and Warren Burger (in 1974) that it is "emphatically the province and duty of the judicial department to say what the law is,"[6] that is only partly accurate. It is also the province and indeed the duty of other branches of government to make constitutional law.[7]

That much is slowly being recognized by constitutional scholars, although their principal emphasis is still upon what courts—mainly the Supreme Court —say and do. Less recognized—in fact, little mentioned in the literature—is the capacity of nonpublic groups (the officers thereof) to make decisions of such basic importance to all Americans that they should be called constitutional in scope. We will discuss each briefly there, leaving the full implications for later exposition.

As for other branches of government, it should be obvious, but is not, that both Congress and the President routinely make constitutional-like decisions. For Congress, such statutes as the Sherman Antitrust Act of 1890, the Employment Act of 1946, the War Powers Resolution of 1973, and the Budget and Impoundment Control Act of 1974, are a quartet of illustrative enactments that fundamentally affect the structure and nature of governmental powers.[8] So too, with the President, whose express powers are noteworthy for their delphic nature. By long-established custom and usage, the chief executive has gathered in that office an independent power to make decisions that are also constitutional in nature.[9] At times, but not always, the courts have validated what Congress and the President have done; and thus given the formal imprimatur of constitutionality on those actions. Most congressional and presidential actions are never challenged on constitutional grounds. Those nonjudicial decisions make up a body of living constitutional law—the law in operation as compared to that in the lawbooks.

American constitutionalism (and democratic dictatorship) cannot be understood without knowing that the 1787 Constitution is continually being updated, not only by the judges but also by other officers of public government. When one comes to the actions of nongovernmental figures, the point becomes more subtle. But it is still evident. Suffice it now to note that the rise, during the past 100 years, of pluralistic social groups within the nation has so altered the milieu in which government operates that a new dimension of private governments must now be recognized.[10] The State in America encompasses both public and private governance. Business corporations are the most obvious examples, but there are others. Decisions by corporate officials so change the environment in which all individuals and institutions act that they, too, basically alter the structure and nature of governmental powers. A corporate decision to go multinational is a prime example. Business multinationalism is slowly but surely changing the nature of American sovereignty. Just as corporations in the nineteenth century went national and thereby altered American federalism, helping to make the states mere administrative districts for centrally established policies, so the twentieth century movement toward larger than national business units is altering the nation-state itself. That is unquestionably a constitutional change of the first magnitude. Corporate decisions are usually made in conjunction with public government. The point is that government cannot be understood today without recognition of the dimension of private governments operating in fact, but not in theory, in close harmony with public government.

To sum up: The Constitution expressly provides for change only by amendment, but is routinely updated by the Supreme Court and by the political officers of government who work cheek-by-jowl with the leaders of the dominant social groups of the nation. The American Constitution, in Woodrow Wilson's terminology, is indeed "Darwinian in structure and practice."[11] Who, then, has the final say in constitutional matters? The answer is simple—and complex. Ultimate power is often asserted by the Supreme Court; as Justice Robert H. Jackson put it in 1953: "We are not final because we are infallible, but we are infallible only because we are final." That, however, is at best a mere half-truth. In many questions of great constitutional concern, the Court not only is not final, it has nothing whatsoever to say about them. We may not like that; we may wish for greater certainty—for a "government of laws, not of men"—but we are not at all likely to get it. "Government by judiciary," perceived by some who should know better,[12] is simply not possible in an industrialized, technologically dominated superpower.

2. The Constitution of the United States is both written and unwritten. It is always in a state of becoming, open-ended and developing. Some provisions, to be sure, are fixed and beyond change, save by amendment. The express terms for congressional and presidential office is an obvious example. The important features of the Constitution are not those few solidified aspects, but the great generalities that gather different meanings through time. The most significant characteristics of the fundamental law are its silences (as in presidential power) and the delphic nature of its litigable provisions. Those features enable succeeding generations of Americans to write their own constitution—which, speaking generally, they have done since 1787. More bluntly, the spurious nature of the written Constitution allows a variety of political actions to be taken to meet unforeseen exigencies in the national experience. Even when the terms seem to be certain, as in the First Amendment ("Congress shall make no law. . . ."), the seemingly absolute language has been diluted by interpretation to make express prohibitions merely relative (to circumstance) statements. That means that the zeitgeist, not "the law," rules. Constitutional law is seldom, if ever, out of phase with the dominant power configurations in the nation.[13] (The zeitgeist, in brief, is "the spirit of the times.")

3. Tension has always existed between a written Constitution with seemingly immutable terms and the idea of majority rule (of popular sovereignty). The Constitution in original concept was distinctly not a democratic instrument. The government it established was a republic, not a representative democracy. As drafted in 1787, the fundamental law was not a means of permitting the people to rule. The people were not trusted. (They still are not.) We have strayed from the original conception; the spread of the franchise means, in theory at least, that government has become representative. The facts are different. The people as such are not represented; interest groups are.[14]

4. The original Constitution recognized only two entities: government and the individual (the natural person) which at the beginning was the basic social unit. No longer is that true. The fundamental, the important social unit in America is the group. The group (the corporation) is productive in the economic system; and politics is best understood as the interplay of social groups. That means that the Constitution has been altered by massive

changes within the body politic. Representation, for example, is of groups, not of individuals.

5. The Constitution, despite much intellectual history to the contrary, is a grant of power. "What the founders were afraid of in practice," Hannah Arendt once pointed out, "was not power but impotence."[15] Further: "Clearly, the true objective of the American Constitution was not to limit power but to create more power, actually to establish and duly constitute an entirely new power center."[16] So it is: the Constitution was drafted to spin off a separate executive from Congress. Government under the Articles of Confederation, dominated by a unicameral Congress, was inadequate. Popular wisdom holds that the powers of the national government were separated to prevent despotism; but that at best is a half-truth (or less).[17] Powers were also separated to have an efficient executive. Since 1787 the cryptic language of Article II of the Constitution (dealing with the presidency) has garnered meaning from experience, so that that branch is by far the most important of the three. That does not mean that the executive is efficient; merely that it is dominant.

There is a larger meaning: The Constitution is—at least, has been—sufficient to any need the American people might face. Despite seeming contradiction, its terms have been no barrier to taking actions considered necessary by the appropriate officers of government. At times, particularly during declared wars, this has meant a "democratical despotism." Actions taken, and approved, during such times of emergency have a way of being used as precedents for similar actions at later periods when no such emergency is perceivable. I do not suggest that constitutional changes are not desirable. Indeed they are.

6. Finally, for Americans the Constitution has definite theological overtones; it is a sacred document, viewed as such by hordes of tourists who pour each year through the National Archives to view the ancient document. An artifact from a bygone age, the parchment upon which the few thousand words are inscribed has a special, albeit inarticulate, meaning for Americans. Some consider it a divinely inspired instrument. Church and State are separated by the Constitution, but State and religion are not. A nation imbued with fervent religiosity, but not true religion, is home to many strange cults. One such, not so labeled, is the cult of the Constitution.

Those who drafted it hammered out its terms on the hard anvil of compromise. Since 1787, they have been endowed with superhuman characteristics. They are often considered to have been larger than life, blessed with a special wisdom that supposedly rings down through the ages and guides governmental conduct today as well as yesteryear—and presumably tomorrow also.

Even though often repeated by lawyers and judges who should know better, these beliefs are naive to the point of being absurd. Thomas Jefferson knew that in 1820. He said:

Some men look at constitutions with sanctimonious reverence and deem them like the ark of the covenant, too sacred to be touched. They ascribe to the men of the preceding age a wisdom more than human, and suppose what they did to be beyond amendment. I know this age well; I belonged to it, and labored with it. It deserved well of its country. It was very like the present, but without the experience of the present; and forty years of experience in government is worth a century of book-reading; and this they would say themselves, were they to rise from the dead.[18]

Why is Jefferson not followed? Reverence for the Constitution and, at times, the Supreme Court is both amusing and necessary. It is amusing because it becomes particularly awkward when the shades of those who wrote the Document are invoked to justify or rationalize present-day constitutional decisions. Constitutional antiquarians delight in poring over the words of men long dead, seeking to find in them a vade mecum, a reference book containing solutions to the pressing problems of the day. That this cannot be done should be obvious to all except the antiquarians—and to those who dislike present-day constitutional decisions because they allegedly were not in the minds of the men of 1787 (or those who drafted the amendments). Professor Michael Kammen has made the point well: There is, he says, "an awkward anomaly in American thought. Although the founders were themselves engaged in a continuous quest for models of legitimacy appropriate to their times and needs, subsequent Americans have sought to validate their own aspirations by invoking the innovations and standards of our hallowed pantheon as unchanging verities. This nostalgic vision of the Golden Age actually conjures up an era when values were unclearly defined, when instability often seemed beyond control, when public rancor and private vituperation were rampant, and institutions frail and unformed."[19]

The antiquarians are latter-day scholastics who search the past for light to throw on the present and the future. They are quite wrong, not realizing that, although the past of course is prologue, the present and the future are not mere extensions of the past. As noted before, Americans live in a social milieu not before known in human history; the received wisdom of the past is at best a flickering light that illumines a bit, but not much. Much more is needed. Hence the wryly amusing aspect of looking to men long dead to solve the pressing problems of the day. If the Founding Fathers intended anything, it was for each generation of Americans to write its own Constitution—precisely what has happened.

That desire to look back—to fly backwards to see where we have been, as the saying goes—may, however, be necessary. Americans and others are not the rational beings they suppose themselves to be. Cold reason alone does not suffice. Hence the religiosity. And hence the human need, as Dostoyevsky wrote in his account of the Legend of the Grand Inquisitor, for miracle, mystery, and authority.[20] The Constitution and its most obvious interpreters, the Supreme Court, fulfill that requirement for Americans. The Founding Fathers—the principal saints in America's Valhalla—are believed to have wrought a miracle (that such a belief is irrational is irrelevant). Mysterious figures from an age not far away as time is computed, but eons ago with respect to the alterations in society, those Founders are vested with an authority, a wisdom they do not deserve. But they help to fulfill deep-felt, subconscious psychological needs. A nation without a personified monarch has little else to employ to stave off fears of the dark unknown and even darker future. Constitutionalism is a secular religion of Americans.

The reverence accorded the Constitution and the Founding Fathers serves another sociological function. In a time of the most rapid social change in human history, there is little other than hedonism for people to grasp save spurious certainties of the past (the myth of the Golden Age). To repeat a previous quote:

No one—not even the most brilliant scientist alive today—really knows where science is taking us. We are aboard a train which is gathering speed racing down a track on which there are an unknown number of switches leading to unknown destinations. No single scientist is in the engine cab and there may be demons at the switch. Most of society is in the caboose looking backward.[21]

So stated physicist Ralph Lapp, who correctly perceived how mankind was acting. What he did not say was that people both had no choice in "looking backward" and did so because of a need to grasp a symbol of certainty in an uncertain world. That that symbol cannot fulfill its function is beside the point. And also cosmically comical.

No doubt other characteristics of constitutions could be discussed. Those listed, however, suffice to show the essentials of the nature and function of American fundamental law. Most important is the idea of the living Constitution. An understanding of it is indispensable. What has been said is not the usual idea of American constitutionalism. A gap has always existed between pretense and reality in our constitutional order.

So, too, with the law: Under the American myth, we are governed by laws, not men. Those who rule are limited, according to this view, by standards or rules external to their subjective beliefs—in other words, by law. Law is considered to be "there," an entity—a body of rules—separate and apart from politics and economics. That emphatically is not true. The law, as Morris R. Cohen said, "is not a homeless, wandering ghost. It is a phase of human life located in time and space."[22] Law is simply not "there"; it is inextricably intertwined with the State. It is not a discrete entity subject to analysis as such, although again, the orthodoxy runs to the contrary.

If that is what law is not, what is it in fact? A few statements may be made in outline form.

1. Law is what authoritative decision-makers actually do, not necessarily what they say they do and surely not necessarily what they are supposed to do. The gap between the law in books and the law in action is, and has always been, large. In government, whether public or private, discretion is the norm. That is especially so for those at the highest rungs of the public and private bureaucracies; and it is of course true for Congress and the courts. We may wish that it be otherwise, but we will not get it.

2. Law, furthermore, is instrumental.[23] Through its use, people both public and private seek to manage a segment of the future. Law, thus, is always looking forward. True it is that people and their legal advisors look to the past —to precedent—for guidance; but that guidance is not controlling. In an age of rapid change, legal principles tend to run in pairs of opposites. A principle of legal uncertainty operates in any human dispute that gets to court. Law does have its certainties, but they are far less than many assume. This, as an aside, may be the reason for the numbers of lawyers in the United States and for the American propensity to go to court—the very fact of social uncertainty often makes for legal uncertainty. Certainty exists only in matters that never get to court, or any other official body, for settlement. Even then, there is often a gap between what the law seems to say and what occurs, as witness the operation of any city government in the United States.

Judges, who are invariably taken from the Establishment,[24] have the function of using law and the legal system to buttress the stability of the system of government in which they operate, and of protecting that system from all except minor and relatively insignificant efforts to change it. Other decision-makers are more important than judges, particularly the bureaucracy. Much of law today is "public" law—what lawyers call administrative law. Surely that will not change in the future. Decisions of bureaucrats, high and low, outweigh by far those of judges, both quantitatively and qualitatively. We live in the "bureaucratic State." That means that law has changed from interdiction —a set of "thou shalt nots"—to instrumentalism, a system in which it is employed by policymakers to achieve desired ends. Put another way, it is the consequences, the results of given "legal" decisions that are important. Who is affected and how? Law, contrary to Aristotle and others, is not "reason unaffected by desire." It is both reason and desire—mainly the latter. Lawyers are forever playing "catch-up" with the enormous societal changes wrought by science and technology.

3. Law is closely entwined with the State; it is not transcendent, above and superior to manmade rules. Those who believe in a transcendent legal order ultimately base their case upon a belief in "natural" law, which in turn rests upon theological (mainly Roman Catholic, in the Western world) precepts. Natural law, however, attains significance only when it is recognized as "positive" law by those who are authorized to speak for the State. Those officers speak at times in terms of natural law or natural justice, but only at times and when convenient, and only as a means of justifying decisions. The positive law of the State always prevails whenever conflicts arise. Again, we may not like that; we may prefer a different legal system but we do not have it—and, what is more, we are not likely to get it. However unpleasant the thought may be, the actions of any government, whether those called democratic or those called totalitarian, are law. It is idle, even mischievous, to assert, for example, that some of the actions taken by Nazis in Germany fell outside the German legal order; they did not, even though quite obviously, as in the Holocaust, they were inhuman beyond measure. Nazi decrees *were* law; and the Nuremburg trials were merely a "civilized" form of victor's justice.

4. Law, finally and to sum up, is an instrument of politics, not separate from the political order. As Professor J. A. G. Griffith has shown, the function of the judiciary is to further the interest of the Establishment—those who wield actual power in society.[25] Those who control the State control, and benefit from, the legal system.

Law creation is a monopoly of the State. Law does not exist separate and apart from the State system. To be law, furthermore, a given precept must be either enforced, or at least be theoretically enforceable. No matter how desirable a given principle may be, unless and until it receives the sanction of the State—its enforceability—it should not be called law. Those who speak of natural law as a body of elementary principles of justice applicable to humans everywhere state an ideal, not the actuality. This may be seen in the United States, a nation where moral behavior is equated with rule (law) following.

Law, however, including constitutional law, has at best a specious morality. Machiavelli spoke of two moralities—the Judeo-Christian and the pagan— and Bagehot of two constitutions, the formal and the living. Law-following is not necessarily "moral." All law reflects power configurations within the nation. It deserves respect, for without it there would be anarchy, but that respect must be tempered by a determination of whether desirable ends are reached. The gap between law as it is and the ideal has always been—and doubtless will always be—large, possibly unbridgable. Law, in sum, is power.[26] To understand that is a necessary first step to an understanding of democratic dictatorship. Another way of saying it is to state that law is a reflection of the times in which it operates. That calls for an exposition of the use of law and legal institutions in American history. That theme will be developed in the context of democratic dictatorship. First, however, some brief discussion of "reason of State" and of the nature of the modern State.

5

"Reason of State" and the Modern State

A republic, we have been told by Machiavelli, must make provision for emergency action; it must be able to govern as does a prince.[1] Though written more than four centuries ago, it is an accurate perception for the United States. The United States Constitution does not have an express provision for emergency action, similar, say, to Article 16 of the present French constitution. But the American fundamental law has always been sufficient to emerging needs. Whether that adaptation came "without loss of essential form," as President Franklin Roosevelt maintained in 1933,[2] is by no means certain. Only the formal Constitution remained the same; the living document was altered then—as it had been altered both previously and since then. One should never confuse formal structures and relationships of the 1787 Constitution with the informal ways that governmental affairs are conducted.

The spare and sparse generalities of the Constitution permit extraordinary needs to be met—but only at a high price: the growing obsolescence of the original conceptions. The United States has survived not because of the Constitution but in spite of it. Emergencies have been met only because of a well-nigh infinite malleability of ambiguous constitutional terms. Crisis government has in fact created new forms, something apparently not foreseen in the Convention of 1787, and not acknowledged by the Supreme Court in ruling on emergency actions. Those who wrote the Federalist Papers argued that the Constitution is equal to any emergency, but they, too, did not consider how the living Constitution can change because of emergencies. Said Justice David Davis for the Supreme Court in Ex Parte Milligan (1866):

The Constitution of the United States is a law for rulers and people, equally in war and in peace, and covers with the shield of its protection all classes of men, at all times, and under all circumstances. No doctrine involving more pernicious consequences was even invented by the wit of men than that any of its provisions can be suspended during any of the great exigencies of government. Such a doctrine leads directly to anarchy or despotism but the theory on which it is based is false; for the government, within the Constitution, has all the powers granted to it which are necessary to preserve its existence.[3]

That is arrant hypocrisy, but it was echoed by Chief Justice Charles Evans Hughes in *Home Building and Loan Ass'n* v. *Blaisdell* (1934) in another prime example of judicial casuistry:

Emergency does not create power. Emergency does not increase granted power or remove or diminish the restrictions imposed upon power granted or reserved. The Constitution was adopted in a period of grave emergency. Its grants of power to the federal government . . . were determined in the light of emergency and they are not altered by emergency.[4]

Rather than create power, said Hughes, emergencies only provide the conditions for the exercise of already existing powers.

This, then, poses the questions starkly: What is an emergency? How may one be identified? What types of powers come into effect? Who is empowered to declare a valid emergency? No ready answers exist. One must resort to history to find guidelines for suggesting answers, or at least ways of thinking about the several questions. In briefest terms, this can be said: An emergency in American constitutional law is that set of conditions perceived by political officers, frequently the executive acting alone but often in concert, actual or tacit, with the Congress, to require actions which under basic constitutional theory are extraordinary, even extraconstitutional. No objective criteria exist to identify the existence of an emergency. To paraphrase Supreme Court Justice Potter Stewart (in another context), the political officers know one when they see one,[5] even though it is impossible to give a single all-encompassing definition save on a level of abstraction that inhibits communication. But the political perception of an emergency, requiring extraordinary action, does not necessarily mean that the perception was correct—a question that Machiavelli, oddly, never confronted.

Government in the United States has always been as powerful as circumstances necessitated, as perceived by the relevant political officers, whether those circumstances were as extreme as secession (the Civil War), massive external threat (World Wars I and II), and economic disaster (the Great Depression of the 1930s); or whether they were relatively minor matters, such as civil disorder (labor strikes in basic industries), natural disasters (hurricanes and earthquakes and contagious disease), or anti-American actions in other (smaller and weaker) nations. Reason of State (raison d'état) is a basic but unacknowledged principle of American constitutional law.[6] Neither Supreme Court Justices nor political officers have called it that in so many words, the capacity of the human mind to delude itself being almost infinitely capable of cloaking harsh reality in more acceptable terminology. Under this view, if one does not admit something exists, then it does not: the delusion thus becomes real. (Even the classical liberal State—often called the laissez-faire or "nightwatchman" State—was always able to meet whatever emergencies were perceived by political leaders, which in the United States and elsewhere, has meant and increasingly means the executive. The consequence, in constitutional terms, is that both of the two American constitutions are relative to specific social circumstances.)

Surmounting emergencies requires either express or inherent capacity for quick and decisive action. That basic Machiavellian principle has never been reconciled in American constitutional theory with the fundamental values of a written constitution—*as it was written*: to establish a government of delegated, limited powers (Rather than expressly recognizing that there are times when it is necessary to do admittedly evil things for the preservation and welfare of the political community,[7] theorists, including the ultimate faculty of American political theory, the Justices of the Supreme Court of the United States, have pretended that doing evil is really doing good—and thus congruent with historical, basic constitutional values.) There has been a tacit refusal to acknowledge a radical dualism in constitutional law; the struggle has been to find a single truth, a seamless web of mutually consistent politico-legal principles that are at once compatible with the original intentions of those who wrote the Constitution and adaptable for the various crises of human affairs.

In a Darwinian world of process and open-ended change, many have searched for Newtonian principles of a static and unchanging constitutional universe. The effort to find a single truth in official behavior means avoiding reality by clothing it in familiar and acceptable garb. Machiavelli's theory, accordingly, was indeed "a dagger plunged into the flesh of the body politic of Western humanity, causing it to cry out and struggle with itself."[8] That struggle still continues. If for "Western humanity" one reads "American democracy," then the question comes into focus: Machiavelli's theory was, and is, a frontal attack on orthodox American constitutional theory. Fully exposed and accepted, it makes the notion of limited government—of a "government of laws and not of men"—a wistful dream, an ideal never realized, an ideal that today and in the future cannot and will not be realized.

Far from vanishing, the historical question of how to take emergency action under a government purportedly limited by law has been exacerbated in recent years. Today the basic question has become: What happens to constitutionalism when emergency government becomes the norm? Under that condition, a republic begins to act routinely by decree; and the purported rule of law outwardly becomes the rule of men. Government by unlimited discretion, if not by diktat, becomes the usual—surely in foreign affairs but also in domestic matters.

Since World War II there have been many arguments over the impact of national security and defense measures upon individual liberties and freedom. Nothing is basically new in these arguments, something that the disputants themselves seem never to understand. They antedate even the organized nation-state known to the ancients; they were posed again in acute and never equaled form by Machiavelli. Since he wrote in the sixteenth century (about city-states mainly, including of course Rome as seen through the eyes of Titius Livy), they have troubled the minds of some of the world's ablest thinkers, who have tried to reconcile conflicting principles of political action in the constitutionalism of nation-states. This has been particularly difficult in those nations that both call themselves democratic and, under popular concepts of democracy, are considered to be such. It is, however, "always a misleading piece of propaganda," says Professor Bernard Crick, "to call governments 'democratic.' It confuses doctrine with theory: we may want the democratic element in government to grow greater, but it is still only an element while it is government at all."[9] Quite right: For purposes of descriptive or explanatory theory, it is better to speak of a "republic" than of a "democracy," of the "republican" concept rather than the "democratic." The word "democracy" has been so perverted by totalitarian nations and is subject to so many varying interpretations, that it is better not to employ it at all.

In the early 1950s, the antics and actions of Senator Joseph McCarthy posed basically the same problems as those which arose three hundred years earlier over the recommendations of Machiavelli, advanced long before the modern system of constitutional government had been developed. Yet McCarthy was only the most obvious exemplar of State action purportedly designed to preserve, at whatever cost, the entity itself. His flamboyance, ultimately self-destructive, cloaked a wider and deeper reality. The thread that connects Machiavelli with McCarthy and today's advocates of the "national security State" runs consistently throughout the intervening centuries—from the decline of feudalism through the rise of absolute monarchy and constitutional monarchy down to the modern constitutional republic. The name for this thread is raison d'état, or reason of State.

Reason of State derives from a paradox that lies at the core of the nation-state system of human organization. However it arose, there can be little question that the nation-state exists to protect, defend, and further the interests of its members (the "citizenry"). In theory, and in its justification by

Machiavelli, it is the ultimate shield, support, and refuge of all its citizens; but
—and this is crucial—it must be preserved even at the expense of the interests
of any one citizen or any small group of citizens. The State must be able to
exercise whatever powers are considered necessary to insure its own safety
and survival and, if thought necessary, its expansion.

Reason of State, or as it is often put, the interests of "society," thus become
paramount—the overriding criterion of public policy. In foreign relations the
State not only may but *must* use any stratagem, employ any mendacity, or
resort to whatever degree of violence is required for its survival *and* the
success of desired policies. In domestic matters it can resort to any type of
oppression, repression, lawlessness, or individual injustice thought necessary
to avert its own destruction or to suppress undue internal disorder.

While in theory it embodies the interests of all, in fact it cannot, because
central to the paradox is that some citizens benefit at the expense of others.
By definition, some must suffer—whether they are citizens of the nation-state
or people elsewhere (or both). The safety of most, therefore, depends upon
the safety of the State, and the interests of the whole as a collective entity—
as a "group-person"[10]—are put before the interests of any recalcitrant member or small group. The State may take a citizen's life—inflict the ultimate
sanction (by conscripting him into battle) if that is considered necessary for the
preservation and protection of the lives of other citizens, or the furtherance of
other interests of the State. It may treat some of its own citizens with cruelty
and injustice, if that presumably will help preserve the type of society which it
maintains for the remainder.

But how can a just society—a society predicated on the great and enduring
concept of "equal justice under law" that is carved in the facade of the
Supreme Court's building in Washington, D.C.—be preserved by committing
injustice? That question poses the paradox at the core of the political order
called the nation-state, particularly that called the United States of America. It
presents the challenge of either recognizing two sets of political moralities, or
of reconciling the conflicts inherent in the paradox by choosing one of the
moralities. There can be no doubt which prevailed in the past and which will
in the future; that, as will be seen, is the pagan, the Machiavellian, morality.

Such an outline of the powers inherent in the State—in the national
government of the United States of America—may appear rather like a description of Soviet or Chinese Communist doctrine, or a disquisition on junta
rule in Chile. Yet long before Stalin or Mao, or even Lenin and Marx, or
before the Greek colonels or the Chilean junta, serious political theorists were
deducing these powers from the very nature of the State organization itself
(the seminal writer, of course, is Niccolo Machiavelli). Furthermore, it is not
easy to comprehend how such powers can in logic be denied to the State. No
one has yet developed a convincing rebuttal to reason of State, save through

ceding State sovereignty in some higher order—either that of the moral law to which past philosophers appealed or that of a world government.(Until either a world government or a world rule of morality—conventional morality, not expedient morality—has been established, the paradox must be faced that a State will be forced at times to bad and unjust means in the interests of a greater value: a good and just society of which it is the guardian. Hence the fact of two constitutions of the United States.)(And it is worth serious mention that even the establishment of a world government would not eliminate reason of State; it would merely move it to a larger frame of reference.)

Communist or fascist governments are by no means alone in their repeated justification of bad means by what they maintain is the nobility of their goals. Machiavelli believed that in the realm of politics, a good end justifies what is morally wrong; in his own words: it is "a sound maxim that, when an action is reprehensible, the result may excuse it, and, when the result is good, always excuses it."[11] The same type of rationalization has been proffered repeatedly throughout history, including that of the United States. Those who drafted the American Constitution were probably cognizant of the paradox inherent in reason of State and a limited government. They were, first of all, keenly aware of the fact that the first duty of a government is to defend itself from external enemies. But they did nothing about it.

The framers wrote a Constitution that does not mention emergencies or reason of State. So they fudged the problem by ignoring it. Only by inference can it be said that the framers perceived a place for inherent powers. Prominent in the Preamble to the Constitution are the goals of insuring "domestic tranquility" and of providing "for the common defense." In the second place, the founders were of course aware of the history of the seventeenth and eighteenth centuries, and thus of the cruelties and oppressions employable by any government in its own defense. In large part, the Bill of Rights—the first ten amendments to the Constitution—may be considered to be a conscious attempt to resolve the dilemma over reason of State. The new government was to have all the powers necessary to defend itself, both against external aggression and internal sedition. At the same time, the clear effort was to limit the exercise of reason of State within bounds compatible with establishing justice and securing " the blessings of liberty to ourselves and our posterity." For whatever reason, however, the framers failed to face frontally the question of reason of State.

To insure the defense of the nation, Congress was empowered to declare war, to raise and maintain a standing army and navy; and the federal government was responsible for guaranteeing a "republican form of government" in the several states. To secure the blessings of liberty, on the other hand, amendments were added to the Constitution (which itself had limitations on government in its original form) in an effort to prevent the new government from using, for reasons of State, many of the methods which monarchies in

Europe had employed. Thus, in the original Constitution, may be found a narrow definition of treason and a careful limitation on suspension of the writ of habeas corpus and in the amendments a guarantee of freedom of expression (speech, press, assembly, and petitioning the government for redress of grievances—all in the First Amendment), a guarantee of right of the people to keep and bear arms (Second Amendment), a prohibition against quartering of troops in private houses in times of peace (Third Amendment), a prohibition against unreasonable searches and seizures by the police (Fourth Amendment), a guarantee of the privilege against self-incrimination (Fifth Amendment), and a guarantee against taking property "without due process of law" (Fifth Amendment). Each of these provisions was a limitation on oppressive practices which governments of the time were accustomed to employ, pleading reason of State, in their own defense against external enemies or internal subversion. (It is worth noting that the framers of the Constitution saw fit to limit the national government only; the states, speaking generally, were free from constitutional restraint in areas of civil liberties.) What was left for inference, and thus the subject of many subsequent arguments, was reason of State itself. (That gap has been filled by the decisions that are part of the living Constitution.) When, then, could extraordinary—emergency—action be taken?

The men who wrote the Constitution were not naive; they knew history and they knew the dark side of man. That the aims of providing for the common defense and the preservation of liberty might be contradictory was fully recognized. Alexander Hamilton provides illustration: In *The Federalist* he pointed out that "even the ardent love of liberty will after a time give way to the dictates" of "safety from external danger." The fear of war would "compel nations the most attached to liberty" to resort to institutions and techniques "which have a tendency to destroy their civil and political rights. To be more safe, they at length become willing to run the risk of being less free."[12] That Hamilton was accurate was demonstrated less than ten years after the Constitution was promulgated, when fears aroused by the French Revolution led to the enactment of the Sedition Act of 1798—certainly one of the most blatant violations of the First Amendment's guarantee of free speech that ever became law. (That the statute was never invalidated—or even ruled upon—by the Supreme Court is impressive testimony of the impotence of the judiciary when reasons of State are at issue.) Since 1798, every great national crisis, and many minor crises, have produced a clash between "reasons of freedom" and "reasons of State," between the claims of liberty and the claims of national security. In addition, absent assertions of national security, emergency government may be seen in economic matters and other areas not considered by Niccolo Machiavelli.

Before beginning a detailed analysis of how reason of State has been applied in American history, attention should be accorded an allied but important matter: the nature of the State in a modern industrialized nation such as the United States of America.

Much is heard these days about "statism" or the State. Government has become a dirty word for many (but not for all). The business press, in particular, regularly castigates the State as the enemy. That is hardly true, but it helps businessmen to speak that way. Indeed, such language serves an indispensable purpose: businessmen can verbally pummel an allegedly hostile and omnipotent government while simultaneously receiving benefits from it. Those benefits come from both protection and subsidy, and, of perhaps more importance, a generally favorable legal system. The corporate executive is able to enjoy the best of two worlds—that of his peers in the boardrooms of the nation and that of those who allegedly regulate him.

What, then, is *the* State? The question is more easily asked than answered. Those who glibly use the terms statism, or the State, seldom take the time to define them. The suggestion here is that the United States is a form of "corporatism—a Corporate State."[13] The term means that public and "private" governments are joined but still apart: both public government and the private governments of the giant corporations (and other groups) retain their identities, but nonetheless are closely connected. By no means is it clear which is the dominant member of the duo, although surely it is accurate to observe with Gianfranco Poggi, that a contradiction is apparent:[14] the State asserts that it is the source of all power relations, but it acts, through the legal system, to guarantee power relations that originate elsewhere (usually in the business community) and that are controlled "privately"—through private control over capital.[15] The State is all-powerful only if seen as a form of corporatism.

The State is an abstraction, to be distinguished from both society and government. Government is the mechanism of the State, the means by which it acts; and society is what is governed, in appearance a collectivity of disparate individuals, but in reality a congeries of interacting groups. Political officers and others seldom are careful when they use the terms. Supreme Court Justices are particularly sloppy in that regard. Often the words are used emotively, in language designed to achieve or to influence a decision—as in the statement that "society" requires such-and-such. An example is a June 1978 decision of the United States Court of Appeals in the District of Columbia. In the course of holding that the National Security Agency cannot be required to disclose in a lawsuit whether it had intercepted overseas communications of specific individuals and groups, Judge Roger Robb called the "state secrets privilege" absolute, adding that "a ranking of the various privileges recognized in our courts would be a delicate undertaking at best, but it is quite clear that the privilege to protect state secrets must head the list."[16] Just why that is so, Robb did not say; nor did he define a "state secret." But that is the way of judges. Judge Robb accepted the assertions of the executive without question. (That means that in such cases—and in many others—the judiciary should be considered an arm of the executive; judges do not readily substitute their views for those of the executive. They are part of the apparatus of the State, despite much loose talk about an "independent" judiciary. Judges are independent, but also part of government.)[17]

In a famous passage, John Maynard Keynes asserted that practical men of affairs are in fact ruled by ideas of long-dead economists and political philosophers.[18] That interesting sentiment is hardly true. Keynes exaggerated "the gradual encroachment of ideas." Burly sinners rule the world—often, to be sure, sinners in buttoned-down shirts and well-pressed suits—and shape the ideas of those defunct theoreticians about whom Keynes wrote. Ideas are created from events, as well as from, probably more than, thoughts of learned philosophers. Those events shape and influence behavior, including what philosophers believe and write. The hard logic of events is more important than Keynes's men of ideas. There may be, to use the cliché, nothing quite so powerful as an idea "whose time has come"; but it should always be remembered that there is nothing quite so impotent as an idea whose time has not come. Most ideas, furthermore, fall on barren soil. Justice Oliver Wendell Holmes, borrowing from John Stuart Mill, once maintained that "the ultimate good desired [under the Constitution] is better reached by free trade in ideas —that the best test of truth is the power of thought to get itself accepted in the competition of the market."[19] Few ideas, however, get accepted; it is the man of action, not the man of ideas, who usually prevails. Later, men of thought come along and tell him what he has done and why, when all along he probably thought only of immediate, tangible goals. Men of action are pragmatists, not ideologists; and while the trouble with pragmatism is that it does not work in the long run and at times in the short run (as we are now perceiving), it nonetheless is America's poor substitute for systematic thinking. Pragmatism, in other words, fails by its own test—it does not work because it does not provide a framework for thinking about human problems. It could work only in a nation of vast wealth and unlimited resources, a situation that is no longer true.

To define the State requires that attention be paid not only to political philosophers, and to the Constitution, but to what occurs in fact in the American political economy. The State is not a thing. It has no physical existence and cannot be touched. Like the business corporation (in legal fiction a constitutional person), it is an artificial being, invisible and intangible, existing only in legal and constitutional theory. The State has a monopoly on the legitimate use of violence and is also the source of law—the positive law, as distinguished from the moral law—and governmental officials act in its name. Even though it cannot be seen, it nonetheless is as real as a natural person. In fact, the

State is even more "real" than you or I, for when its will collides with those of natural persons, it *always* prevails in any matter considered important by those who wield effective power in America.

The State, therefore, is more equal than individual members of the citizenry; it is superior. That is so even though the citizenry—the people generally—are the units of the society symbolized by the State. And of course the State differs from the fifty states of American union—hence the capital *S*, to help distinguish it from, say, Nebraska or Massachusetts.

Not mentioned in the Constitution, the State nonetheless exists as the ultimate power in the nation. An abstraction, its survival or well-being motivates political officers to take extraordinary actions. The meaning for American constitutionalism is profound: Despite the accepted notion to the contrary, popular sovereignty—ultimate power in the people—is more fantasy than fact. The Constitution of the books begins with the words, "We, the people . . ."—a shorthand expression for popular sovereignty—but the Constitution in operation has always been otherwise. The people are subordinate to the State. At most, as Hannah Arendt observed, the people have power only on election day—when they choose the ruling elite. Said Miss Arendt: "The most the citizen can hope for is to be 'represented'"—but "representative government has in fact become oligarchic."[20]

Power in America rests not in the people as such, but in an elite structure. The elite rules in the name of the people—but their decisions tend to favor the relative few rather than the many. Government "of the people" there is, but surely not "by the people" and not necessarily "for the people." There is, in other words, a class society in the United States now (and in the past and doubtless in the future). The myth is different, but this nation is not now, nor has it ever been, "classless." Those classes are now becoming rigidified in something akin to a caste society. The people, furthermore, rather than being a monolith are a congeries of disparate publics, publics that often conflict.

The Constitution in operation—the living Constitution—recognizes the State as the overarching social reality. Not mentioned in the formal Constitution, it exists, like the business corporation, even though it has "no anatomical parts to be kicked or consigned to the calaboose; no soul for whose salvation the person may struggle; no body to be roasted in hell or purged for celestial enjoyment."[21] More nearly a method than a thing, as a metaphysical entity it is a legal fiction that itself can do no act, speak no word, and think no thoughts —but in whose name those in government speak and for whose benefit men may die and property be seized. The State is an invention of lawyers, used to fill in one of the gaps in the original Constitution. The analogy to the corporation is not an accident: symbiotic interlocks between government and business make it necessary to define the State as encompassing at least the giant corporations.

Everyone lives in the shadow of the State. Whatever a person wants to do, alone or (increasingly) as a member of groups, depends in final analysis on receiving approval from the State, tacit or expressed. The myth of individualism speaks to the contrary, but it is not based on fact. In some degree, that has always been so in the United States. Even in the heyday of the "negative, nightwatchman State," the living Constitution permitted actions in circumstances that ordinarily would have been clearly invalid under the formal Constitution. At times, however, the formal and the living Constitutions meet and merge in Supreme Court decisions.

Surely that is also true for other nations and other political communities, such as the city-states about which Machiavelli wrote. Machiavelli's importance cannot be overemphasized. He stood, as Ernst Cassirer put it, "at the gateway of the modern world. The desired end has been attained; the state has won its full autonomy. . . . The sharp knife of Machiavelli's thought has cut off all the threads by which in former generations the state was fastened to the organic whole of human existence."[22] In sum, the political world—the State—stands alone, entirely independent, not only from formal religion but also from ethical considerations. It is amoral. And supreme. There has always been, however, a close connection between the State and religion, even though the Constitution commands, according to the Supreme Court, separation of church and State. Religion plays an important, albeit unacknowledged, role in the survival of the State. As Hannah Arendt said, "politics and the state needed the sanction of religion even more urgently than religion and the churches . . . ever needed the support of princes."[23] More tersely, "politics is now religion."[24]

Machiavelli stood at the gateway of the nation-state. He wrote at a time when political communities began to integrate out of the ruins of feudalism and of the Holy Roman Empire. The Florentine's ideas had been known for some time, but, in Western thought at least, they had been ignored or hidden for centuries. His basic message—reason of State—far antedated him. No historical evidence exists to negate the view that group values—that of the political community (the State), whatever the size—have not always prevailed. What Machiavelli did was to let the dirty little secret of human governance out of the bag in which it had lain hidden. Political theory—political science—and constitutional theory have not been the same since.

If humans ever lived in a "state of nature," surely they did not as atomistic individuals. No doubt the lives of people in prehistoric times were poor, dangerous, and short—indeed, that is true for much of the world today. Man is a herd animal. He runs in packs, always has, and no doubt always will. Man emphatically is thus a political animal. That has long been ignored, both because "politics" has been denigrated and because the ideology of much of the Western world for at least two centuries has been individualism. The "autonomous" man does not exist as such. Everywhere a person is caught up in group activity, of varous sizes and natures—from the family to society. Group activity inevitably means politics, not necessarily the refined and bureaucratized forms it takes today, but political activity nonetheless. There is no group so small or so insignificant that someone does not try to dominate it; and no group that does not interact with other groups.

Modern society is the organized society, the collective society, one dominated by groups, large and small, public and private. Ours is truly the age of collective action. That is not new. The solitary individual has never existed; although there are degrees of personal solitude and isolation. Even Thoreau, the saint in the Valhalla of American individualists, was not a solitary man when he spent a few months at Walden Pond. He always could, and in fact often did, repair to the family home for sustenance. (The very few hermits and other solitaries merely are rare exceptions to the general rule.) The fact of "private" collectivism has substantial consequences for American constitutionalism: in economics it is the organization rather than the individual that is productive, in politics the group dominates rather than the individual, and we live and act in the bureaucratic State.

Furthermore, no group is so small or so insignificant that someone, or a small segment of that group, will not control it in fact, however much it may say it follows "democratic" principles. From the smallest group within America, up to and including the largest—the nation itself—Robert Michels' "iron law of oligarchy" operates.[25] Who says organization says oligarchy, Michels told us; and nowhere is that not true. The question is not whether an oligarchy exists, but who in fact controls—those in formal authority, or those who, behind the facade of authority, in fact greatly influence or control the decisions of groups. Normally, a difference exists between those with ostensible power to make decisions and those who in fact exercise that power. That means that the political sovereignty of the individual does not exist. A person is important in politics only as a member of a group; and that group in turn is controlled by a few of its members. Once again, this runs contrary to the accepted wisdom, particularly among lawyers, who prefer not to confront the obvious fact of control by oligarchy—an elite, in other words.

If group activity means political activity, then it is at least amusing, and perhaps ludicrous, for politics to be denigrated. Everyone, whether in public life or not, plays politics. In a highly organized, bureaucratized society, politics is the norm. It ill becomes someone to damn another for playing politics, as is often done, when all do it in one way or another. The most characteristic feature of the modern State is just that: Politics. Those who accuse others of playing politics are doing just that—playing politics; it is one of the more effective ploys of emotive use of language in group behavior.

The science or art of politics, however, is the most difficult of all human activities. Max Planck, so the story goes, began his education in economics (a branch of politics) but soon dropped it because of its difficulty and intractable nature. He turned to physics and, as all know, eventually produced the quantum theory. Planck found the laboratory problems of theoretical physics less difficult than the human problems of political economy. Compared to politics, the wonders produced by science and technology are relatively insignificant. Putting men on the moon was a tremendous technological achievement, but the astronauts got there only because the political system and administrative apparatus were sufficient to the need. The organizational abilities that produced the first atomic bombs were as remarkable in their own sphere as was the bomb itself. Harnessing men in collective efforts, that is, surely is as difficult as harnessing technology—more so, indeed, for many of the problems produced by science and technology get no adequate political response. The reaction to the climacteric of mankind is, thus far at least, feeble and unavailing.

To Machiavelli and others (Hannah Arendt, for example) man realizes his potential only by participation in the political community—the State.[26] That point is not argued here; one accepts or rejects it as a matter of faith, based on a subjective conception of what "potential" means, not as a matter of empirical proof. Any comprehensive discussion of raison d'état—of Machiavellianism—in this country or elsewhere, must perforce devote attention to the état as well as to the raisons. For it is the nature of the State itself that creates the reasons—the interests—which are to be furthered.

To speak of the State one must consider the question of power—those who wield it, in whose interests, for what ends, by what means. Power, a political concept, is difficult to define. It is the ability or capacity to influence or control the actions of others; or, as Professor Roberto Unger put it, "Power is the capacity to command, to subordinate the wills of others to one's own will."[27] Power always exists; there is no such thing as a power vacuum. In politics as in the physical world, nature abhors a vacuum. Power is exercised by identifiable people who operate through institutions.

A theory of the State being a theory of power, it also, Professor Ralph Miliband tells us, must encompass a view of the nature of society and of how power is exercised in that society.[28] But the State is more. Miliband is only partially correct when he asserts that the State "is not a thing, that it does not, as such, exist. What 'the State' stands for is a number of particular institutions which, together, constitute its reality, and which interact as parts of what may be called the state system." Certainly the State is not a physical thing, and the interacting institutions that constitute it are more than public government itself. The State is a metaphysical entity—an overarching being that is greater than the arithmetical sum of its parts. Although it is a legal fiction, nonetheless in law it is as real as any natural person.

The State is not synonymous with government. Governmental officials speak on behalf of the State, for the State cannot speak for itself (just as a corporation, despite Supreme Court pronouncements, cannot speak for itself). People give their allegiance to the State, rather than to the (transient) government of the day. People identify with it (the State), but government is the direct recipient of their obedience. Therefore, defiance of government is defiance of the State, permitted only in exceptional circumstances (as when constitutional limitations are violated). Small wonder, in these circumstances, that there is confusion in the literature, particularly in judicial opinions. Little attempt is made to distinguish between State and government. At times, moreover, government officers act in ways close to that of Louis XIV: "*L'État? C'est moi!*" All Presidents of modern vintage have so acted; from Franklin D. Roosevelt on, an unbroken pattern of identifying the chief executive with the State may be seen. So, too, with some of their predecessors, notably Wilson, Theodore Roosevelt, Lincoln, and Jackson.

As with any collective organization, the State, in Gierke's label, is a "group-person" with drives and interests of its own that transcend those of the individuals, natural and artificial, within the society it symbolizes.[29] It is more: it is a "super-group-person," the ne plus ultra of social organizations. Other groups exist, but within society; they are not identified with society. Corporations. Unions. Veterans' legions. Farmers' groups. Educational institutions. Ethnic groups. Religious groups. But they—each one—are secondary, not primary. The State is *the* primary group.

The State in the United States consists at the very least of the following: (a) A set of interacting institutions, reflecting configurations of power within society, operating within a limited territory; (b) a theory of power and its exercise, with emphasis upon those who can define the axiomatic in public policy; (c) a metaphysical entity that is greater than the sum of its parts; and (d) an organization with definite religious attributes. The last is discussed first.

We cannot escape history, nor should we want to. Adherence to the past, however, is merely a necessity rather than a duty. The modern State cannot be understood without knowledge of the context from which it grew. In the Western world, where our ideas were born and flourished, the State always had a close connection with religion. That is true even today, when the constitutional separation of church and State, supposedly by a high and impregnable wall, is more ostensible than real. In modern America, as in the ancient world, there is an interdependence of State and ritual, of governance and myth. An essential function of religion is to provide an excuse and justification for the exercise of power by some over others in the political order. That becomes clear when to the orthodox views of religion (of the church) are added concepts relating to the "rule of law." Of the two, orthodox religion undoubtedly is of lesser importance; it has become religionism, or religiosity, in which the facade hides a darker reality: the language of political officers is often couched in terms of morality, but their actions follow realpolitik.

One need not look very far or very deep to find convincing evidence that, far from being separated, religion and the State are closely connected. The Supreme Court has tried to erect, so the Justices assert at times, an impenetrable wall between Church and State—but that refers only to the church as organized religion—and not always then. Through a typical bit of judicial casuistry, the Court permits some aid to religious organizations—for example, public financing of school textbooks and buses, grants for the construction of buildings—but those are rationalized on the basis that the monetary aid is not to the church but to the students. That makes sense to the judges, but little to others. But it is the law. My point is not to argue the matter, but to show that the supposedly solid wall between State and religion is far from that. Other examples could be given to show the religiosity of the government. The Supreme Court itself is not immune, for each of its public sessions is opened by a marshal intoning "God Save This Honorable Court!" Prayer breakfasts in the White House; chaplains in the Congress; "In God We Trust" on our coins—all these, and more, evidence the close connection of religion to the State.

Formal religion helps to legitimize the actions of government. It sanctifies them, giving them an authenticity they would otherwise not have. Here the civil religion of the Rule of Law (or of the shibboleth of a "government of men and not of laws") serves to reinforce support given by formal religion. Americans are the most legalistic of all peoples, the most litigious. They call upon judges to decide many problems that other nations settle politically. "Legalism" is the operative ideology of the legal profession; legalism means rule-following.[30] Law is considered by lawyers (and others) to be separate from politics and economics. Morality furthermore, is equated with legalism—with rule-following. "We find," said the late Professor Alexander Bickel, "our visions of good and evil in the experience of the past, in our traditions, in the secular religion of the American republic."[31]

The law surely has, as Professor Sanford Levinson has argued, a "specious morality,"[32] but, nonetheless, it is the prevalent belief-system of most modern legal thinkers. It is, in Bickel's phrase, "the value of values." There is a large intellectual problem here, as yet unresolved: the specific content of the values is left undefined. Bickel's is essentially a procedural viewpoint: "right" or "correct" procedure, followed by government officers including judges, is thought to produce "right" or "correct" answers. "Due process of law," viewed historically, is the core principle. That, however, is far from enough. Content must be put into the process, the procedure. That the Supreme Court has done by redefining "due process of law" to mean *what* government does as well as *how* it does it. The point, however, is that the secular or civil religion of the law reinforces formal religion in underpinning the modern State, which cannot be understood absent these two religious attributes.

The nation-state, the characteristic form of political order today, has still another secular religion—nationalism, which is often reduced to a jingoistic chauvinism or patriotism. And it has a basic legal concept—sovereignty— without which it could not exist. The myth in the United States is that popular sovereignty exists; that is, the people rule. But that is not now, nor has it ever been true; and it will be even less true in the future. Sovereignty is ultimate power; and that rests in the State, as articulated by government officers. Who controls, manipulates or greatly influences those officers is one of the important questions about the living American Constitution, a question far from fully answered.

Both nationalism and sovereignty—and the nation-state itself—arose out of the ruins of the Roman empire and what had, in the Western World, been an attempt to join temporal and spiritual forces in one social system—the Holy Roman Empire. That it was neither holy nor Roman nor an empire is a truism. But nonetheless the origin of the modern State can be found there. The State grew from religious soil: Western Christendom was the grand concept. That concept foundered with the growth of feudalism and ultimately with the severance of the formal church from the State. Not always, to be sure, for in some nations—Great Britain is a good example—the head of State is also the head of the State's religion (the Anglican church). But sufficiently: the coming of Protestantism meant a split between church and State.

Protestantism was political and economic as well as theological. Max Weber hypothesized a close connection between the rise of capitalism and the Protestant revolution;[33] and no doubt there was some relationship, even though one should be chary of assigning a unilinear cause-and-effect connection to the development of any important social institution (such as capitalism). The economic freedoms of a capitalistic order meant political freedoms as well—for only the bourgeoisie, not the masses. Protestantism also doomed the idea of an international, unified Christianity under one head (the Pope), and provided the ideological base for new States as they were created. One has only to recall the invocation of the Deity in the Declaration of Independence to realize that the United States was created under an ideology of Protestant religion.

Protestantism's significant contribution to modern views of the State and of nationalism cannot, therefore, be minimized. The United States was settled in part by religious dissidents— Quakers, Huguenots, and others who fled persecution in Europe. That they had curious notions of religious freedom does not diminish the point. They wished to be free from the papacy, but did not accord others a like freedom, either of worship or of disbelief.

The State in America has always been the object of a curious mixture of patriotism and piety, with an overlay of a notion of special mission. Religion, accordingly, is a socially indispensable instrument, whether it is the formal religion of the familiar churches or the secular religion of the rule of law and nationalism. It promotes solidarity and cohesion, and as such is a utilitarian cement. Americans have an irrational love for their country, deep felt and abiding; but only an ill-disguised contempt for their governments. One consequence is that Americans look more to the State than to God for sustenance, both material and moral. "We are a religious people," Justice William O. Douglas asserted in 1952, "whose institutions presuppose a Supreme Being."[34] That may be so, but we are also a nation that with its religiosity comes close to being a theocracy. The Constitution and the Supreme Court are best understood as religious institutions. Can it be an accident that the piece of ancient parchment is revered by tourists who throng through the National Archives? Or that the Justices, like priests, wear black robes and conduct their affairs in deepest secrecy? The State, finally, shares with religion the capacity to impart meaning to death. As Max Weber suggested, the soldier's death on the battlefield is a consecrated one.[35] One need only recall the incessant propaganda of most wars to see that. (A basic trouble with the Vietnam conflict was that, for various reasons, death was meaningless and purposeless.)

So religion and the State are closely intertwined—but not church and State. People look to the State for relief from some, perhaps all, of the pains of living. More and more, the State is the Earth Mother from whom all blessings flow. In this, the President, far from being "de-imperialized" in the post-Watergate era, is taking on the character of a secular Pope. The executive offices of the President resemble the papal bureaucracy; it is the American Curia, a center of governing power in the United States, insofar as any such center exists. Can it be pure happenstance that a born-again Baptist now resides in the White House? Or that successive Presidents invoke the Deity in public statements? Those calls upon God serve an indispensable social purpose—that of bringing an aura of legitimacy to public actions.

Power is exercised within the United States by both public and private governments. Public government—that which most people readily acknowledge to be the government, indeed, the only government—interacts with an aggregation of decentralized social groups, of which the giant business corporations are by far the most important. Formal law is (must be) pronounced by public government—Congress, the administrative agencies, the courts. The content of that law is often the resultant of a parallelogram of conflicting political forces. Rules of law are in final analysis a reflection of the political order—rather than vice versa. Much that should be considered to be law, however, in that it affects the values of Americans, never reaches the plateau of formal promulgation. Informal interactions between the organs of public government and prominent social groups may (often is) never be formally codified. But it is law—"living" law.

This also means that many decisions issued by public government are in fact effectively controlled, or greatly influenced, by the private groups of the nation. That can be seen, for example, in agriculture, where the Farm Bureau has enormous power; in veterans' affairs, where the American Legion and Veterans of Foreign Wars exercise great influence; in communications, where the radio and television networks tend to set the policies; in air transportation, where scheduled airlines often control what the Civil Aeronautics Board does; in the procurement policies of the Pentagon, where large weapons-systems producers have an inordinate amount to say—indeed, in the entire range and nature of the regulatory activities of government.

An appropriate name for this development is "the corporate State, American style." Corporations, large and small, business and nonbusiness, are closely connected to, and interlock with, government. Groups, thus, are able to stave off most regulations of significant adverse impact. Furthermore, they are often recipients of large grants and other subsidies; government largess of one type or another is a significant factor in the operation of the American economy.

Business, the strongest of the social groups, not only strongly influences or even controls the organs of government, particularly the administrative agencies, but also is able to define what is taken for granted in public policy. It is axiomatic, for example, to protect the property of Americans abroad, particularly that of corporations. No one argues about that. It is done by public government as a matter of course. And accepted by the people, who also accept the slogans of those who wish to maintain the status quo. Speak about public health programs, for instance, and the cry of "socialized medicine" goes up—from the doctors, from the drug companies, from the politicians, from the press. The people agree: Socialism is considered to be a bad nine-letter word. Use of it serves to cloud argument, to blur the issues, and to make rational public dialogue impossible.

That government (public) and business are entwined closely together is fast becoming a commonplace. Many thoughtful observers admit it, the difference between them being in the normative conclusions they draw from it. Some see no dangers, and in fact like it. Others perceive massive harm to human freedom, and warn against it. Our point here is neither to condemn nor to applaud, but merely to describe. A peculiar form of corporatism is being built —has been built—by the ever increasingly close associations between government and business (and other social groups).

It should not be thought that this is a new development, one that has sprung fully grown in the past few years. Quite the contrary; the roots of American corporatism may be found throughout American history. But it was by a particularly sly way that business could simultaneously take, even demand and receive, the benefits of governmental activity while damning government as the enemy. Social Darwinism, the prevailing ideology of the late nineteenth and early twentieth centuries, had its major prophet in Herbert Spencer. Justice Holmes said, in 1895, that no thinker other than Darwin himself had exerted a more powerful impact on American thought.[36] Spencer thought "government a necessary evil"; but his adherents in the business world, while accepting the Spencerian verbalism, nevertheless readily employed government for their own ends. (They still do.) The "survival of the fittest" in effect became the survival of those who could most effectively get government to do their work for them—one way or another.[37] John D. Rockefeller could utter homilies to Sunday school classes, but he was also one of the most ruthless of the Robber Barons who did not hesitate to bend government to their will. "The growth of a large business is merely the survival of the fittest," Rockefeller told a Sunday school class, adding: "The American Beauty Rose can be produced in the splendor and fragrance which bring cheer to its beholder only by sacrificing the early buds which grow up around it." This, said Rockefeller, "is not an evil tendency in business. It is merely the working-out of a law of nature and a law of God."[38] (Note, again, the invocation of the Deity.)

At the same time, Rockefeller and other tycoons controlled legislatures and were able to persuade the Supreme Court to read Social Darwinism into the Constitution. If, that is, the fittest survived, those who suffered must be left to suffer the consequences of failing to succeed. State power was "negative," particularly in Supreme Court decisions, toward the have-nots of the nation. They were considered to be weak or lazy and thus not deserving of help. The meaning is clear: Social Darwinism meant a theory of power, which emphasized a concept of the State as the instrument to punish wrongdoings, but with the corollary that services were to be denied as illegitimate. The close affinity to some modern thinking about many of the welfare programs is obvious. The point need not be labored further, save to repeat that power is shared between public and private governments and that the beneficiaries of State power, throughout American history, have tended to be those who in fact needed it least. (Welfare programs, it seems clear, are a means by which social discontent is siphoned off, allowing those with wealth and power to continue in their privileged positions.)

In the United States, political power is group power. Narrowly based elites pursue goals aimed at enhancing the well-being of their groups. Each elite seeks to control a segment of public government. Public policy thus becomes the resultant of the pulls and tugs on conflicting group forces. Government is both the target of group activity and a group with drives and interests of its own. When dangers are sufficiently obvious, some groups may be forced through operation of the State to suffer. But not usually. Individuals suffer in the United States, not groups. The individuals come and go, the groups continue; individuals are mortal but groups often are immortal.

Power in America is exercised for the benefit of elites, and of them, of the ruling or governing class.[39] The myth has it that ours is a classless society—

which it has never been. Only because we had in the past an ever-expanding granary from which to draw the sustenance of life was enough left over for the masses. The masses, furthermore, are kept quiescent through welfare and other ostensible income-distribution programs—ostensible because reality conflicted with the appearance. A small percentage of people have always controlled the bulk of the nation's wealth.

In many respects, it is easier to say what power is not. In the first place, power does not rest with the people, save in the myth. The organs of public government—Congress, the executive, the courts—exercise formal authority; it is they who put the commands of the State into writing. But that emphatically does not mean that they alone control the decisions that are made. Those, even with the courts, are influenced, even controlled by others (the elites who head the nation's social groups). Finally, there is no spokesman for the overall public interest who is able to make commands stick. True, the President does assert a power to state what is in the public interest—to speak for the nation generally, as the only elected official from the entire nation— but those attempts are diluted, even blocked from elsewhere—from Congress, from the interest groups, from other nations.[40]

One further point deserves mention: The American corporate State is a metaphysical entity at once superior to, and dominant over the sum of its parts. It is, in brief, the "super-group-person." The joinder of public and private governments into the corporate State has created something new under the constitutional sun.

The development may be seen with special clarity in some Supreme Court opinions. *Missouri* v. *Holland* is an example: there, Justice Holmes in the course of upholding a treaty with Canada, had this to say: "When we are dealing with words that also are a constituent act, like the Constitution of the United States, we must realize they have called into life a being the development of which could not have been foreseen completely by the most gifted of its begetters. It was enough for them to realize or to hope that they had created an organism; it has taken a century and much sweat and blood to prove that they created a nation. The case before us must be considered in the light of our whole experience and not merely in that of what was said a hundred years ago."[41] (The "they" in that quotation refers to the framers of the Constitution.) Holmes was there stating, in his usual lean style, an organismic conception of the nation. Just as the Court had in 1886 made the business corporation a constitutional person, so now Holmes had made the State a real person—a group-person.

The conception has had—always has had although it has never been spelled out—enormous consequence for American constitutionalism. By making a group—corporation or State—a real person, with a real will, it becomes as real as the Leviathan of Thomas Hobbes. It is not an automaton, as said Hobbes, but a living reality. When the State's will collides with that of other wills, it carries with it the claim that, being superior, it must prevail. That is precisely what has happened. The State is the one true group that assimilates all others, and it provides the philosophical base for the assertion of mere personal power unfettered by prohibitory rules of law.

That is abstract, but it is not a hypothetical fear. Whenever the rights of natural persons, asserted in litigation, collide with the rights of the State, the State always prevails in any matter considered important. Although the Constitution speaks in seemingly absolute terms, the language is not to be taken literally. Interests are "balanced" by the Supreme Court.[42] Save in marginal cases, the balance is always struck in favor of the State. We may not like to believe it, or even think about it, but Benito Mussolini put the matter in starkly realistic terms: "The highest personality is that of the Nation. . . . The Fascist State, synthesis and unity of all values, interprets, develops and actuates the whole of the life of the People. . . . For Fascism the State is an absolute, in whose presence individuals and groups are the relative."[43] Small wonder, then, that a perceptive and thoughtful commentator such as Professor Bertram Gross can speak seriously of the rise of "friendly fascism"[44] in America. The theoretical foundations of it have been established by the judiciary in its constitutional interpretations. The Court has managed, without design, to make the State a real person, whose will is superior to that of the natural person. The Hobbesian Leviathan lives.

One has only to read some representative opinions of the Supreme Court to validate the point. Two illustrations will suffice, one dealing with freedom of expression (protected by the First Amendment), and the other with searches and seizures (the Fourth Amendment).

In March 1966, David Paul O'Brien and three companions burned their Selective Service registration certificates (draft cards) on the steps of the South Boston Courthouse as a symbolic protest against the Vietnam conflict. O'Brien was arrested by FBI agents and convicted under a statute that made it a federal crime knowingly to destroy or mutilate a draft card. Sentenced to prison (for five years), he appealed to the Supreme Court. There a Court headed by an allegedly activist and liberal Chief Justice Warren upheld the conviction. For the most specious reasons, with only one dissenting vote, the Court said that the "Government's substantial interest in assuring the continuing availability" of draft cards outweighed O'Brien's first amendment interest in freedom of expression.[45] The State prevailed, even though no one could seriously maintain that O'Brien's conduct really jeopardized any actual State interest.

The point may be put in another way. The judiciary in any modern industrial society, as Professor J. A. G. Griffith of the London School of Economics has shown, "is an essential part of the system of government and . . . its function may be described as underpinning the stability of that system and as protecting that system from attack by resisting attempts to change it."[46] In the *O'Brien* case, the Supreme Court in effect acted as an arm of the executive, punishing those whose conduct was thought to be inimical to the interests of the State. In 1966, when the incident occurred, and in 1968, when the Court rendered its decision, the tide of public opinion was running in favor of American participation in Vietnam. So the Court could tap the zeitgeist in upholding the State, it ran no risk of massive disapproval.

The other case deals with a Mrs. James, the recipient of aid to families with dependent children. Could her home be visited by social workers—in effect, searched—without a prior warrant? The answer given by the Court was yes. When the State's treasure—at least a part of it—is concerned, then the Fourth Amendment's requirement of warrants for searches must give way.[47] Again, the Court, in effect, acted as an arm of the political branches of government.

The meaning is twofold. First, the State does win when its will collides with that of natural persons. Only when the matter is trivial do the judges come down on the side of the individual. Leviathan is triumphant. Second, when making such decisions the Court acts as spokesman for the State—not baldly, to be sure, but as a clear inference to be drawn from the many decisions like the *O'Brien* and *James* cases. The Justices update the Constitution, always keeping in mind the paramount need to protect the State. The legal act of making a Constitution in 1787 drew together the disparate individuals and groups that make up society and turned that association into a legal or juridical organization, at once separate from society and superior to its constituent parts. A nation of groups is outweighed by the one group—the State. This conjunction of public and private governments into a politico-legal type of syzygy is the consequence. (Syzygy is a biological term, meaning two bodies joined together but retaining their separate identities.)

To summarize: an exposition of democratic dictatorship must of necessity focus on the nature of the State with raison d'état the controlling principle; an evaluation of the raisons requires knowledge about the State. Suggested in this chapter is that the United States is the American version of the corporate State; this requires analysis of both raison d'état and raison de groupe. Government and groups are connected in a condition of syzygy; both retain their separate identities, but are firmly joined together. Neither could exist without the other. The State is a "super-group-person," a metaphysical concept, but it means that the apparatus of the State is both public and private governments.

In some respects, sovereignty is splintered, but only ostensibly so, between the leaders of public and private governments. Those leaders cooperate more than they conflict. The routine details of their cooperation constitute the social basis for the "living law" of the corporate State. The United States, as Professor Michael Kammen has shown, is the contrapuntal civilization.[48] Dualism—

"biformities"—characterize it. The "collective individualism" of the American people is becoming a type of democratic despotism. Tension exists between the idea of popular sovereignty, and a written Constitution of the books, and the Constitution in operation. Says Kammen: "Our Constitution seems to foster fragmentation of power while our economic-technological system seems to encourage consolidation of power. Thus the imperatives of pluralism under conditions of large-scale technology commonly conflict with principles and practices of constitutional democracy."[49]

Finally: as with all groups, however large or small, the State is controlled by an elite structure—or, rather, a series of cooperating elites. Democratic elitism may be the label for this, however contradictory it may seem.[50] The elites rule for the benefit, not of the people as a whole, but for the interests of their own groups and particularly for the ruling or governing class. Sociologically, the United States is a caste society.

Those on the bottom rungs receive enough for minimal sustenance, plus just enough of the luxuries of an industrialized nation to stifle dissent and to keep the masses quiescent.[51] To the extent that this has been successful in this century, it may be traced to what was once viewed as an ever-expanding economy. But with the economic pie becoming static, or at least smaller relative to the population, then it may no longer be possible to buy off discontent with minimal material rewards. With that comes social discontent at the very least; social turmoil is more likely.

6

The Past as Prologue:
Two Moralities in
Public Behavior

Few studies have been made of crisis government in the United States. Of those, the author usually concentrates upon the obvious: all-out war, plus, at times, economic depressions. That focus led the late Professor Clinton Rossiter, the leading student of "constitutional dictatorship," to conclude that applying that label to the American experience is "little more than a convenient hyperbole." Rossiter believed that one had to stretch the point considerably "to say that any American government has ever been a constitutional dictatorship."[1] He was correct only in part; his perspective was too narrow, his analysis too sketchy. American government, as Franz Neumann said, has always been "precisely as strong" as it had to be.[2] This chapter outlines how emergencies, actual and perceived, large and small, have been dealt with in the past. It is illustrative, not exhaustive; some emergency situations are not included, there being no need to document the conclusions further.

The organizing principle comes from Machiavelli: "I claim that republics which, in imminent danger, have recourse neither to a dictatorship, nor to some form of authority analogous to it, will always be ruined when grave misfortune befalls them."[3] Precisely. The dangers that have triggered extraordinary responses are, however, not confined to "grave misfortune." They go far beyond those contemplated by Machiavelli and discussed by Rossiter (who mentions the Civil War, World Wars I and II, and the Depression of 1933). All types of emergencies, *as perceived by political officers*, should be considered in order to see that two moralities of public behavior in fact are applied. Included are wars and rumors of wars (cold wars), internal subversion (actual or possible), economic depression, labor strife, actions of dissident groups, the use of force to protect American lives and property, and natural disasters. Or, as Hannah Arendt has cogently said, "Necessity, since the time of Livy and through the centuries has meant many things that we today would find quite sufficient to dub a war unjust rather than just. Conquest, expansion, defense of vested interests, conservation of power in view of the rise of new and threatening powers—all these well-known realities of power politics were not only the causes of most wars in history, they were also recognized as 'necessities,' that is, as legitimate motives to invoke a decision by arms."[4] She speaks of war, but our canvas is wider and deeper. Violence (war), as we will see, is not always necessary; those who control the State have other weapons at their command. Our list, plus hers, may not include all, but it does contain most situations when extraordinary political responses occurred (the use of violence being an extension of politics). The governing principle is that a given situation must be perceived by the ruling elite, or elites, to be an emergency before action is even contemplated; the response is pursuant to what we call the principle of the economy of means.

Two moralities? Exactly. The Constitution makes no express provision for emergency action. Equally truistic is the fact that the fundamental law has never been a barrier to any action deemed necessary during emergencies perceived by the political officers of government—usually the President but often that officer and Congress acting together, plus, at times, officials in the state governments. The one exception is the *Steel Seizure Case*,[5] which in 1952 struck down President Truman's seizure of the steel mills during the Korean War. That decision, however, is a sport and should so be considered.

The meaning is—or should be—clear: a dualism runs through American constitutional history. Not only is there the distinction, already mentioned, between the law in books and the law in action; there is also a need to see that government officials, including judges, at times speak in terms of one morality (and often adhere to it) but act in terms of another. Thus Justice David Davis, writing in 1866 in *Ex parte Milligan*, a case involving court-martial of an alleged spy when the civilian courts were open, asserted:

The Constitution of the United States is a law for rulers and people, equally in war and in peace, and covers with the shield of its protection all classes of men, at all times, and under all circumstances. No doctrine involving more pernicious consequences was ever invented by the wit of men than that any of its provisions can be suspended during any of the great exigencies of government. Such a doctrine leads directly to anarchy or despotism, but the theory of necessity on which it is based is false; for the government, within the Constitution, has all the powers granted to it which are necessary to preserve its existence; as has been happily proved by the result of the great effort to throw off its just authority.[6]

That is a nice sentiment, were it true; but it is not, as this chapter will demonstrate. Not only does the government have all the powers "necessary to preserve its existence," it has all the powers necessary to protect the values of those who wield real power in the nation. Furthermore, it simply is not true, unhappily, that the Constitution protects "all classes of men, at all times, and under all circumstances." In 1942, for example, in *Ex parte Quirin*,[7] the case of the Nazi saboteurs, the *Milligan* decision (and Davis' florid prose) were neatly overturned. So it goes in American government; there are indeed two moralities in our constitutional history, but those moralities at times meet and merge (as in the *Quirin* decision); and at other times, one of the moralities is conveniently ignored.

What, then, are the two moralities? Here we again revert to Machiavelli; and more specifically, to Sir Isaiah Berlin's brilliant interpretive essay, "The Originality of Machiavelli."[8] Berlin's interpretation—there are more than twenty others—is that the Florentine proposes a radical dualism—"two incompatible ideals of life, and therefore two moralities." First is the morality of the pagan world, whose virtues are "courage, vigor, fortitude in adversity, public achievement, order, discipline, happiness, strength, justice, above all assertion of one's proper claims and the knowledge and power needed to secure their satisfaction." (This is what Machiavelli called *virtù*, not translatable as "virtue" but as "manliness.") Much of American history reflects the furtherance of those values; although even some of these—what Berlin calls virtues of the pagan morality—are not followed rigorously. In more times than Americans like to think, raw government power has been and still is exercised when considered necessary by ruling elites. (Moral degeneracy under *both moralities* occurs in both foreign and domestic affairs.)

At the same time, there is another morality, says Berlin (interpreting Machiavelli): that of the Judeo-Christian tradition, whose ideals are "charity, mercy, sacrifice, love of God, forgiveness of enemies, contempt for the goods of this world, faith in the life hereafter, belief in the salvation of the individual souls as being of incomparable value—higher, indeed wholly incommensurable with any social or political or other terrestrial goal, and economic or military or aesthetic consideration." This is the language in which public officers often speak. It is, in brief, the facade of American constitutionalism. The harsh reality lurking underneath is at least pagan, and at times morally defective action (under either morality).

The point Sir Isaiah makes is not that one morality is superior over the other (although Machiavelli of course adhered to the pagan morality), but that there are two goals of human endeavor, both believed in by human beings, but not compatible with one another. That causes intellectual confusion—and a gap between pretense and reality in official behavior. The reality of official behavior, in short, is this: At times those human goals merge in Supreme Court opinions (and other governmental actions). In those instances, the Court usually chooses the first (pagan) over the second (Judeo-Christian) morality, but rationalizes its decisions and writes it opinions in terms of the second. So, too, with other government officers.

That is a harsh accusation. To show that the pagan morality, despite disclaimers to the contrary and despite the religiosity of the American populace, has always prevailed requires documentation by illustrative episodes in our national history. These examples will, I believe, conclusively demonstrate a factual basis for the accusation. We Americans like to think that we are different, that in some way we escaped the iniquities of other nations. But that is fantasy. Americans now and in the past, have always been ready to do whatever was considered necessary to meet threats, actual or imaginary. Crises are of varying dimensions. The accusation, to be sure, does not comport with the orthodox view of Americn constitutionalism. I aim to show, not only that dualism runs through our history, but that the pagan morality is now, and has been in the past, dominant—when the need was perceived by those who wield actual power in the constitutional order. The second point is that in American history, following the pagan morality was always limited in time and space. To that extent, Professor Rossiter was correct.

Machiavelli is relevant to the United States despite the popular wisdom about him, because it was he who first made the radical dualism in government affairs so plain, the one who in his writing (*The Discourses* and *The Prince*) plunged a sword "into the flank of the body politic of Western humanity, causing it to cry out and struggle with itself."[9] The pain of that sword's thrust is still with us, five centuries after Machiavelli lived; it is a pain, a contradiction if you will, that has never been directly confronted or unified in our constitutional history. Of course the dualism is disturbing to people, including judges (for example, Justice Davis in the *Milligan* case), who insist on finding a single truth, or who otherwise evade this awkward duality. Not that the Florentine preferred a "prince," despite the belief to the contrary; he recognized that "republics are to be preferred if you can get them."[10] But republics must, and do, make provision for emergency measures; and even democracies act, when their leaders consider it necessary, contrary to the Judeo-Christian morality. If there is a single truth to be distilled from our heritage, it is that the pagan virtues prevail. I do not expect that to be liked; but it cannot be gainsaid. Justice Davis, in sum, was simply wrong.

Can one, then, distinguish between the circumstances fit for republican— i.e., democratic—rule and those suited for personal rule? That was the central concern of the much maligned Machiavelli. And that should be a fundamental concern of American constitutional scholars in the future. It is *the* crucial question, as yet unresolved and seldom even asked for the American constitutional order. Other, subsidiary questions include: Who decides that emergencies exist? How? In whose interests? Under what criteria? How are they terminated?

In what follows, it will be shown that no middle course is possible between the two moralities. One or the other is ascendant, depending on the environment in which governments operate. So long as that environment is, in a word, salubrious, then "democracy" and the second morality prevail. Further, as Rossiter cogently said, even during times of true all-out emergency, the institutions of the State still operate. It goes without saying that they do so for most Americans during times of limited emergency action—limited in time and space. Will that continue? It depends entirely upon the circumstances, domestic and planetary, in which government will operate. Since we have postulated an imminent climacteric for humankind, the short answer to the crucial question facing the American constitutional order is that the pagan morality will continue to prevail; and that Americans will indeed be fortunate if they merely have an authoritarian, as distinguished from a totalitarian, government. The remainder of this book will spell out some of the aspects for that grim conclusion. In addition, possible alterations in social and legal institutions will be suggested as a means of alleviating the Orwellian world that is rapidly approaching. In a nation avowedly Christian, pagan virtues have prevailed. Will that continue?

Look at what we do, not what we say, quipped John Mitchell, President Nixon's first Attorney General, in a rare and possibly unthinking burst of candor. (Mitchell was the first Attorney General to be jailed for crimes committed in office.) Precisely. We should look at what government officers do, not what they say—certainly not what Supreme Court Justices have said—when dealing with examples of extraordinary, emergency political behavior. As we will see, when the Court does rule on issues concerning emergency actions, it tends with few exceptions to uphold their validity. The meaning will become clear: Americans have one, and only one, Constitution—and it is the one that is in consonance with the pagan virtues which Machiavelli extolled. The further meaning is that the judiciary, particularly the Supreme Court of the United States, operates in effect (but not in theory) as part of the "executive juggernaut"[11] during all-out and even lesser emergencies. Even in times of limited emergencies the Court, in interpreting the sparse words of the Constitution, has been able to uphold actions that a layman would have thought contrary to the meaning of the words of the Constitution. The judiciary, moreover, has not been a consistent barrier against actions that are morally degenerate under either the pagan or the Judeo-Christian conception.

The assertion that we have but one—a pagan—Constitution may not be liked. It will probably be denounced as wrongheaded. The facts are there, however, for those with eyes to see. What are those facts? Consider the following, chosen from the welter of history, not to fit a theory but as data that make the conclusion of a pagan "living" Constitution unavoidable. Only when the interests of the State, as determined by spokesmen for the State, consider a given situation not to require the application of pagan virtues have they been replaced with Judeo-Christian standards. The dualism in American constitutional history is between the living and formal constitutions, not in public behavior itself. It is also a dualism between public and private governments—between, that is, sovereignty split between what all concede is government and decentralized centers of economic power—mainly the giant corporations.

One of the options open to American policymakers is the calculated use of violence. This, as Professor Abraham Sofaer has shown, has been true since the beginnings of the nation.[12] Presidents since George Washington have used violence, usually without a declaration of war, when deemed necessary. No provision is made for that in the Constitution, save perhaps in a controversial interpretation of the "commander-in-chief" clause of Article II, under which the president is the head of the armed forces. The meaning of that delphic language is far from clear. Does it make the President merely the civilian chief of the military, which means in essence tactical control of the troops, or does it vest him with an independent power to commit the military forces whenever and wherever he deems it necessary? Chief executives—for example, Lyndon Johnson and Richard Nixon—of course maintain that the latter is the true meaning. Commitment of more than 500,000 troops to Vietnam was based on the President's reading of that clause. And that despite the fact that Article I clearly and expressly gives to Congress the power to declare war. Presidents from Washington to Gerald Ford—with some exceptions— have used military force on numerous occasions without a declaration of war. On the record of custom and usage—the Constitution in operation—the formal Constitution has been neatly amended. That the President does have an independent power to use violence in war has become obvious—and, in the atomic age, necessary. With intercontinental missiles and nuclear bombs, the power of making all-out war is now presidential, not congressional. Even lesser, "brush-fire" wars have now been recognized by Congress as a matter of executive discretion, as attested by the War Powers Resolution of 1973 and President Ford's employment of armed force in the *Mayaguez* incident in 1975.

The United States has been fortunate in one large respect: It has been able to use violence, even to the extent of all-out war, with relatively minimal restrictions on civil liberties. There are exceptions to that statement, to be sure. The American Indians could by no stretch of imagination believe that only minimal restrictions were laid on them. So, too, with American young men, who despite the seemingly plain language of the Thirteenth Amendment ("Neither slavery or involuntary servitude, except as a punishment for crime whereof the party shall have been duly convicted, shall exist within the United States, or any place subject to their jurisdiction"), have nonetheless been marched to the front, there to fight and die (at times) for their country. A layman might be pardoned the view that such plain language prohibited compelled military service; but lawyers have ways of taking clear words and defining them as they wish.

One need not relate in detail all of the instances of raison d'état in the use of violence. Three illustrative examples will suffice: the Civil War, World War II, and Vietnam. Each illustrates some basic principles about democratic dictatorship, including the following: (a) The President takes such action as he deems necessary to meet the threat (actual, in the case of the Civil War; probable, for World War II; nonexistent, for Vietnam); (b) Congress and the President act together, with Congress being by and large a rubber stamp for executive actions; (c) the courts, including the Supreme Court, erect no barriers to whatever actions the President takes, particularly when approved, tacitly or overtly, by Congress; the judiciary in effect exhibits either a self-imposed impotence or upholds presidential action; (d) save for a relative few, civil liberties were not disturbed; the populace at large is not involved (this has important consequences relating to the extent to which violence can be used); deprivations, save again for a few, are economic rather than physical (personal); (e) violence is limited in time and space—in time, to victory or as in Vietnam, defeat; in space, to other lands, save in the Civil War; and (f) with some notable exceptions (as in the use of the atomic bombs and the scorched earth policy pursued in Vietnam), violence has been employed only to the extent necessary to achieve postulated goals; that may be called the principle of the economy of means in the use of violence. Let us take each of the calculated uses of violence and detail some of the actions taken.

THE CIVIL WAR

"Is there in all republics this inherent and fatal weakness? Must a government of necessity be too *strong* for the liberties of its people, or too *weak* to maintain its own existence?"[13] So asked President Abraham Lincoln on July 4, 1861. On the historical record the answers are clear: a nation—this nation—can fight a successful total war and still remain a "republic." Lincoln proved that; as did President Franklin D. Roosevelt; and, indeed, as did Presidents Kennedy, Johnson, Nixon, and Ford, in the unpleasantness that travels under the banner of Vietnam. At best, the Constitution is bent in such circumstances; at worst, it is simply ignored. Nuclear war adds a different dimension, however. If that happens, a rigid dictatorship will be immediately invoked, and will remain as long as considered necessary—which will doubtless be a very long time indeed. The Constitution will not only be ignored; it will in effect be abolished.

The pattern was set in the Civil War. Civil wars are like religious wars—bloody and total. So it was in 1861 to 1865. Whether Lincoln acted constitutionally, and whether a state (or group of states) could secede from the Union on their own motion, are questions which were settled on the battlefield and in the law courts. He did act constitutionally, and states cannot secede. This much we know; but that much Lincoln did *not* know when he took unprecedented actions in the eleven weeks between the fall of Fort Sumter and the convocation of Congress on July 4, 1861. Why Lincoln waited so long to

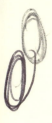

summon Congress into session can be explained only by the theory that he wanted to act without interference from that branch. He wanted, in other words, to get the job done as he saw the needs. Thus he established an irreversible pattern during the early weeks of combat. Only Lee's surrender kept the Union intact; and only the Supreme Court, acting in effect, if not in theory, as an arm of the executive, made Lincoln's unilateral actions constitutionally valid. Whether or not he wanted it, he became a dictator.

Lincoln came to office with "little more than an acute understanding of his obligation to see to the due execution of the laws."[14] But he had also sworn to uphold the Constitution; and in his inaugural address promised Americans that he would preserve the Union. Lincoln had a mystical view of the nation, and was prepared to go to whatever lengths were necessary to keep it intact. He acted to protect a society, not merely its Constitution. Congress was not in session when the guns at Sumter began to rumble, thus permitting the President to proceed on his own and assume a number of powers that Congress did little to alter until Lee laid down his sword at Appomattox. The law, constitutional or otherwise, was no restraint. Said Lincoln: "It became necessary for us to choose whether, using only the existing means, agencies, and processes which Congress had provided, I should let the Government fall into ruins, or whether, availing myself of the broader powers conferred by the Constitution in cases of insurrection, I would make an effort to save it, with all its blessings, for the present age and for posterity."[15] But those "broader powers" do not exist as such in the Constitution; Lincoln had to draw upon Machiavellian principles, upon a concept of raison d'état, to justify his actions. Lincoln, in brief, was a dictator, albeit a limited and even (outside the South) a popular one. His use of extraordinary powers provided the basis for subsequent presidents to do likewise—for example, Woodrow Wilson and Franklin Roosevelt. Even the disgraced Richard Nixon asserted that chief executives had powers that he (Nixon) traced to Lincoln (among others).[16]

What, then, did Abraham Lincoln do? He saw his duty as that of dealing with a gigantic mob and of dispersing it, the government being faced "by combinations too powerful to be suppressed by the ordinary course of judicial proceedings or by the powers vested in the marshals."[17] First, however, what did he *not* do? The answer here is easy: he did not call Congress into special session when Fort Sumter was fired upon; he did not want a formal declaration of war (and in fact never got one).

Lincoln, acting on his own as a "self-appointed" constitutional dictator, took these actions in the eleven week period:[18]

1. He called up 75,000 of the state militia by executive proclamation, to suppress the rebellion and guarantee execution of the laws. This was on April 15, 1861, after Sumter had fallen. At the same time, he called upon Congress to convene in special session on July 4 "to consider and determine

such measures as, in their wisdom, the public safety and interest may seem to demand." That was as cavalier a refusal to bring Congress into operation immediately as the nation had ever seen.

2. On April 19, by another proclamation, the President blockaded the ports of the seceded states, followed the next day by an order that nineteen warships be added to the navy "for purposes of public defense." One would think, on reading the Constitution, that such actions, if taken, would require Congressional approval, particularly the latter. (More than 100 years later President John Kennedy blockaded the ports of Cuba in the Cuban missile crisis, drawing on powers first asserted by Lincoln.)

3. On May 3, Mr. Lincoln went even further: he invaded the expressly granted Congressional powers to "raise and support armies" and "to provide and maintain a navy," by calling for volunteers for the army and enlarging both the army and navy. Says Professor Rossiter: "This amazing disregard for the words of the Constitution, though considered by many as unavoidable, was considered by nobody as legal." It was an example of the pagan morality —of raison d'état—in its purest form; the President acted contrary to law for the survival of the nation—as he saw it.

4. Public money was spent in total disregard of the constitutional requirement that "No money shall be drawn from the Treasury but in consequence of appropriations made by law."

5. President Lincoln suspended the writ of habeas corpus, by proclamation again, this time authorizing the Commanding General of the Army to suspend it when deemed necessary. When in 1861 Chief Justice Roger Taney held (sitting alone "on circuit") that the suspension was invalid, the decision was simply ignored. Lincoln in effect thumbed his nose at the Chief Justice in a classic example of judicial impotence when faced with executive intransigence.

When Congress finally convened, it speedily ratified the presidential actions. What lessons are to be drawn from the experience? One is that peacetime government by and large did continue, save for the extraordinary actions. This exemplified the principle of economy of means. Another is that precedents established by Lincoln were remembered and used by later presidents in other situations. Third, the Supreme Court acted in fact, but not in theory, as an agent of the executive. When the blockade of Southern ports was challenged (in the *Prize Cases*),[19] the Justices of the Supreme Court had no difficulty in finding constitutional justification for Lincoln's actions—there and elsewhere. Said the Court: "Whether the President in fulfilling his duties as Commander-in-Chief, in suppressing an insurrection, has met with such armed resistance, and a civil war of such alarming proportions as will compel him to accord to them the character of belligerents, is a question to be decided by *him*, and this Court must be governed by the decisions and acts of the political department of the Government to which this was entrusted. . . . He must determine what degree of force the crisis demands." The Constitution had been neatly amended. Raison d'état became an operative principle of our fundamental law. In the interval between April 12 and July 4, 1861, a new principle thus appeared in the constitutional system of the United States, namely, that of a temporary dictatorship.

Strong words, those—but only partially accurate. They are accurate in the judicial approval of presidential power, inaccurate in calling it a "new principle." The principle had existed, but in narrowly circumscribed conditions, since the beginnings of the republic. President George Washington, for example, used military force in times of perceived crisis, without regard to Congress or to the Constitution. But it took Lincoln and the bloodiest civil war in modern history to weld the principles into the Constitution. Machiavelli's first (pagan) morality became a part of our law. We have been living with it ever since. FDR outdid Lincoln in excercising discretionary powers. And Vietnam capped it off with raison d'état applied to a situation far removed from America's shores and not even remotely an actual danger to the country.

WORLD WAR II

We will get to Vietnam in a moment. Let us now summarize FDR's actions before and during World War II. The "before" part is particularly instructive. We now know, with the publication of Stevenson's A Man Called Intrepid[20] how President Roosevelt in fact committed the nation to war on the side of Great Britain two years before Pearl Harbor. It was much more than that attributed to him by Rossiter: ". . . the President not only gave repeated verbal support to the democratic cause, but also pushed the American people right to the brink of war (where they belonged anyway) with such extraordinary exertions of executive initiative as the call for the Lend-Lease Act, the occupation of Iceland, and Atlantic Charter, the initiation of the American convoys (particularly the extension of the neutrality patrol almost to England in April 1941), the 'shoot at sight' order of September 1941, and the destroyer deal of 1940."[21] Stevenson tells us that Roosevelt was cooperating closely with Great Britain during that period, secretly accomplishing acts that can only be called acts of war.

My point is not to criticize FDR's actions: World War II, as some have argued, was a "just" war if ever there was one.[22] Assuming that it was, the essential point is the President following the first (pagan) morality well in advance of a declaration of war. That is presidential lawmaking carried to its extreme. It shows, however much we may believe the contrary, that the written Constitution is no barrier to a determined chief executive and an acquiescent or pliable Congress. We had government by secret decree.

Consider, in that respect, the following statement of presidential powers made by Roosevelt to Congress on September 7, 1942: He first demanded that Congress repeal a provision of the Price Control Act of 1942 concerning ceilings on food prices, and then went on to assert:

I ask the Congress to take this action by the first of October. Inaction on your part by that date will leave me with the inescapable responsibility to the people of this country to see to it that the war effort is no longer imperiled by threat of economic chaos.

In the event that the Congress should fail to act, and act adequately, I shall accept the responsibility, and I will act.

At the same time that farm prices are stabilized, wages can and will be stabilized also. This I will do.

The President has the power, under the Constitution and under Congressional acts, to take measures necessary to avert a disaster which would interfere with the winning of the war. . . .

The American people can be sure that I will use my powers with a full sense of my responsibility to the Constitution and to my country. The American people can also be sure that I shall not hesitate to use every power vested in me to accomplish the defeat of our enemies in any part of the world where our own safety demands such defeat.

When the war is won, the powers under which I act automatically revert to the people—to whom they belong.[23]

That is as classic a statement of what John Locke called the "prerogative"[24] as can be found in American history. ("Prerogative" is a synonym for raison d'état.) Powers admittedly belonging "to the people" were seized and used with the President telling Congress that even though he had a duty to execute the laws, he was going to disregard one of them if it wasn't repealed at once.

That the President was a (temporary) economic dictator cannot be doubted. Production for war, consumption, and supply were all under the direct control of the executive branch. Congress was a rubber stamp. And the Supreme Court was a nonstarter; when it did act, it supported the President. Consider the following, each of which is an illustrative instance of presidential power:

Power over war contracts. Presidential power over industrial production, whether by overt act or delegation from Congress, was almost complete. Government by decree became routine under the First and Second War Powers Acts. Congress, in effect, threw up its collective hands and told the President: "Do it your way. Win the war. That's all that is important." Even so, one episode, early in the war, illustrates both the extent of presidential power and limitations on it.

Early in 1942, members of the Negro community, led by Philip Randolph, head of the Pullman Porters Union, quickly saw that blacks—again—were not getting a fair share of the jobs in war industries. Randolph then went to the President and asked him to rectify that unhappy situation, only to be met with the reply—FDR at his charming best—that "Dr. Win-the-War" had replaced "Dr. New Deal"; therefore, Randolph and his fellow Negroes should wait until the war ended, at which time FDR promised to aid them. Randolph replied that that was not good enough, whereupon the President sent Mayor Fiorello LaGuardia, a certified liberal, to reason with him. No success. Then FDR sent his wife, Eleanor, to ask Randolph to back off. Again, no success. Randolph said that either the President ordered the end of racial discrimination in war industries or he (Randolph) would lead a Negro march on Washington. Roosevelt thought, Roosevelt consulted with aides, Roosevelt capitulated. Executive Order 8802 was issued in 1942, inserting a non-discrimination clause in all war contracts.[25]

What lessons are to be drawn from that little-remembered episode? First, the President—as he did on numerous other occasions—simply legislated the clause. He did not consult Congress (except to note that it was highly unlikely, what with the Southern hold on the critical committees, that Congress would act). FDR did what was necessary to fulfill the interests of the State. That his action, which has since become law in the Civil Rights Act of 1964, comported with standards of decency merely indicates that at times the pagan and the Judeo-Christian moralities come together.

The second lesson is important to note: a democratic or constitutional dictator, such as President Roosevelt, does not have absolute power. He must, of necessity, have the people with him. FDR could have, but doubtless did not, draw on Machiavelli, who said: "A republic or a prince should ostensibly do out of generosity what necessity constrains them to do."[26] It was a grudging generosity, a *necessary* generosity, that Roosevelt tendered to Philip Randolph. The President managed to let the blacks think he was doing them a favor, exemplifying again a Machiavellian principle: "Prudent men always and in all their actions make a favor of doing things even though they would of necessity be constrained to do them anyhow."[27] That is an example of the necessity of decency—employed when a sufficient number of the populace becomes disgruntled. Absent urgent circumstances, such as an actual invasion of American shores, Presidents cannot be absolute dictators; they must and do take into consideration the felt necessities of the times—internal pressures as well as external dangers.

The Japanese-Americans. Three ethnic groups of people have been dealt with particularly harshly under the Constitution. Negro slavery was recognized in the Constitution and not abolished in law until after the Civil War (Lincoln's Emancipation Proclamation had no legal effect whatsoever). American Indians were systematically either exterminated or removed to harsh and inclement areas. The native American was not considered to be a "person" under the Fourteenth Amendment, thus protecting his life, liberty, and property from arbitrary governmental action. The forced evacuation of Indians will be treated later (it is another example of raison d'état). Our present interest lies in the third group—the Japanese-Americans and treatment of them during World War II.

Some 112,000 people of Japanese ancestry, 70,000 of whom were native-born American citizens, were summarily and arbitrarily removed from the West Coast, mainly California, and sent to the interior of the United States. Concentration camps were built for them—tarpaper-covered shacks surrounded by armed guards and barbed wire fences. How was it done? Why was it done? Both are easily answered.

On February 19, 1942, President Roosevelt issued Executive Order 9066, giving the Secretary of War "and the military commanders whom he may from time to time designate" discretionary authority to establish military zones within the United States "from which any or all persons" might be excluded. The Japanese-Americans were not named as such, but obviously the order was designed against them: within a few months the Army had forcibly removed the 112,000 people. The excuse? "Military necessity." And that, despite the fact that no case of espionage or sabotage was ever proved against any of the evacuees. That mass deprivation of civil liberties was bad enough in itself—Attorney General Francis Biddle noted in his autobiography that he was glad that he was not called upon to justify it in law—but even worse was the fact that the Supreme Court, in manner supine, bowed to the executive (and subsequent Congressional) judgment and upheld the evacuations.[28]

Justice Hugo L. Black, writing for the Court in the leading case of *Korematsu v. United States*,[29] opined that "Hardships are a part of war, and war is an aggregation of hardships"—as pusillanimous a statement as ever came from the High Bench. The action by FDR was racism pure and simple, as Justice Frank Murphy noted in his dissenting opinion. Justice Robert Jackson, who had been FDR's attorney general, put the matter in realistic terms: "The chief restraint upon these who command the physical forces of the country, in the future as in the past, must be their responsibility to the political judgments of their contemporaries and to the moral judgment of history."[30] On that score, the political judgments were all on FDR's side; the moral judgment of history is that it was the worst example of the pagan morality in action that the nation has ever seen.

Add to *Korematsu* the case of General Yamashita.[31] To quote Machiavelli, again: "It is a sound maxim that reprehensible actions may be justified by their effects, and that when the effect is good . . . it always justifies the actions."[32] Yamashita was the Japanese officer in charge of the Philippines when those islands were invaded by American forces. Atrocities were admittedly committed by Japanese troops. Could he then be tried as a war criminal? The answer would be easy, could it have been proved that he ordered, or, knowing about the atrocities, did nothing. Neither was true. Nevertheless, he was tried and sentenced to death. He counsel took the case to the Supreme Court, which again turned away, wringing its hands in impotence: By a 6 to 2 vote Yamashita's trial was validated and he was executed. The verdict of history: Judicial murder.

Who, however, should worry about a now-forgotten enemy general officer? The answer came in Vietnam. Those—"the best and the brightest"[33] —who got the nation into and kept it in the Vietnam conflict were susceptible to the same type of reasoning the Army and the Supreme Court used in condemning Yamashita. Under any theory of command responsibility, it was not only Lieutenant Calley, but his superior officers, who were guilty at My Lai. How high up the chain of command that responsibility should have gone is debatable. Surely to the Commanding General of the American Forces in Vietnam. And possibly even higher—to the Secretaries of Defense and of State, the Joint Chiefs of Staff, the President himself.[34] If Calley was guilty, as he was, then under the *Yamashita* principle numerous others should have been held to be guilty of war crimes and adjudged accordingly. (That they are not merely means that the *Yamashita* decision was an example of "victor's justice," rather than the rule of law. The end was thought to justify the means.)

The Case of the German Saboteurs. In early 1942 a clutch of German soldiers was landed by submarine on the east coast of the United States. Their purpose: to sabotage as much of the American war effort as they could. Soon picked up, the question became one of what was to be done with them. FDR wanted them tried by military tribunal and executed. He asked his attorney general, Francis Biddle, for an opinion on the legality of such action.[35] Biddle wrestled with the problem, came up against the Civil War case of *Ex Parte Milligan*, but nonetheless did his master's bidding. Said the President privately: I want those men tried and I want them executed, and I don't want a writ from the Supreme Court telling me that it cannot be done.[36] A military tribunal was set up, the men duly tried, and sentenced to death. Their lawyer took the case to the Supreme Court. The Court met, but without knowing where the men were or even if they had been executed; the Court decided, in *Ex Parte Quirin*, that they could be tried by military tribunal; their sentences were upheld, but no opinion was written. Some were executed. Several months later, the Court tackled the problem of writing an opinion, giving reasons for the decision. Chief Justice Harlan Stone admitted it was a most difficult task, but it was accomplished. So much for "the rule of law."

The lesson: the judiciary—the Supreme Court—became in fact an arm of the executive, doing the president's bidding (in fact but not outwardly). As in the *Prize Cases* during the Civil War, the Court read the principle of raison d'état into the Constitution. Machiavelli's pagan virtues were ascendant—and triumphant.

VIETNAM

What occurred in the most obvious of emergencies—wars, declared or otherwise—means at the very least that despite the constitutional theory of separation of powers, an independent President exists in fact. If that be so with respect to the Civil War and World Wars I and II, it was equally so for two other modern episodes—Korea and Vietnam.

Korea first, but briefly. Was it necessary? Yes. How do we know that? The President said so. (Whether it really was necessary is at best disputable.)[37] The lesson? Raison d'état once again, this time a major external conflict carried out on the President's orders alone. Congress, of course, went along: It appropriated money and it enacted other necessary statutes. But the initial decision was that of the President, and his alone. For the first time since the Civil War, the nation found itself in a large conflict, not technically a war because Congress did not so declare it, on lands far away. The importance of Korea for conceptions of presidential power cannot be overemphasized. Previous external forays by American military forces were far smaller and far more localized. Was it legally wrong? The answer as given by the State Department: No. Although some reliance was placed on the United Nations Charter and the Security Council's resolution asking support against North Korean military action, principal emphasis was upon the constitutional powers of the chief executive: "The President, as Commander in Chief of the Armed Forces of the United States, has full control over the use thereof. He also has authority to conduct the foreign relations of the United States. Since the beginning of United States history, he had, on numerous occasions, utilized these powers in sending armed forces abroad."[38] But never, the State Department neglected to say, to the extent of the Korean engagement. The powers of the President took an immense jump; his prerogative became complete a few months later whan Secretary of State Dean Acheson told Congress: "Not only has the President the authority to use the Armed Forces in carrying out the broad foreign policy of the United States and implementing treaties, but it is equally clear that this authority may not be interfered with by Congress in the exercise of powers which it has under the Constitution."[39] In sum: an independent President, restrained only by politics and the President's own sense of self-restraint.

Not that Acheson (or the lawyers of the State Department) were correct: They were not, on any theory of constitutional interpretation. But they got away with it; the troops were committed, and thousands of Americans and untold thousands of Koreans and Chinese died as a result. Nevertheless, the most important aspect of Truman's action was to set a precedent *in practice*, a precedent that was drawn upon either expressly or tacitly by Presidents Kennedy, Johnson, Nixon, and Ford. But—and this is a large qualification— actions by those Presidents, speaking generally, had to be "ratified" in effect by Congress. Actions similar to those which Lincoln took to put down a rebellion and Wilson and Roosevelt took to fight declared wars, the five Presidents (Truman, Kennedy, Johnson, Nixon, and Ford) continued in far different circumstances. The Constitution bent with the need as perceived by the chief executive (and not opposed by a complaisant Congress).

We come thus to Vietnam. It began in 1946 when President Truman was persuaded to help the French regain colonies lost to the Japanese; continued under President Eisenhower, when the French were defeated and the United States came within an eyelash of using nuclear bombs; and then began a steady escalation, first under President Kennedy and then under President Johnson. President Nixon started a withdrawal, completed by his successor. Each chief executive, beginning with Truman, saw in Indochina what in fact was not there: a major American national interest that required protection. So the Establishment decreed what Presidents put into official form: Using powers at best controversial and nebulous, more than 500,000 troops were eventually sent to Indochina.[40]

This is not the place to evaluate the collective madness that inflicted the American policymakers, save to say that by no stretch of one's imagination could one believe the United States was in fact threatened by what was essentially a civil war in a remote corner of the earth. But some 55,000 Americans were killed, and untold thousands of Vietnamese and Cambodians died, because governmental leaders, since rewarded by the system, made the greatest blunder in American history. One is reminded of Justice Jackson's pungent remarks (quoted above) in the *Korematsu* case: "If the people ever let command of the war power fall into irresponsible and unscrupulous hands, the courts wield no power equal to its restraint. The chief restraint upon those who command the physical forces of the country, in the future as in the past, must be their responsibility to the political judgments of their contemporaries and to the moral judgments of history." That the war power did fall into irresponsible and even unscrupulous hands during the Vietnam conflict is as certain a proposition as can be stated. The ultimate tragedy? As Machiavelli put it, it is "a sound maxim that, when an action is reprehensible, the result may excuse it, and when the result is good, always excuses it."[41] In Vietnam neither the end nor the means were morally good—under either the pagan or the Judeo-Christian morality. The United States will live under the shadow of that for many years. The individuals—the Kennedys, McNamaras, Bundys, Johnsons, Rostows, Kissingers, Nixons, Rusks, Alsops, etc.—may have come out of the mess without outward deprivation; but their deeds will live in infamy. The nation—the world—will never forget what they did. Americans will bear the burden of their misdeeds for decades. (Much, for example, of the economic inflation of the 1970s can be attributed to Vietnam. The United States tried to fight a major war and create the Great Society at the same time, and failed in both. The social cost was enormous, the financial cost we still endure. It is called inflation.)

For present purposes, the significance of Vietnam was the assertion of raison d'état in wholly new circumstances, with the President getting away with it. The Constitution was neatly amended; the war powers became presidential. As Professor Richard P. Longaker has put it: "when the United States became deeply involved in Vietnam in the mid-1960s there was no firm grounding, in either post-World War II precedent or practice, for the proposition that Congress needed to 'authorize' the use of troops abroad if their use was to be constitutional. On the contrary, the presidential position was that while any formal support that Congress might wish to extend in a given instance would be welcomed, the *independent* power of the executive was sufficient."[42] (Emphasis added.) That position means that the executive branch considers itself dominant in theory as well as in fact. That is raison d'état run riot. Without any perceptible danger and merely on the executive's assertion, a major war was fought. And lost.

Where, then, were the courts and Congress, those ostensible checks on the executive? They remained in operation, of course, as did other American institutions. Indeed the civil rights movement—the push of black Americans for better treatment—reached its apex during the time that escalation took place. But the courts, displaying the typical lack of courage of judges or perhaps the fact that judges are taken from the Establishment, simply refused to rule on the validity of Vietnam.[43] Well enough, one might say, for could the judiciary have done much even if it had wanted to? The answer is no. But what about Congress? The answer is that Congress could have blocked the appropriations necessary to wage war, but consistently refused to do so. Not until 1973, and then only when a rising tide of domestic discontent was being felt throughout Capitol Hill, did Congress act.[44] So long as those who were drafted and sent to Vietnam came mainly from the blacks and other disadvantaged groups, Congress was quite content to go along with the executive. (A question worth asking and exploring, but only posed here, is whether there was a relationship between Great Society welfare programs for the disadvantaged and the overwhelming employment of young males from that segment to fight the war. Was the Great Society a way of paying black, and other, Americans for their sacrifices?)

In net, then, the President can use force and even (as in the Cuban missile crisis) anticipatory force. This is more than the pagan morality put into American constitutional law. When the President is wrong, as all were in Vietnam, the action is immoral under any criterion. Machiavelli would probably not have approved the Vietnam adventure. For when extraordinary action is taken, the President labors under an obligation to succeed. The action was "reprehensible," in Machiavelli's language, and the result was even worse. Success did not come.

The several presidents went astray on their perception of the "public good" and how to attain it. John Locke in his *Second Treatise of Government* defended use of the prerogative, basing it on the ancient principle salus populi suprema lex (the welfare of the people is the supreme law), in these well-known words: "This power to act according to discretion, for the public good, without the prescription of the law, and sometimes even against it, is that which is called the prerogative. . . . There is a latitude left to the executive power, to do many things of choice, which the laws do not prescribe."[45] The executive, when he undertakes these extreme actions, must insure that the public good is being furthered—that he acts because, and only because, the welfare of the people is in fact at stake. That is precisely what went wrong in Vietnam; or, rather, what was inherently wrong in the first place. The "public good" was not being furthered by military action; the welfare of the American people was not in jeopardy. There was, in sum, no crisis except one manufactured by American policymakers.

Presidents *must* act in the face of crisis, actual or impending, of that there can be no doubt; but they labor under the burden of being correct; their analysis of the situation must be accepted by both their contemporaries and by historians.

The lesson of Vietnam, put bluntly, is simply this: If one is going to employ military force—to exercise it according to the dictates of raison d'état—then be sure than one wins. This, be it said, is not an argument for going into Vietnam in the first place. Far from it. That ill-starred adventure was wrong from the beginning, wrong under both the pagan and the Judeo-Christian moralities. It was the exemplification of evil in public affairs.

Consider, however, two military episodes not so different from Vietnam, but which ended in victory: The 1848 war against Mexico[46] and the Spanish-American War.[47] Both were imperialistic adventures, taken not for reasons of national security but to expand territory (and consequent riches). Both were opposed, and stoutly, by many people. One need only cite Thoreau's imprisonment for not paying taxes to help support the Mexican War, during which time he wrote his famous essay on civil disobedience, to note the discontent within the nation not dissimilar to that during the 1960s over Vietnam. The United States won: the end justified the means. That Mexico did not agree is shrugged off. So, too, with that "splendid little war" (Theodore Roosevelt's term) against Spain: Not only the engagement with Spain but particularly the savage suppression of the Filipinos after the war have now been washed out in the aura of victory. Again, for Americans, the ends justified the means; even though the means were reprehensible, the effects were good under the pagan morality—however bad they may have been under the Judeo-Christian morality. It seems that for most people, losing is the greatest sin of all.

Some actions of American leaders—the Mexican War and the Spanish-American War could fit this category—do not, however, jibe with either morality. Perhaps the best example of this in American history is the systematic mistreatment of the native American Indians. That history of amoral actions, taken for the basest reasons, deserves brief discussion, for it is a record of democratic dictatorship as it has usually been pursued in the United States against a limited number of people in a limited area.

AMERICAN INDIANS

Until recently, Indians were "nonpersons" under the Constitution. From the time that Europeans first landed on American shores, the natives they found here were systematically driven from their ancestral homes, their lands confiscated, their lives terminated in the steady drive westward. The Fifth Amendment to the Constitution, promulgated in 1791, states in part that "no person shall be deprived of life, liberty, or property without due process of law." The Indians were deprived of all three with only the semblance of law. Treaties, when made, were consistently broken. Only by asserting, as we have (chapter 4), that law is what officers of the State do in fact, can American action against the Indians be said to be legal. That does not mean that the law permitting anti-Indian actions comported with either morality. The reason? In effect, and in fact, the Indian was not a person within the meaning of the Constitution. He did not exist in the law.

So much for written constitutions. The extermination or banishment of Indians is a series of examples of raison d'état in action. But one would be hard put to perceive either the pagan morality or the Judeo-Christian morality in action. Official acts against Indians were at best amoral; at worst they were evil. Even after the Fourteenth Amendment was added to the Constitution, containing a similar due process clause and also an equal protection clause ("no state shall deny any person the equal protection of the laws"), Indians were still nonpersons. It is only in recent years, and then only partially, that they have come under the aegis of the Constitution.

Greed, pure and simple, was the motivation. The Indians had what the white men wanted. The whites had superior resources and took what they wanted. The Indians not killed were herded onto reservations in the most desolate parts of the country. Americans would like to forget those unsavory episodes, particularly when lecturing about treatment of blacks in South Africa; but they cannot—or at least, should not. This is not to justify the actions of present-day Afrikaaners, but merely to point out that our own history is none too pristine when it comes to those considered to be aborigines. Greed, be it said, is not part of Machiavelli's pagan morality.

Of particular interest also is the indisputable fact that the Supreme Court, that ostensible barrier against arbitrary governmental actions, was no obstacle at all to brutal treatment of the Indians. Even when Congress during this century in what may have been a spurt of latent guilt, enacted a statute allowing some Indians to sue the United States in certain instances, the Court found a technical means to invalidate the statute. In this, the Justices in effect acted as arms of the executive, which argued that there was no "case or controversy" —no adversary proceeding—and thus could not be heard by the Supreme Court.[48] But there is nothing in the Constitution—or the statutes, for that matter—which says that there must be true adversary proceedings in federal court. It is a self-imposed limitation on the judiciary, used when the Justices so desire, the end result of which meant that the Indians were left without a remedy. So much for the written Constitution and a Supreme Court.

Enough has been said about the use of violence, in declared wars and otherwise, to validate the existence of two moralities—one of public action and one of public statement—and also to show that at times even the pagan morality is transgressed. To round out the discussion, reference should be made to other instances in American history where raison d'état (and raison de groupe) have been employed. This will illustrate the range and nature of emergency actions taken by government, for diverse reasons. We have seen that the modern State is a combination of public and private power—hence, raison de groupe, which should be seen then as part of raison d'état. Included in the following exposition are such matters as economic depressions, control of dissident groups, terrorism, antisubversive measures, forced movement of people, and (historically) labor strife. Each deserves fuller treatment, but since each exemplifies the conclusions that can be drawn about the overt use of calculated violence by the State, the discussion will be relatively brief.

Following that exposition, conclusions will be summarized, built around the theme that the pagan morality is dominant. In addition, the role of courts and legislatures will be emphasized; it will be shown that, despite separation-of-powers theory to the contrary, each branch of the federal government has participated in and cooperated with the others in emergency actions.

ECONOMIC DEPRESSIONS

Ebbs and tides in economic matters have characterized the United States since its beginning. The system, loosely called capitalism, is based mainly on private ownership and control of the means of production and distribution. For whatever reason, and no doubt the reasons are multiple, those who control private enterprise have seldom been able to achieve a stable economy. The net result is that destitution has periodically swept the country, hitting all save the favored few. Until 1933, government eschewed intervention to assist economic recovery. President Herbert Hoover is the classic, but by no means the only, example. He could sit in the White House, dining sumptuously, while knowing that people were hungry and desperate—and doing nothing. Like the British during "the great hunger" in Ireland,[49] he—outwardly, at least—thought with the Social Darwinists that government help went not only against the grain of laissez-faire economic theory, but was basically wrong. The economy would recover by itself, was the general idea. (It is grimly amusing, perhaps, that a nation of avowed pragmatists elected to the presidency a man who so sedulously followed an ideology.) Hoover did little. The most important governmental action in his administration was the Reconstruction Finance Act, by which federal funds were allocated (through loans) to business, which—so it was hoped—would then employ some of the millions of men in dire penury. In economic terms, it was on the basis of the "trickle-down" theory, by which those at the top are helped, and it is expected that eventually the benefits would seep down to those at the bottom. (That notion still has adherents, but is as invalid today as it was during Herbert Hoover's tenure in office.)

The governmental posture changed abruptly, as is well known, when Franklin D. Roosevelt replaced Hoover. His was the first administration in American history to try to alleviate a depression through governmental action. Roosevelt employed crisis (warlike) techniques in meeting a critical danger to the entire nation. He proposed, "not prudence, but the deliberate assumption of risks in the hope of great gains."[50] Whether those gains were sufficient to the need is not the point here; it is probable that the nation emerged from economic depression only with the coming of the war economy of the late 1930s and early 1940s (carried on since then during various periods of the Cold War.) The point, rather, is the type of action that FDR took during a period in which, as Professor Rossiter put it, Roosevelt "was as much the government of the United States in . . . grave national emergency as Lincoln and Wilson had been in those of the past."[51] Take, for example, these statements from his inaugural address in 1933:

I am prepared under my constitutional duty to recommend the measures that a stricken nation in the midst of a stricken world may require. These measures, or other measures as the Congress may build out of its experience and wisdom, I shall seek, within my constitutional authority, to bring to speedy adoption. But in the event that the national emergency is still critical, I shall not evade the clear course of duty that will then confront me. I shall ask the Congress for the one remaining instrument to meet the crisis—broad Executive power to wage a war against the emergency, as great as the power that would be given me if we were in fact invaded by a foreign foe.[52]

Of note in that statement is the need for delegation of power from Congress. The President, however, may have been speaking only for the public (and Congress); perhaps he did not really believe that he had to await the deliberations emanating from Capitol Hill. On March 6, 1933, two days after that inaugural address and three days before Congress was summoned into emergency session, FDR referred to the existence of a national emergency and ordered a bank "holiday," forbade the export of gold and silver, and prohibited transactions in foreign exchange—a pure example of presidential dictatorship. His authority for that? A dubious reading of the Trading with the Enemy Act of 1917—a World War I measure aimed at foreign exchange matters. His authority *in fact*? Raison d'état: The nation was in dire straits; its very survival was at stake. That Congress speedily ratified those actions (on March 9, 1933), and gave the President even more authority, does not belie the fact that FDR acted contrary to law as it was then known. His actions comported with both the pagan and the Judeo-Christian moralities. Survival of the nation, compassion for its people, were his motivations.

During the Hundred Days following Roosevelt's inauguration, the President and Congress worked closely together, so closely that Congress could be called a rubber stamp for presidential edicts. Separation of powers was forgotten; the chasm between the two political branches of government, Congress and the executive, was completely bridged—but only for a time. The National Recovery Act provides apt illustration.[53] The Act was the first major attempt to deal with the depression. Codes of fair competition of business were issued by government, after being drawn up by industry groups. In time, growing opposition in Congress, fed by interest groups in the nation, led ultimately to a series of Supreme Court decisions that struck down New Deal legislation.[54] The NRA was prominent among them. The declaration of policy in the NRA was typical of other statutes, in declaring a national emergency: "A national emergency productive of widespread unemployment and disorganization of industry, which burdens interstate and foreign commerce, affects the public welfare, and undermines the standard of living of the American people, is hereby declared to exist."

NRA operated for only two years. It was noteworthy for the fact that governmental power, for the first time in American history, was overtly delegated to industry groups under the supervision of the administration. The statute was an express move toward a corporate State; for the first time, American formal law expressly recognized the close connection between government and business. When the Supreme Court declared the NRA unconstitutional in 1935, what was begun under it—close government-business cooperation —continued informally. What did not continue was the public check in the program: the fact that the decision of industry boards had to be approved by government. In terms of political theory, pluralism was given a mighty boost, but as will be discussed, it simply does not work adequately. It does not work because each group pursues narrowly conceived goals—for its own interest, a sort of raison de groupe, one might say—without an overall authoritative spokesman for "the public interest." The President tries to do this, but cannot, because interest groups have conquered Congress and the bureaucracy. Without them, the President is reduced to negotiating "treaties" with them. In Machiavelli's terms, the President is not a prince. Democratic dictatorship does not go that far.

Nonetheless, the President does have certain emergency economic powers, although these come from Congress. Absent such an obvious and all-out economic crisis as the Great Depression, no chief executive would be able to rule by fiat. So President Harry Truman learned in 1952, when during the course of the Korean conflict he ordered seizure of the steel mills when a strike was threatened. Congress had not authorized that seizure; and even though the nation was at war, the war was undeclared. A majority of the Supreme Court simply could not find an emergency of sufficient urgency. Truman could only muster three of the nine Justices, the dissenters adhering to a theory of inherent emergency powers in the President. In all probability, however, the dissenters' view will prevail should another President consider crisis action to be necessary. Also worthy of note is the fact that the Court did not say that if Congress had authorized the seizure, it would have been valid. Justice Hugo Black's opinion for the Court concentrated on precisely that issue—the fact that Congress had not done so. The lesson, then, is that the President and Congress acting together will find no barrier in the Constitution for seizures of basic industries during times of strife.

The important lesson to be drawn from FDR's antidepression actions is not only that, after some preliminary decisions otherwise, they were constitutionally valid, but that measures taken then have become permanent techniques and institutions of government. In sum, the Great Depression added greatly both to presidential power and to the constitutional power of government generally.

Were the New Deal economic measures an example of the pagan or the Judeo-Christian morality, or both? At first glance, one would think that the compassion inherent in the New Deal programs exemplified the second (Judeo-Christian) morality. But is that really true? I suggest not: The New Deal, in final analysis, was a means by which "the system" was preserved;[55] its programs enabled those who had always been in actual power in the United States to remain in power. Discontent was "bought off," so to speak; the economically disadvantaged who were coming dangerously close to an all-out onslaught on the system were given social security and other financial aid, farmers were allowed to couple permanently to the federal treasury, and labor was allowed to organize and bargain collectively. That is the first (pagan) morality par excellence. It also illustrated the principle of the economy of means: just enough was done to buy off social discontent. The New Deal, finally, made a necessity out of decency, a principle which, as we have already said, Machiavelli approved. FDR seemed to act "out of generosity," but "necessity" constrained him (and the power structure for which he spoke).

CONTROL OF DISSIDENT GROUPS

The dissident has never been suffered gladly in the United States. Only when dissent takes innocuous forms—as, say, Thoreau at Walden Pond—is the person tolerated (for Thoreau the tolerance has become, for some, veneration). An "open" society has been much more conformist than is extolled in the myth.

How, then, is the dissident controlled? Usually through use of the law and the legal system. Radicals and deviants, with some exceptions, are not shot down, and they are rarely victims of emergency legislation. The process is much more subtle. Injunctions are issued by judges always taken from the Establishment; Congressional and state legislative committees inquire into their actions; and at times they are tried in an outwardly lawful way and convicted of criminal activity. Examples? In 1920 a man in Connecticut was sent to jail for six months for having said that Lenin was "the brainiest" or "one of the brainiest" political officers in the world.[56] Jump a few decades to the 1970s, where in North Carolina some civil rights advocates were arrested and convicted on trumped-up charges, and given savage prison sentences.[57] "The hidden underbelly of American politics," says Professor Murray Levin, is the

deeply felt intolerance that springs from our intense commitment to Americanism, the irrational and compulsive need to defend the assumptions of John Locke and Adam Smith, the anti-Semitism, the nativism, the anti-intellectualism, the vigilantism, the racism, the xenophobia, the pursuit of self-interest under the guise of superpatriotism, and the profound antiradicalism that can be observed "in extremis" during the hysteria of such matters as the Red Scare of 1919-20, and McCarthyism have always been and are today the working assumptions of millions of Americans.[58]

Repression of dissidents is not an aberration; it is as American as apple pie.

The seductive nature of much of this lawful governmental action is exemplified in the 1959 Supreme Court case of Barenblatt v. United States.[59] There the Court upheld Barenblatt's conviction for contempt of Congress when he refused to answer questions about possible Communist party affiliations. He had argued that the First Amendment's freedom of expression provisions inferentially included a right to remain silent. Not so, said the Court in a 5 to 4 decision: Congress has the power to investigate Communists and "the balance between the individual and governmental interests here at stake must be struck in favor of the latter." "In the last analysis," said Justice John Harlan for the Court, Congress's power "rests on the right of self-preservation, 'the ultimate value of any society.' . . . Justification for its exercise in turn rests on the long and widely accepted view that the tenets of the Communist Party include the ultimate overthrow of the government of the United States by force and violence, a view which has been given formal expression by the Congress." That, in sum, is a form of thought control, wholly lawful because it was uttered by a majority of the Supreme Court. It boggles the mind to determine how Barenblatt's silence had anything to do with any proposed overthrow of the government, imminent or deferred.

Dealing with alleged subversives deserves lengthier treatment. Before turning to that question, however, the essential lesson of the Red Scare of 1919-1920, McCarthyism, and similar episodes in American history is this: They are not the exception; they are the rule, when considered necessary by political elites.

ANTI-SUBVERSIVE MEASURES

Much that has been said thus far in this chapter deals with actions that are known (or should be known) to any knowledgeable person. The situation differs, however, when one enters the shadowy world of subversion. By definition, those considered—usually, but not always, by the executive—to be harmful to the body politic operate in clandestine ways. How, then, may a nation purportedly devoted to constitutionalism and to limited government deal with individuals or groups who would wreak harm on the nation? Or who would be considered to have that potential?

The question is easily asked and can be bluntly answered: Action accords with the pagan morality; public statements, including those of judges, speak in terms of the Judeo-Christian morality. The problem obtruded early in American history. In 1798, Congress passed the Alien and Sedition Act— perhaps the most repressive piece of legislation ever enacted by that body. Seldom enforced and never considered by the Supreme Court, that act was ultimately erased from the statute books. The point is that repression of people considered subversive began quite early after the republic was formed. The nineteenth century, while ostensibly a time of freedom of expression, generally was in fact anything but that. Dissenters in America have always had a hard time; only when their dissent—their speech and actions—are not inimical to the established order were they—are they—permitted.

Schenck v. United States and Abrams v. United States, 1919 decisions by the Supreme Court,[60] provide apt illustration, as does the more recent decision in Dennis v. United States.[61] Schenck is the first significant freedom of speech decision by the High Court in American history—a fact important in itself. How explain the failure of the Court to rule on the Alien and Sedition Acts or to rule on any other suppression of speech—there were many— during the nineteenth century? The answer is easy—but only on technical grounds for everything except the Alien and Sedition Act. The First Amendment by its express terms limits the federal government only; in an 1833 decision the Court had held that the Bill of Rights was not applicable to the states. That lasted until a breakthrough was made in 1925. That, however, is a technical reason. Can it be said that the federal government did nothing about freedom of speech, except that one 1798 statute, prior to the First World War? Were state governmental officials the only ones who trampled on that freedom? The Alien and Sedition Act has been mentioned; but other federal actions effectively stopped that freedom of expression that Americans today take for granted. And not only in war—as in Civil War. It is true that internal subversion was not a real concern of a nation that was protected by two oceans and the British navy, and that saw domestic development as its main task. So the states did what was necessary, and did it effectively. The Haymarket episode which made a martyr of Governor Altgeld is an example. But *In re Debs*, a Supreme Court decision upholding imprisonment of a labor leader, surely is another—and that *was* federal action.

It was only when the nation lost what some native chauvinists call its innocence and plunged deeply and irretrievably into world affairs, first in the Spanish-American War, and then more importantly in World War I, did federal action limiting expression become prominent. Here *Schenck* and *Abrams* are significant; they began the modern theory of the philosophy of the First Amendment. Articulated by Justice Oliver Wendell Holmes, that, in sum, is the theory of the "marketplace of truth." First, however, the meaning of *Schenck*: There, Justice Holmes created, for the first time, the "clear and present danger" test for governmental actions impinging on speech; there he said that the First Amendment did not protect a man falsely shouting "Fire!" in a crowded theater; there, Mr. Schenck and cohorts went to jail for exercising their constitutional freedoms; and there, Holmes *for the first time in American history* tried to carve out an area of constitutionally *protected* speech. That is the meaning of the test—clear and present danger—enunciated by Holmes. Schenck went to jail, but a chink had been put in what had been an impregnable wall of the right to suppress expression for the good of the State. It is worth mention that at the very time that the Court was making grand pronouncements about protected speech, Attorney General Mitchell Palmer was conducting his notorious "Palmer raids," broadside deprivations of civil liberties by the Department of Justice against aliens merely suspected of subversion or disloyalty.[62]

Americans—the nation of an alleged but not actual melting pot—have long had a fear of alien ideologies and thoughts. Avowed pragmatists, they thereby (at least tacitly) conceded the power of ideas. Those fears were puerile at best: a few puny and insignificant "anarchists" or "syndicalists" could hardly have brought down the republic. Nonetheless, those who expressed the "alien" ideas, whether in time of war or not, were savagely repressed—by both federal and state governments, and the Supreme Court bowed supinely to the executive and Congressional (and state governmental officials) reading of the First Amendment.

Dennis v. *United States*, decided in 1952, clearly illustrates the point. At issue was the question of whether leaders of the Communist party could be prosecuted under the Smith Act (making it unlawful knowingly to advocate the "duty, necessity, desirability, or propriety of overthrowing or destroying any government in the United States by force and violence.") No *overt* anti-government (antistate) actions were shown. At most, Dennis and cohorts published materials calling at some indeterminate future time for a Communist victory at the ballot box. They did not agitate for revolution, but at most merely predicted that at some time a revolution would occur. For this they went to jail. The episode is a clear example of raison d'état, at the bidding of the executive branch, and of (at best) the pagan morality in action. Probably it did not comport even with the pagan morality, for no evidence was produced to prove that the Communists were an actual harm—a clear and present danger—to the State. It was a political trial, for political purposes,[63] and the fact that subsequent Supreme Court decisions watered down the impact of *Dennis* means little insofar as State action against those said to be subversive are concerned.

The *Dennis* case illustrates a long line of actual, but seldom acknowledged, repression—of thought control. At no time in American history has speech deemed inimical to the vital interests of the State been permitted. The seemingly clear language of the First Amendment does not mean what it says: "Congress shall make no law. . . ." means, in fact, as seen in official actions, that Congress may make *some* laws. (So, too, with the states.) Only when the interests of the State are not considered to be endangered, as when a young man paraded in public during the last months of the Vietnam conflict, with the slogan "Fuck the Draft" printed on his leather jacket,[64] is speech upheld. Dualism—two moralities—once again. We—public officers—say one thing and do another. And the Supreme Court participates.

ESPIONAGE

There is a code term for much of this: "national security,"[65] in the name of which many actions are taken. (The term in many respects is a synonym for raison d'état.) The banner of national security flies high when, for example, the House Un-American Activities Committee pillaged the country in a largely bootless quest for subversives (mainly communists). The plea of national security was even used—to no avail—when it was learned that the Nixon White House had ordered the burglary of the office of Daniel Ellsberg's psychiatrist. Many crimes, surely under the Judeo-Christian morality but also under the pagan morality, are committed to using the justification of national security. In most, but not all, of these the President (plus Congress) prevails; the Constitution is no barrier.

An as yet unsettled constitutional question—whether a warrant is needed in electronic surveillance of persons suspected of conducting foreign intelligence—reveals some of the conflicting currents that eddy around the incanta-tion by government officials of the magic words, "national security." We have already seen in Judge Roger Robb's 1978 decision in *Halkin* v. *Helms* that the "state secrets privilege" is absolute, and therefore that American citizens cannot complain in court about having their overseas telephone and telegraph messages intercepted and read by American intelligence agencies. Does that mean that suspected spies from other countries can be wiretapped without a judicial warrant? The answer is by no means clear at this time: the Supreme Court has yet to rule on the question. Of the lower courts that have, the deci-sions go both ways.

Under the terms of the Fourth Amendment, a warrant must be obtained before a search may be made. In 1972, the Supreme Court unanimously held that the amendment prohibited wiretaps of domestic individuals or groups without a warrant; but Justice Lewis Powell, speaking for the Court, carefully noted that its ruling did not extend to intelligence gathering by foreign powers.[66] Two United States Courts of Appeals have wrestled with that problem, only to produce contradictory answers. The Third Circuit main-tains that no warrant is required, but the District of Columbia Circuit seem-ingly held to the contrary.[67] The law, thus, is unsettled. Only when the Supreme Court, possibly anticipated by Congress, rules on the issue will the formal law become clear.

In the meantime, the living constitution—the pagan morality—is said by high officers in the executive branch to permit warrantless wiretaps in matters involving foreign intelligence. The magic words, "national security," are invoked to justify, for example, electronic surveillance of an American citizen (and government officials) convicted for passing secrets to a foreign power. As we have said, national security equals reason of State—thus far, as deter-mined by the President. Constitutional dualism, again. Two moralities in operation at the same time.

EVACUATION OF PEOPLE

Still another example of democratic dictatorship, of the operation of raison d'état, may be seen in the forced evacuation of people. We have already noted the brutal treatment of American Indians; those not killed were herded on reservations on land no one else wanted. And we have also discussed the World War II internment in concentration camps of the Japanese-Americans, the bulk of whom were American citizens. Two examples of more recent vintage are illustrative: the islands of Bikini and Diego Garcia.

When the United States decided in the late 1940s to test some atomic bombs, the site chosen was not American territory, but the atoll of Bikini.[68] People resident there were forcibly removed and relocated hundreds of miles away—all in the name of American national security. Thirty years later, lasting radiation after-effects still did not permit the return of the natives.

Diego Garcia is less well known.[69] A spit of land in the Indian Ocean, once under Britain's sovereignty, it became a military base for the United States. But first the people who lived there had to be evacuated and relocated against their will. Those still alive now live in nauseous slums on Mauritius.

The lesson is clear: When considered necessary, the United States government will move people against their will in order to further a view of national security. That is raison d'état in pure form. Whether it was in fact vitally necessary to explode atomic bombs at Bikini or confiscate the property of the people on Diego Garcia is another question, one that is not even asked, publicly at least, by American officials or the American press.

The State in the United States (and elsewhere), is, despite theory and ideology to the contrary, the corporate State—a fusion of public and private power into a transcendent entity at once superior to and greater than the sum of its parts. Government in the United States is a peculiar amalgam of public and private power, exercised by public and private bureaucracies that are closely interlocked in fact—but not in theory. Private enterprise in America refers to ownership of shares in corporation, not to their control and not to the functions they perform; those functions are public. Once that is perceived, then the concept of raison d'état must of necessity encompass raison de groupe.

Which groups? The giant business corporation (and smaller ones, too), for certain. Trade Unions. Universities. Farmers' organizations. Veterans' legions. Churches. Political parties. Those are the principal, but far from the only, ones. Each is a bureaucracy—a private bureaucracy that often performs public functions. As such, they are entities that have survival and aggrandizement as principal goals. We now concentrate on one of them—the business corporation—but what is said can and should be applied to the others as well.

The overriding criterion for business judgment is profit. In the name of profit, which economists such as Milton Friedman believe should be the sole motivation of corporate managers, many crimes—of omission and commission—have been committed. Corporate growth is the desired end: "The way to achieve and retain business greatness," Osborn Elliott said in *Men at the Top*, "is always to be striving for something more."[70] In getting that "something more" corporate officers have often played fast and loose with the law. Enough now is known about "white collar crime" or what Ralph Nader calls "crime in the [executive] suites," to know that criminality, if not pervasive, is far from unknown in the business world.

Examples are legion, but need not be multiplied to make the point—that men, otherwise pillars of rectitude, at times will take actions to further the interests of their firms even though they know they are breaking the law. For example:

1. The "electrical conspiracy" cases of the early 1960s when executive of major electrical firms were convicted for price fixing.[71]

2. The little-publicized portion of the Senate Watergate Committee's work, which revealed widespread corporate violation of the election laws.[72]

3. Bribery by Lockheed (and other U.S. aircraft companies) of officials in other nations in order to sell airplanes.[73]

4. Knowing delivery of faulty aircraft brakes to the Navy by the B. F. Goodrich Company.[74]

5. Innumerable violations of antipollution laws by corporations.[75]

The list could be expanded, if not indefinitely, then certainly to the extent that a book would be needed merely to list the many peccadilloes, large and small, of corporations. Corporate executives did and still do these deeds, all for the greater glory of the enterprise. The law responds at best in a halting manner.[76] When the perpetrators are caught and convicted, their sentences usually are light to the extent of being ludicrous. One example, not from the United States, shows the pattern: Hitler could not have gone his evil way without the quite willing help of I. G. Farben, a German chemical conglomerate. When, after the Second World War, some Farben executives were tried at Nuremberg, their sentences were "light enough to please a chicken thief"[77] —even though their deeds were as bad as the Nazis at their worst.

The lessons are at least twofold. First, corporate crime is a way of aggrandizing the firm itself; hence, the term raison de groupe (or, in this instance, raison de compagnie). The men who acted illegally or immorally did so not for personal gain so much as for the good of the company. (Speaking parenthetically, this is an example of "the banality of evil" [78]—Hannah Arendt's term for Adolf Eichmann's actions.) Their identifications and loyalties, in other words, went to the company rather than to the nation (which, it may be noted, is one way of saying that citizenship of the corporation is now becoming as important, at times more so, as citizenship of the nation-state).[79]

Second, quite often, and particularly in international business affairs, the corporation and the government work together. Government supports, and seldom calls a halt to corporate activities abroad. Examples, again, are legion. One will suffice to show the pattern: the United Fruit Company in Central America, a company that for years was the effective government of several Central American nations—with the full knowledge and indeed support of the United States government. Major General Smedley D. Butler, Commander of the Marines, let the dirty little "secret" out of the bag when in 1935 he wrote in *Common Sense* magazine:

I spent thirty-three years and four months in active service as a member of the country's most agile military force—the Marine Corps. . . . And during that period I spent most of my time being a high-class muscle man for Big Business, for Wall Street, and for the bankers. In short, I was a racketeer for capitalism. . . . Thus I helped make Mexico and especially Tampico safe for American oil interests in 1914. I helped make Haiti and Cuba a decent place for the National City Bank boys to collect revenues in. . . . I helped purify Nicaragua for the international banking house of Brown Brothers in 1909-1912. I brought light to the Dominican Republic for American sugar interests in 1916. I helped make Honduras "right" for the American fruit companies in 1903. In China in 1927 I helped see to it that Standard Oil went its way unmolested.[80]

The bitter fruit of those decades of repression and authoritarianism is now being reaped in Nicaragua and other Latin American nations.

Back, however, to United Fruit. The tale has been well told by Thomas P. McCann, UF's vice president for public relations, in his 1976 volume *An American Company: The Tragedy of United Fruit*.[81] McCann tells us that "once you get to know it from the inside, you realize that a company is a living organism, just like a family." That "living organism" called United Fruit Company was for a period the most powerful economic and political force in Central America. It won its way by force, bribery, and political subversion — all with the acquiescence and often with the ready cooperation of the State Department and the military forces. The Central Intelligence Agency used UF ships in the abortive Bay of Pigs fiasco. The close connection between business and government is nowhere better seen than in the relationships between U.S. and UF. For United *Fruit* one could say United *States*, and vice versa, for their interests coincided. The United States, despite hortatory pronouncements to the contrary, did not look with favor at democratic governments south of the border. It still does not — as witness Chile, Paraguay, and Brazil, among many.

As with international business, so with domestic matters during the nineteenth century: the corporation, which through a piece of remarkable lawyer's verbal sleight-of-hand became a constitutional person in 1886, was able to draw upon all segments of government for protection from the rising demands of the working class. The history of the American labor movement is one of oft-times savage repression. An oversupply of labor, coming mainly from unrestricted immigration, meant competition for what were mostly unskilled jobs. Corporate managers, aided by their minions in government, began an enormous growth in number and size of corporations in the post-Civil War period. One labor historian, Richard Lester, concluded in 1947: "During the depression from 1873 to 1879, employers sought to eliminate trade unions by a systematic policy of lockouts, blacklists, labor espionage, and legal prosecution. The widespread use of blacklists and Pinkerton labor spies caused labor to organize more or less secretly and undoubtedly helped bring on the violence that characterized labor strife during this period."[82] Nonetheless, workingmen continued to struggle and to organize — and eventually were able to persuade state legislatures to pass laws regulating wages and hours, only to run into the barrier of the Supreme Court. The Justices, as John R. Commons said in 1924, operated for at least fifty years as "the first authoritative faculty of political economy in the world's history."[83] Soon after discovering that a disembodied economic enterprise, the corporation, was a person, they invented a new legal and constitutional concept: "substantive due process of law."[84] Following that, they effectively watered down the Sherman antitrust law, passed in 1890 in a legislative effort to control giant business.

Substantive due process transformed judicial review from a seldom used, innocuous instrument of governance into a powerful tool. That tool was used by the courts to favor business enterprises, thus again exemplifying a close connection between business and government. For a half century, judges at the trial level issued injunctions against strikes and the Supreme Court declared wage-and-hour legislation unconstitutional. The latter deserves brief discussion. What happened was this: The Justices of the Court, seeing in the Constitution two due process clauses—one limiting the federal and the other state governments—altered by judicial fiat that concept from what had theretofore been a *procedural* matter. The principal question historically was: did government officers follow the proper ritual (procedure) when limiting private activity? If so, then all was well. That was the ancient conception, with roots running at least as far back as the Magna Carta. "Substantive" due process means that judges look not only at the ritual but also at the content—at what is done. In brief, it enabled the Justices, as Commons said, to substitute their views of wisdom of legislation for those of Congress and the state legislatures.

More specifically, the Court found lurking in the undefined term *due process of law* the idea of freedom of contract, which it said was of the liberty protected against regulation by government. The Constitution states: "Life, liberty, and property" shall not be taken without due process of law. The Court redefined the nature of liberty in the United States. In economic terms, that was laissez-faire run riot. In political terms, it meant that judges became the ultimate arbiter of economic policy in the nation. They had an open-ended, self-asserted power to read their ideas of good social policy into the Constitution. That they did, by protecting the corporation through outlawing adverse regulation. The meaning of this is simple: raison de compagnie became enmeshed with raison d'état.

Lochner v. *New York*[85] is illustrative. In that famous case, decided in 1905, the Supreme Court invalidated New York's statute imposing a sixty-hour limit on employees of bakeries. With typical casuistry, the majority of the Court found that the law intruded on both the company's *and* the worker's freedom to contract. "The interest of the public," said Justice Peckham, would not be "in the slightest degree affected" by the statute, a clear instance of meshing the interests of the company with the interests of "society." Peckham simply refused to recognize what all knew, or should have known, that necessitous men cannot be free men; and thus that the liberty he protected was really that of the business firm *only*, not of the worker who was only too willing to receive the benefit granted by the legislature. Numerous other cases in the 1887-1936 period attest to the same conclusion. It was only when hydraulic forces of social discontent reached a point where it was seen by all, including the Supreme Court, that social legislation—labor legislation—was a necessary price to pay to buy off that discontent did the Supreme Court shift gears and suddenly find that Congress, and the state legislatures, could indeed legislate in socioeconomic matters. Not that it has mattered all that much for the public at large; the raison de groupe of the companies has now become the raison de groupe of the unions—which often, indeed usually, cooperate with business more than they conflict. The Justices, it should be noted, have never extended laissez-faire to prohibit government aid to business. They had only one eye, and that was cocked against regulation—another example, if one is needed, of the interlocks between business and government. Many public subsidies of business never got to court.

All of that is clear enough—at least, for those with eyes to see. An even more obvious example of the use of State power against the labor movement may be seen in the campaign against "Wobblies"—the Industrial Workers of the World (IWW). Founded in 1905, the IWW went beyond seeking mere economic gains; it wished to reorganize the American political economy. Cooperative labor groups would control production, distribution, and even exchange. The IWW acted by trying to organize workers at the lowest rungs of the labor force. The reaction from government (prodded by the corporations) was quick and savage.[86] In 1917, for example, with the approval of President Woodrow Wilson, their headquarters were attacked by federal officials, their records confiscated, and their leaders arrested on charges of sedition, espionage, and interference with the war effort. Found guilty, the IWW leaders were imprisoned, even though there was in fact no evidence against them. The Wobblies were smashed.[87]

The point, I think, has been made: Companies (and other groups) pursue narrow goals of self-interest; that is raison de groupe. When they are able to use the mechanism of the State—the official organs of government—in their behalf, then raison de groupe becomes meshed with an overarching concept of raison d'état. The morality? Not better than the pagan morality of Machiavelli, and often far worse. Some of the actions taken in the past by corporate managers (and other leaders of groups) do not comport even with that morality; they are indecent by any criterion. The further point is that the State, as should now be obvious, must be considered to be a fusion of public and private power.

Since Watergate catapulted Richard Nixon from the presidency, a myth has grown of the omnipotence—the great power—of the press, accompanied by a corollary that the media (owners and reporters alike) are in an adversary relationship with the government. Neither idea is accurate. The *Washington Post* is credited at times with bringing Nixon down; but that is only a part of the actual story. Watergate was at least a four-legged stool. The press was there, to be sure; but so, too, were the Senate Watergate Committee, Judge John Sirica, and the Special Prosecutor. If any one episode can be said to have struck the lethal blow against Nixon, it was the Senate Committee's disclosure that the President had bugged the Oval Office of the White House —and, presumably, that John Dean's testimony could be proved or disproved. The *Post* was early on the story, and kept it alive; but its power is not nearly so great as some assert.

If that be so for Watergate, how about other examples of the purported power of the press? The same may be said. The mass media, as Tom Bethell observed in *Harper's Magazine* in 1977, "can best be understood as departments of the federal bureaucracy."[88] (Perhaps a fifth leg should be added to the Watergate stool—the federal bureaucrats who resisted attempts by Nixonites to subvert government.) The media are not the nemesis of government; they are its surrogates. The news leak from within government was the main staple that fed the media's coverage of Watergate; and is today a main resource for reporters. The unidentified "sources" that sprinkle a news story, in print or via electronics, usually are some public officials willing to talk, but only anonymously.

That willingness may be for one of two purposes: an official's notion of where the public interest lies (this is the "whistle blower") or, far more often, attempts by government to manipulate public opinion. The latter is the more important for present purposes. Government manipulation of the press is a standard technique of high officials. Reporters tend to accept the official line on any particular matter. This is best seen in reporting of wars. As Phillip Knightley has documented in *The First Casualty*,[89] correspondents are in fact arms of the military forces with whom they associate. War is not a game. The military demands and gets total commitment, even from the press. The press may be free, but that freedom is to do what is expected, even demanded, of reporters. To "get along" the reporters "go along"—usually quite willingly.

Nowhere was this better seen than in the Vietnam conflict. But it is also prevalent throughout government, whose officers are adept at "stroking" what is often a quite willing press corps. Companies, too, with their public relations departments and calculated news releases, gain favorable publicity from a compliant group of reporters. Thomas McCann's book on United Fruit Company is revealing in this regard.

Evidence that the press is not in an adversary relationship with either government or business need not be piled up. There are reasons for that coziness. The media are private businesses, businesses with three goals— making a profit, marketing through advertising the output of consumer goods, and training the people for loyalty to the American politico-economic system.[90] Only the "underground" press and some little-read (and sometimes suppressed) political tracts operate otherwise. No segment of the mass media speaks out against the "system"; they are, in brief, house organs for the Establishment. The public's "right to know" is asserted by mass media spokesmen, but followed only when it does not conflict with those goals. Small wonder that the media are considered to be a part of government, for they are. Those who represent the State can, speaking generally, rely upon a quiescent, even servile, press corps when episodes falling within the category of raison d'état are undertaken. No overt system of censorship exists in the United States simply because there is no need for one. A pervasive system of self-censorship, at times but not always done at the request of government officers, fills this need. One example will show the pattern. When a few years ago reporters learned that a ship owned by Howard Hughes, the *Glomar*, was in fact a CIA-financed attempt to raise a sunken Soviet submarine, William Colby, Director of the CIA, prevailed upon all the mass media leaders to kill the story.[9] Only when columnist Jack Anderson refused to go along with the voluntary censorship did the press (and television) report the news. Seymour Hersh, the *New York Times* reporter who learned about *Glomar*, refused to answer questions about his part in the matter, as did Clifton Daniel, head of the *Times*' Washington office. Daniel stated (to me) that a person would have to be naive to believe that the press did not do such things often. Our "free" press is often a servile press.

That means, as Jacques Ellul has said, that all governments, including those that call themselves open, are participants in a pervasive program of propaganda.[*] Propaganda is "the expression of opinions or actions carried out deliberately by individuals or groups with a view to influencing the opinions or actions of other individuals or groups for predetermined ends and through psychological manipulations." Its goal is to maximize power by subordinating groups and individuals, while reducing the material cost of power. It may readily be seen how important the mass media are. Without them, propaganda could not be carried on. Says Ellul: "the study of propaganda must be conducted within the context of the technological society . . . Propaganda must be seen at the center of the growing powers of the State and governmental and administrative techniques. . . . In the midst of increasing mechanization and technological organization, propaganda is simply the means used to prevent these things from being felt too oppressive and to persuade men to submit with good grace."

Propaganda techniques are accompanied by acquiescence in permissiveness in personal behavior—but only so long as the vital interests of the State are not jeopardized (or even involved). No State, even those considered to be democratic and humanist, can do without propaganda as a means of governing. The mass media are primary instruments in that all-pervasive system. The "underground" press and a few little-read weeklies and monthlies, with no influence, vary the pattern. Take another example: *The Nation* published accounts of the planned Bay of Pigs invasion months before it happened, but no one heeded. The *New York Times* censored itself when one of its reporters stumbled on the story.

Franz Neumann was correct: Government in the United States has always been as strong as conditions required. It is not hyperbole to apply the label of "constitutional" or "democratic" dictatorship to the United States. The qualification is not that in numerous circumstances, some of which have been outlined in this chapter, American government was dictatorial; rather those actions were qualified by being limited in time and space. That is the principle of economy of means in operation; nothing was done beyond what was considered necessary by those wielding actual power in the nation. The victims were a relative few; the beneficiaries were many, particularly when through the use of propaganda those who spoke for the State were able to convince most people that extraordinary actions were required. Emergency actions, save in such instances as natural disasters, are always taken for the furtherance of those who control the State.

Two morallities exist in the United States. One is the first morality of the Judeo-Christian virtues; that is inherent in the sparse words of the formal Constitution—the Document in 1787, plus its twenty-six amendments. The other is the pagan morality, not expressed in the Constitution in so many words, but nonetheless both present *and* overriding. Whenever the two moralities come into conflict, it is, whether through judicial interpretation or political action, always the second, the pagan, morality that prevails in any situation deemed important by those who wield effective control in the United States. A dualism does exist in our constitutional law and history, but that ambivalence fades away when necessary. The morality of the *living* constitution always controls the often conflicting morality of the *formal* Constitution. When the two moralities come together in Supreme Court decisions, as in the Civil War and Second World War cases, they mesh into one Machiavellian principle.

This is not to say that all actions are moral under one of the two moralities.[93] Some are evil; they do not comport with either morality. They go beyond the Machiavelli of *The Discourses* to resemble the Machiavelli of *The Prince*. Amoral under either criterion are such actions as the near genocide of the native American Indians, the incarceration of American citizens of Japanese descent, the brutal treatment of the Wobblies, the Vietnam "war." Others could be listed, but need not be. Some things cannot be justified, even though (as with the Japanese-Americans) upheld by the Supreme Court, under either morality. One is tempted to agree with Lord Acton when he said in 1906: "Weighed in the scales of Liberalism, the instrument the Constitution, as it stood, was a monstrous fraud."[94] He went on to say: "And yet, by the development of the principle of Federalism, it has produced a community more powerful, more prosperous, more intelligent, and more free than any other the world has seen." Quite possibly, Acton was correct in the first quoted sentence; but his second is far from accurate. This nation grew powerful and prosperous and relatively free not because of the Constitution but in spite of it. He simply misread the meaning of the principle of federalism.

In the development of the two moralities, the dominance of the pagan morality, the judiciary (the Supreme Court) has had only an ostensibly powerful role. The political officers of government, interacting with the officers of the principal social groups, are far more powerful than are lawyer-judges. Judges are hampered by two major factors. First, they must await the accident of a lawsuit before they can act; and second, they must depend on the willingness of political officers to put their decrees into operational reality.

One final conclusion: People generally do not object to exercises of raison d'état. Rather, they applaud. The American people like the pagan morality. That is so even though masses of them dutifully go to church each week. They prefer not to think about any excessive use of power unless and until their own personal values are transgressed. It was only, to cite but one example, when middle-class whites felt the impact of Vietnam (the manpower pool of poor whites, blacks and other disadvantaged having been depleted) that social discontent reached the point where political officers had to draw back from that misadventure. That is just another way of saying that, in general, the American people are as Machiavellian as their political and economic leaders.

Part III

THE IMPLICATIONS: CONSTITUTIONAL CRISES

If there are crises—a climacteric—looming dead ahead in socioeconomic matters, there are and will be large consequences for the constitutional order. Some have long been apparent; others are just now coming into view. Part III develops facets of the constitutional crisis. A discussion of the end of the idea of liberal democracy precedes an essay on "Caesarism"—presidential government. The final chapter develops reasons for the inability of government to govern adequately. The net conclusion of part III is that the American constitutional order is changing rapidly into governance under the "Constitution of Control"—a translucent layer on the palimpsest of 1787, plus a pervasive system of economic despotism emanating from corporations and other "private" centers of power.

7

The Myth of
Liberal Democracy

"The politics of the future," Napoleon once observed, "will be concerned with the art of moving the masses."[1] So it is: The Napoleonic future has arrived. Mass "democracy" has indeed come in the United States—but only seemingly. Never have so many had the franchise—and never have so few deigned to cast their ballots. Do they know something intuitively that their "betters"—the ruling elite—know but do not tell? Never has so much outward obeisance been paid to egalitarian ideas—and never has the class—caste?—society in America seemed so obvious.

The masses can be and are moved, but manipulatively. Those who ruled in the past—they of wealth and family and position—still rule, and in their own interests. The masses—the growing lumpenproletariat—are controlled but at a price: the tradeoff is a relative trickle of material goods that, in the light of history, actually is large (opulence compared to other nations), and a growing permissiveness in personal relationships. The masses have never been free in actual fact, so they really are giving up nothing—and they know it—when they accept, even demand, material gains and personal liberties that do not challenge the power of the State or of the ruling elite. Aldous Huxley's prescient *Brave New World*,[2] published almost a half century ago, is one text from which those who wish to learn should start their journey of understanding the political (constitutional) changes that are occurring and that are well-nigh certain to take place in the future. Can, to cite only one example, there be any real difference between Huxley's soma pills for the "proles" and marijuana (now legalized for all practical purposes)?

Chapter 7 deals in main part with the growing merger of liberal democracy with "totalitarian" or "authoritarian" democracy. The latter terms will likely grate on the sensitivities of many Americans, who have been conditioned to think in terms of the antithesis of democracy and totalitarianism.

Americans like to call their government democratic, even though that label is both misleading and inaccurate. It is idle, even mischievous, to indulge in the pretense that the people rule or that they even have any substantial opportunity to choose their rulers. The Trilateral Commission, that little-known but influential "private" group of academics, politicians, and business-men from the United States, Europe and Japan, believes that democracies are becoming ungovernable. The main reason is a shift in personal values that is occurring "away from the materialistic, work-oriented, public-spirited values toward those which stress private satisfaction, leisure, and the need for 'belonging and intellectual and esthetic self-fulfillment'."[3] One should take the Trilateralists seriously, for it was from that organization that President Jimmy Carter came and from whose ranks he filled many of the top posts in his administration (Mondale, Blumenthal, Vance, Brzezinski, Brown, Chris-topher, Bowie, Richardson, Linowitz, Woodcock, Gardner, among others). They assert the growing ungovernability of democracies because of the "com-bination of challenges" that have created "a situation in which the needs for longer-term and more broadly formulated purpose and priorities, for a greater overall coherence of policy, appear at the same time that the increasing com-plexity of the social order, increasing political pressures on government, and decreasing legitimacy of government make it more and more difficult for government to achieve these goals."

Reading between the lines: What does that mean? It is a call for elitist government; and if need be, for a government that controls a planned society. Another word for that: authoritarianism. The Trilateralists are closet authori-tarians, who boldly and baldly disapprove of "the democratic challenge to authority." They also disapprove of "value-oriented intellectuals who often devote themselves to the derogation of leadership, the challenging of author-ity, and the unmasking and delegitimation of established institutions."[4] This, it is said (quite seriously), is as serious a challenge to democracies as those posed by "aristocratic cliques, fascist movements, and communist parties." The message, unstated but clear, from the Trilateralists to those intellectuals: "Shut up; shape up or ship out." That is an odd position for any group said to be concerned about the health of democracy. To unmask an established insti-tution, to challenge authority, to derogate leadership is said to be a menace. One would think that the members of the Commission would be more careful in hiding their preferences.

For so many of their members to be, or to have been, in positions of power and authority in government gives one pause. They assert a belief in democ-racy but believe instead in some type of controlled society. That is authori-tarianism. The larger meaning should also be clear: If it ever existed—which by no means is an historical certainty—liberal democracy, for whatever reason, is dying. Social conditions in the United States eat away at its under-pinnings; and the intellectual support for an increase in authority may be found in the Trilateral Commission's 1975 book, *The Crisis of Democracy*. (For them to publish their views so openly evidences a confidence that those views will prevail. That is not a conspiracy, be it said. The Commission is merely the executive committee for the Corporate State, American style.)

The end of belief in liberal democracy may be clearly seen in the rise of the executive and the bureaucracy to power, as well as the manifest illiberality of "the masses."[5] At about the time (May 1975) that President Gerald Ford won his famous "victory" in the *Mayaguez* incident off Cambodia the constitutional principle of separation of powers died a silent and unheralded death. As with previous constitutional revolutions, few realized it; no one marked its passing. Quite the contrary: Congress and courts are apparently stronger than they have been for decades. The appearance clouds a gloomy reality; despite occasional bursts of activity and of seeming power, both are, or soon will be, in an increasingly emaciated state, hollow shells propped up with the form and facade of power. In fact, the very exercises of power, those in which Congress and even the courts ostensibly have prevailed, are creating counter-vailing reactions undercutting those efforts. The twentieth century belongs to the executive, in the United States and elsewhere. The age of parliamentary government is over. Behind the facade of supposedly separated powers in the United States lurks government by decree, by fait accompli, ready as it has in the past to be employed when the need exists. That the need will exist, and soon, is fast becoming obvious except to those intellectually blinded by adherence to long-dead concepts of progress and the perfectability of man and an unthinking faith in Micawberism. The social conditions of liberal democracy are vanishing, swept over by the onslaught of changes traceable to the scientific-technological revolution.

The process is far from complete. It is a tendency, albeit an unmistakable one, that marks a sea change in American constitutional government. With-out the midwifery of constitutional amendment, an independent executive is being created, limited not by those external standards called law but only by the exigencies of politics. The constitutional system of checks and balances is being replaced by a pervasive system of executive powers, presidential and bureaucratic. Discretion with only ostensible checks is the norm. A generation ago Professor Edward S. Corwin noted the death of a Constitution of limita-tions (of rights) and its replacement by a Constitution of powers.[6] The informal Constitution, as Woodrow Wilson saw,[7] had long been different. But Corwin did not develop, although he was aware of it, the passing of the dominance of the legislature. He also concentrated upon the formal exercise of powers, rather than upon those who in fact had effective control over the formal actions of government.

In foreign affairs the death of the time-honored principle of separated powers is most obvious. Despite an occasional contrary instance, the executive reigns supreme, with only minimal restraints. An occasional Congressional action—the War Powers Resolution of 1973 is an example[8]—that purportedly stays the executive is merely a switch of the tail of the giant beached whale that is Congress. At times that tail can be lethal, as Richard Nixon and some of his merry men learned, but not often or even usually. The Congressional whale, as a rule, is gasping out its feeble efforts to regain the ocean of political power without placing substantial restraints on the executive.

The appearance is otherwise. Those who gain their (superficial) knowledge almost entirely from reading newspapers or—worse—from television, believe with some reporters and even some academics, in a resurgence of legislative controls. But that is not and will not be true. No committee (rather, two committees) totaling 535 people can hope to do more than strike an occasional blow against the executive, which has both the expertise and the will to govern—qualities lacking in Congress. (The executive includes both the presidency and the bureaucracy.) So, too, with the courts, including the Supreme Court: Some observers who should know better maintain that governing power has been captured by the judges.[9] Again, the media help to perpetrate and perpetuate this impression. But again, it simply cannot be true. Judges are not self-starters; and making policy through litigation surely is no way to run any nation, let alone the superpower that is the United States of America. Government by judiciary is not possible—now or in the future.

In the modern age, foreign and domestic affairs are increasingly intertwined, so that public policies cannot be neatly separated, as once they were, into two categories (even though it is still done for purposes of convenience, bureaucratic, academic, and journalistic). Further, it is indisputable that Americans do live in a "global city," with the result that "foreign" affairs have become ever more important. Hence, there should be little wonder that separation of powers is dying the same death that "dual" federalism suffered with the rise of the Positive State.[10] The Positive State is the shorthand label for a national government with assumed responsibilities for the socioeconomic well-being of the populace. The formal constitutional structure remains, but as a facade— mostly front and little substance. So, too, do the fifty states remain, but principally as administrative districts for centrally established policies (public and private). The quaint ceremonies on Capitol Hill, both legislative and judicial, continue. Decisions issue from Congress and the Supreme Court. But when one looks beneath the counterpane of formal constitutionalism, and also at the manner in which judicial decisions are "obeyed," then it is undeniable that the American people are slipping without constitutional amendment and little argument into "Caesarism"—government by the executive.[11]

The obsequies, to be sure, have not yet been paid, but the main thing that remains is to give the ancient principle of separation of powers a decent burial. Even though it is the chief contribution of the United States to the art of governance, its day has passed—finally and irrevocably. For as it now exists, it is a barrier to efficient, and an inadequate check on despotic, government. Separation of powers, as it evolved, is based upon at least two untenable assumptions: first, that of a Newtonian universe, a clocklike governmental mechanism, in which each part both aids and simultaneously restricts the other; and second, that each branch will represent different and conflicting social classes. That the Constitution is Darwinian, not Newtonian, has long been known.[12] Government, in short, is a process, an open-ended system always in a state of becoming. The Constitution is rewritten by each generation of Americans. What was all right in 1787 and even in 1850 cannot, and will not, because of the inexorable force of circumstances, be satisfactory in the latter part of the twentieth century.

The second—the "living"—Constitution makes it clear that ancient notions, derived from Montesquieu, no longer are sufficient to the need. This in large part is attributable to the second invalid assumption: Separation of powers, as Franz Neumann has said, can be a valid principle of government only when there are balanced social classes represented in the several branches.[13] But that is precisely what is not true in the United States today: Each of the branches, including the judiciary, is the target, even the captive, of the governing class in the nation. Not recognized in the formal Constitution, this becomes clear in the informal Constitution. The most meaningful separation today is not between Congress and the executive, but between government and decentralized centers of social power (that inevitably become political power), in the entity we have previously called the corporate State. There is, in short, a *seeming* separation of powers, which in fact vanishes when one penetrates beneath the facade of formal constitutionalism. Nowhere can this be better seen, to cite only one example, than in the way in which the alleged populist, President Jimmy Carter, drew upon members of the Establishment for his major executive branch appointments; and in the way that Congress and the courts respond to the interests and desires of the managers of the corporate communities of the nation (and other interest groups).

There is, to put it bluntly, a specter menacing the nation: Government by fiat, by fait accompli. It takes many forms—a growing assertion of presidential "inherent" powers by executive branch lawyers; sweeping delegations of power from Congress to the bureaucracy, including the President; discretion unfettered by external constraint; corporate leviathans that plan and control the economy—and it marks the end of whatever representative government has meant in the past, if indeed it meant anything save in the myth.

The men of the American revolution considered that the principle of separated powers was their greatest innovation for the republican government. Since 1787, and particularly since the *Federalist Papers* were written to influence ratification of the Constitution, it has become accepted—almost beyond argument—that powers were separated in the Constitution to produce conflict among the branches and thus to prevent despotism.[14] That is only a half-truth: A separate executive was created by the men of 1787 as much in an effort to promote efficiency as to prevent despotism, for under the Articles of Confederation it became clear that the national government could not be efficient.[15] Government by legislature, then and now, is not sufficient to the need. Furthermore, it has not been adequate to prevent despotic government, when in the past the need arose for quick and even ruthless action. That despotism may often have been benevolent, and limited in time and space, but it was despotism nevertheless.

Separation of powers, finally, is a profoundly conservative technique of governance. It is obvious that powers under the Constitution were never sharply divided, with each branch having its own independent set. The powers, rather, were blended, with the principal attribute being one of "check." To the extent that separation of powers has had meaning in American history, it was to prevent or delay actions which either the President or Congress wanted to take. Delay, not prevention, was and is the general rule; that delay usually results in a compromise between the executive and Congress. Delay, furthermore, never came in any situation that was an emergency.

Historically, the federal courts erected barriers to some congressional action, principally from about 1890 to 1937. When, about forty years ago, the judges abdicated their lofty position of an authoritative faculty of political economy,[16] it has been politics and politics alone that has been the guiding force in American public policy. Lawyer-judges on the Supreme Court still make their ostensibly portentous pronouncements on segments of public policy, but the tide of history has swept by them. Public policy in the United States emphatically is seldom judge-made. At times, as in the *Abortion Cases* of 1973, the Supreme Court does have a major role to play; but those times are noteworthy for their rarity rather than their frequency. The myth is otherwise, and many in the professoriate and legal profession believe the myth. But it is not true, nor can it be true: Just as government by legislature is not possible in the latter part of the twentieth century, so too with the judiciary. Judges have neither the competence nor the institutional capacity to govern, save in isolated parochial instances. A "government of laws, not of men" is an improbability, and perhaps an absurdity, in the late twentieth century. At best, it is an ideal; the spotted actuality is far different. Men rule; not laws. That we will call in subsequent discussion the rise of the Constitution of Control.

The constitutional theory of separation of powers must consider the growth of new centers of power—the bureaucracy, within public government; the corporation and unions and universities, within the amorphous confines of "private" government. The point is that the historically meaningful separation —which paradoxically is rapidly becoming a fusion—is between public and private government, not between Congress and the executive, and the Supreme Court.

Changes take place in the formal structure of government because of the extraordinary radical nature of the social structure. Not radical in its conventional sense, but because men of business and of science are so transforming the environment in which governmental institutions exist that it bears no resemblance to the puny collection of thirteen allegedly sovereign states that brought the United States of America into existence two centuries ago. Law, including constitutional law, is a reflection on the power configurations of society at any given time. It has a force, not of its own, but as an instrument of those who are in fact the effective power-wielders in the community. Law has been instrumental throughout American history—not a set of interdictory rules but a means by which those who govern can realize their desires.

The core concept of government is not, as many have thought, "due process of law," nor is it "representation"; rather, it is the "public" or the "national interest," as perceived and conceived by the bureaucracy, high and low. Foreign and domestic policies are not built upon abstractions. They are the result of practical conceptions of national or public interest arising from some immediate exigency, or standing out vividly in historical perspective. Predicated on secrecy and a monopoly of governmental expertise in a society where knowledge plus skills equals power, the bureaucracy, topped by one man who is both the head of State and head of government, reigns triumphant. The occasional skirmish lost to Congress or the courts merely signifies increasingly insignificant guerrilla tactics used by those branches.

Power became concentrated in the bureaucracy and the President by slow accretion since 1787, plus sudden volcanic bursts occasioned by emergencies—external wars and internal distress, economic and otherwise. What Madison called "the very definition of tyranny"[17]—the concentration of governmental power in the same hands—has now been created. The second, the invisible, the "living" Constitution has as its central core a concept of benevolent despotism. As David Wise has recently documented, a form of an American "police State" now exists;[18] technology increasingly is employed against individuals and groups thought to have that degree of dissidence to threaten the ruling elites. Justice Felix Frankfurter noted in 1952: "Much that should be rejected as illegal, because repressive and envenoming, may well be not unconstitutional."[19] The need for further controls will become more critical in the future.

My point is not that of Wise or even of Frankfurter; I do not say that government today is repressively despotic, although numerous current examples can easily be found, but, rather, allude to its latent powers which are usually used when the political branches of government are in agreement and used to further the interests of decentralized power groups. Watergate, if it proved anything, showed that the President must have Congress with him—or at least not against him—when he undertakes adventures on the unruly sea of illegality. The further point is that the social conditions of the immediate future will provide a reason for exercises of "benevolent despotism." When this happens, as it will, the people will not care; as with the Germans under Hitler, they will think that they are free. Americans will have, in Auguste Comte's words, "popular dictatorship with freedom of expression."[20] And they will not care. Indeed, most will probably applaud.

Why does the ideal of liberal democracy persist? It has no factual basis. In the hearts of most Americans and in the language of government officials and in the communications media, it is paradoxically both dead as a correct theory or model of the body politic and simultaneously cited with a frequency that reveals its viability as an idea. When totalitarian nation-states, such as East Germany, call themselves democratic, there is something important afoot that bears scrutiny. The "something" is the growing merger of liberal with authoritarian (or even totalitarian) democracy.

In the United States at least, and perhaps elsewhere, the liberal ideal persists because democracy is a method of peacefully compromising and reconciling conflicting interests. In lawyers' language, democracy thus is a *procedural* concept; it is assumed without stating that the goals of the nation are commonly accepted, even though they may be inchoate or vague, and that conflicts, when they arise, will be about the ways—the procedure—to achieve those goals. Using constitutional language, everyone may agree that the nebulous term, "due process of law," without which life, liberty or property cannot be taken by government, is a desirable goal. When disputes arise, by following the proper procedure the correct answers are presumably learned—and the people abide by them. Consensus develops on the rules of the game, not on a sense of purpose as to what can be achieved by playing the game. Force has no role other than exercised by the State to enforce the decisions made procedurally. That is the judicial and legislative process. Legislatively, the procedure is one of bargaining and of tradeoffs—in other words, a crude form of barter economics.[21] Those who fail to attain their desires are expected to bow to the "will of the majority."

As such, democracy is a secular religion. When joined with nationalism (patriotism), and the "rule of law," it is perhaps *the* religion of the American people. That is so even though millions regularly attend church and ostensibly adhere to the tenets of an organized religion. These people are not religious, in the true Judeo-Christian meaning of the term; rather, they are imbued with a deepset religiosity that enables them to go through the motions of adherence without doing much about it. One has only to remember the quaint ceremonies that are performed each July 4th or the nationwide celebration of the 200th anniversary of the Declaration of Independence to realize that something much more basic than mere politics is at play. Democracy is like the flag; it is a symbol of deepest values, mystical hopes, ethical maxims, of desires that are not even illogical. They are primordial, the product of primitive drives. "We live by symbols," Justice Oliver Wendell Holmes once said,[22] and "democracy" is one of the most enduring of them. "Man cannot live with himself, with his state, or with his state of affairs," says Professor Murray Edelman, "unless he continuously re-creates his past, his present, and his future in the light of his significant symbols."[23]

Another factor is that the United States developed throughout its history in the name of the people. The wealth and the power and prestige of the nation thus have been tied to an incessant repetition of the slogan or symbol, so much so that it is deeply embedded in the psyche of individual Americans. That there were unequal rewards and that freedom at times was slavery (for those of African descent) or "wage slavery" (for the workers who were exploited) did not minimize the symbol.

Furthermore, that development did permit, when viewed comparatively with other governments, a person to maximize his individual freedom. That was particularly true before the closing of the frontier, which came about 1890. The opportunity still exists as an ideal, in the sense of some social mobility between the classes of American society; but a class, even caste, society is being built.

Finally, the ideal persists because it is convenient for politicians and pundits to use it to flatter the masses. Responsibility can thus be avoided. Moreover, opponents, foreign and domestic, can be put down in the mystical name of the people. The public interest, as defined by public officials, thus becomes the overriding, but never defined, criterion of policy.

But the ideal, while it persists, is in fact stoutly resisted by those who manipulate the levers of power in the nation. When attempts are made to bring the people into the decisional process, the result is a posture of massive resistance, or worse, by those who effectively control them. One example will suffice to make the point.

When in 1966 the Congress, in a burst of political myopia, legislated that there should be "maximum feasible participation" by the local people in the "model cities" program, it quickly became evident that local politicians would not give up their positions of power easily. The consequence should have been easy to predict, but was not—the program soon bogged down in administrative battles over who would control. This led Daniel Patrick Moynihan to write a book with the expressive title: *Maximum Feasible Misunderstanding.* The opposition, led by Edmund Burke, of the ancien regime to the French Revolution provides a classic instance of resistance to popular will.[24] Burke was unwilling to agree that changes were necessary, and thus legitimate, in the distribution of wealth and privileges. He defended elitism with fervor, the elite being a small propertied class, against what he considered to be mob rule and anarchy. To him, order and hierarchy, privilege and inequality, were typical of all social systems and accordingly of all governments.

In the United States today, Burke has been resurrected as the patron saint of a group of intellectuals called "neo-conservatives."[25] They include, but are not limited to, those who routinely write for *The Public Interest* and for

Commentary, both of which may be called the house organs for the movement. Their names are familiar: Daniel Patrick Moynihan, Nathan Glazer, Daniel Bell, Irving Kristol, Robert Nisbet, Sidney Hook, Seymour Martin Lipset, Samuel Huntington, James Wilson, and the late Alexander Bickel, among others.

These are the modern Burkeans who see the mob storming the gates of the citadel and who are rushing to protect the status quo ante. Like Burke, their writings are couched in mellifluous prose; but also like Burke, they are in essence apologists for the ancien regime, if that term can be used, in the United States. Once they called themselves, or were called, "liberals" (in the modern sense of the term), but they have become disillusioned and now flay away at those who perceive the need for and agitate for, as the neo-conservatives put it, equality of *condition* as well as *opportunity*. They defend property and privilege, position and prestige, and even go so far as to perceive a danger to the State when those who are disadvantaged attempt to employ the institutions of the ancien regime, mainly the courts and the legislatures, to alter social affairs.

In other words, the intellectual counter-revolution to what Tocqueville long ago saw as a movement toward equality[26] has achieved respectability. In much the same way that Julien Benda perceived during the 1920s, in his *The Treason of the Intellectuals* [27] these "clerks" are thrall to those who wield real power in the United States. They lend their talents to the preservation of the status quo—not all of them, to be sure, but enough and with sufficient influence on others to make the counter-revolution an obvious clear and present danger to those who wish this nation to achieve true democracy. This means that it will be even more idle to talk about democracy in the future. It cannot and will not be attained, however much one may desire it in the abstract. Those in power and their intellectual apparatchiks pose too great a barrier.

But if "democracy" is more a slogan than a description of reality, then its employment becomes a means of organizing the masses. When the leaders pretend that the will of the people is sovereign—this, in fact, is the stated theory of the Constitution—it is done for a purpose. That purpose is to attract the support of the people. Observe the language of Professor J. L. Talmon, on the demise of liberal democracy.

Totalitarian democracy early evolved into a pattern of coercion and centralization not because it rejected the values of eighteenth century liberal individualism, but because it had originally a too perfectionist attitude toward them. It made man the absolute point of reference. Man was not merely to be freed from restraints. All the existing traditions, established institutions, and social arrangements were overthrown and remade, with the sole purpose of securing to man the totality of his rights and freedoms, and liberating him from all dependence. . . . it saw man as the sole element in the natural order, to the exclusion of all groups and traditional interests. To reach man *per se* all differences and inequalities had to be eliminated. And so very often the ethical ideas of the rights of man acquired the character of an egalitarian social ideal. All the emphasis came to be placed on the destruction of inequalities, on bringing down the privileged to the level of common humanity, and on sweeping away all intermediate centres of power and allegiance, whether social classes, regional communities, professional groups or corporations. Nothing was left to stand between man and the State. The power of the State, unchecked by any intermediate agencies, became unlimited. . . .[28]

The suggestion is that liberal democracy and totalitarian or authoritarian democracy, which Talmon maintains were derived from the same premises in the eighteenth century, are in the modern era meeting and merging. That they have not completely done so thus far is attributable less to design, or inherent merit, than to a unique and unrepeatable set of socioeconomic circumstances. But there are definite, unmistakable present portents of precisely that merger in these United States.

What, then, are the two types of "democracy"? There are some 200 definitions of the word "democracy,"[29] but the present remarks are confined to two basic types—liberal and totalitarian. (I agree with Professor Bernard Crick that no useful purpose is served by using the word as if it meant something identifiable.[30] Certainly it does not.)

Professor Talmon asserts that the basic difference between the two types of democracy does not revolve around the affirmation of liberty by one and its denial by the other (the totalitarian), as some believe.[31] Rather, they differ in their attitudes toward politics. Liberal democracy postulates that politics is a matter of pragmatic adjustments; and also concedes that there are a range of private activities, including collective actions, outside of the sphere of politics proper. But totalitarian democracy is predicated on the belief that there is only one truth in politics. It could be called a form of political messianism. Everything is "political," for all human thought and action has direct social significance. Pragmatic adjustments have no part to play. Politics is considered to be the application of the one truth to society. In some respects, it might be said that liberal democracy is inductive, working from a congeries of atomistic individuals, out of which the common good is by some mystical means achieved; whereas totalitarian democracy is deductive, with politics being the application of ideas deduced from the one central guiding truth. Both schools, Talmon tells us, "affirm the supreme value of liberty." But one finds it in the State applying no coercive sanctions, but allowing the free reign of individual spontaneity to rule; and the other thinks in terms of the absolute necessity of the furtherance of the collective—the societal—purpose.

Talmon's views are mentioned simply to indicate that what is said in this chapter is by no means a sharp break with the past. The merger of parallel lines of democratic development runs back at least 200 years. John Kenneth Galbraith, in several of his books,[32] proposes a principle of convergence in discussing the industrial institutions of the United States and the USSR. The term is borrowed and extended to have a shorthand term for the coming convergence of liberal and totalitarian democracy into an indigenous form of authoritarian democracy, American style. This is the principle of political convergence.

No useful purpose is served by repeated employment of the word "democracy" as if it meant something precise. Emphatically, it does not. Those who wrote the Constitution of 1787 disliked democracy; constitutional history since then has, in recent years, broadened the franchise. Never have so many people had the right to vote; and never have so many neglected to exercise it. They do not exercise it because they know, intuitively or empirically, that voting is often, perhaps usually, a sham. It, with the slogan of "democracy," is a way of organizing the masses. They were given the appearance but not the substance of power.

Power in the American political order rests now, has always rested, and will always rest in an elite structure, not in "the people." Jeb Magruder, an aide to President Nixon, candidly acknowledged as much: "We didn't spend much time on the disadvantaged for the simple reason that there were no votes there. . . . We don't have a democracy of the people. We have a special-interest democracy."[33] We are a nation of competing (and cooperating) elites. Presidents deal with the leaders of elite groups, strike bargains with them, and eventually produce a policy statement. No one really believes in democracy as the "voice of the people," no one, that is, in any position of power or responsibility. As an anonymous aide to President John F. Kennedy said in 1970: "Everyone believes in democracy until he gets to the White House and then you begin to believe in dictatorship, because it's so hard to get things done. Every time you turn around, people resist you and even resist their own job."[34] In sum, "elites, not masses, govern America."[35] It is a basic fact that government is always by the few, however much those few purport to rule in the name of the many. The symbol, or myth, is one of mass participation—a government of the people and by the people—but the *reality* is otherwise. The United States is not immune to the iron law of oligarchy. That, however, does not mean that government is adequate to the need, present or future.

8

Caesarism Triumphant: Presidential Government Comes to Stay

During Richard Nixon's tenure in the White House, Professor Arthur Schlesinger suddenly discovered that Americans had an "imperial presidency."[1] Why that flash of revelation had not struck him earlier—say, in the Kennedy-Johnson years, is a minor and unexplained mystery. As long ago as the Civil War, William Seward knew that Americans elected "a king" every four years, and as long ago as 1898 historian Henry Jones Ford called the presidency the first "elective kingship" in the world.[2] As with lawyers, historians must in each generation rediscover the past. In any event, Seward was not speaking in hyperbole; he was accurate in general. This chapter will show that the President is more than first among equals in the American government, despite orthodox constitutional theory to the contrary. And it will also show that Amaury de Riencourt was not far off the mark when he observed in 1957:

In truth, no mental effort is required to understand that the President of the United States is the most powerful single human being in the world today. Future crises will inevitably transform him into a full-fledged Caesar, if we do not beware. Today he wears ten hats—as Head of State, Chief Executive, Minister of Foreign Affairs, Chief Legislator, Head of Party, Tribune of the People, Ultimate Arbitrator of Social Justice, Guardian of Economic Prosperity, and World Leader of Western Civilization.[3]

Riencourt miscounted the President's hats, but the nine he listed summarize what the chief executive has become—and will increasingly be in the future. Not entirely, to be sure, for there is a difference between the "textbook" presidency[4] and the actual powers of the office; but enough to know that any President, today and more so in the future, will be a latter-day Caesar. The

President, in sum, is becoming not only a monarchical figure; he is slowly and not so obtrusively taking on the character of a secular Pope.

The Constitution gives remarkably little attention to the executive. What the presidency has become is largely the result of external demands pressing upon a government whose other organs, legislative and judicial, are simply not up to the needs of modern America. The President fills a power vacuum (as in the physical world, so in politics: nature abhors a vacuum).

Congress has contributed to the growth of presidential powers by delegating large chunks of authority to the President and agencies within the executive branch. Congress is only too willing to make general policy and allow the details to be filled in by bureaucrats. This means that some 400 laws are passed each year by Congress; but the bureaucracy issues some 20,000 administrative regulations. The task of filling in details of statutes has taken over much of the actual governing power. Some bureaucratic decisions are as important as the original statute. And a decision not to enforce a law can cripple it. Day-to-day operations of government of course cannot get attention from either Congress or the courts; hence, the rise in recent decades of the "bureaucratic State."[5]

The delphic terms of the Constitution's Article II do not begin to detail the President's many powers and duties. "The executive power" is vested in "a President of the United States of America," but nowhere is it defined. Whether it is itself an independent grant of power and, if so, how much, are questions that have not yet been answered. Lawyers argue over them, but their conclusions reflect those whom they represent; those for Congress take one position and those for the executive take a directly contrary position. That is what passes for professionalism among lawyers. The Supreme Court has not rewarded Americans with a definitive assessment of what "the executive power" means. We are left with an empty vessel into which Presidents can pour nearly anything. So, too, with the "commander-in-chief" power. Does it mean more than mere tactical control of the troops in the field? Again, the question is unresolved. Open-ended and undefined, it is limited only by politics, not law.[6]

The President can pardon criminals, even before conviction, as the world learned in 1974 when Nixon was transformed from an "unindicted co-conspirator" to an elder statesman by a mere stroke of his successor's pen. Of much more importance, the President can "make treaties," but must get concurrence of two-thirds of the Senate. That requirement has resulted in most international agreements today being "presidential," with no need for Senate action. And he appoints to public office, often with the concurrence of the Senate. He is required to give Congress information "on the state of the union," and recommend laws that should be passed. Finally, "he shall take care that the laws be faithfully executed," and "shall receive ambassadors and other public ministers." Save for his power of veto, which can be overridden, that's all there is of any substance. On the flimsy foundation of a few dozen words, enormous constitutional powers of the President have been built—by design and at times by raw grabs for power. The Supreme Court, when it has ruled, which is not often, has generally approved the extension of powers, finding in the silences of the Constitution ample grounds for presidential action.

Those who wrote the Constitution deliberately left the President's duties, responsibilities, and powers vague, possibly so that the office could garner preeminence through experience. As Woodrow Wilson said in 1908, the office permits a man to be as big a man as he wants to be[7]—which is about half right: it permits him to be as big a man as the political system allows (quite a different thing). But it no longer permits him to try to be small. The United States will have no more Buchanans in the White House. Each new occupant will inherit two centuries of customs and usage, enormous delegations of power from Congress, and a growing capacity to exercise political muscle. The Constitution's sparse generalities simply do not convey the range and nature of "the most powerful single human being in the world today."[8] He is that because the Constitution and Congress have vested in him, and him alone, the immense responsibilities of office. No other major nation, let alone the minor ones, allows one person to be both head of State and chief of government. That little discussed, but vastly significant status means that the President can lawfully take action without consulting anyone. In net, the result is that the President is more primus inter pares (first among equals), more than "equal in origin and equal in title" to the other branches of the federal government. He is primus. Period. By merely occupying the office, a President has political clout, as Jimmy Carter has demonstrated.

Since the Watergate scandals, and the resignation of Richard Nixon, many have asserted a resurgent Congress and a decline in the presidency. They consider the post-1974 period similar to Andrew Johnson's and Warren Harding's tenures. That is hardly true. For a brief period after the Civil War, Americans did have a congressionally dominated government, but that did not last long. The Harding-Coolidge-Hoover trio in the 1920s was more a time of governmental inaction than of congressional superiority. When Franklin Roosevelt became President in 1933, his entry into the White House marked a new (and continuing) birth of presidential power. That primacy continues, despite recent congressional efforts to stem it, and will not cease in the future.

Government today could not operate without a strong chief executive. No President since Herbert Hoover has been "small"; and none will be in the future. Even Dwight Eisenhower, often considered a caretaker President, was exactly as strong as conditions demanded. After all, he sent an Army airborne division into Little Rock, Arkansas, to integrate the public schools, an action unprecedented in American history.[9] So, too, with Jimmy Carter, who ran for office on an anti-Washington and weak government platform, but who found that he could not operate under those premises. The American people demand presidential leadership. If the American system is to work at all, that is indispensable.

That the system works badly is, or should be, obvious. Only a well-nigh infinite capacity of the human mind for self-delusion allows some to say, with pretentious smugness, that the system is working well. Take Watergate and Nixon, which has led many observers to trumpet that "the system worked." Surely the correct analysis is that it worked only by accident. Consider the following unplanned events and ask whether, if any one of them had been absent, Nixon would have had to resign:

★ ★A guard who inexplicably found a door taped open in the Watergate complex;

★ ★A radio, to be used to alert the burglars, that had been cut off to save batteries, so no warning came;

★ ★A police car out of gas; so that an unmarked car, without the usual flashing lights, was sent to investigate the burglary; the lookout did not identify it as a police car;

★ ★Editors of the *Washington Post* assigning the story to the Metropolitan Desk rather than the National Desk; had it been the latter, it would have been a two-day story at most, and likely buried deep inside the *Post* near the goiter and hemorrhoid ads;

★ ★Two zealous young reporters who were given their heads by the *Post* and who received vital but unrecognized assistance from a veteran police reporter (who told them what to do);

★ ★A series of "leaks" from within government, which kept the story alive;

★ ★A federal judge who gave savage sentences to perpetrators of what was in fact a third-rate burglary; the far larger crime was the White House "cover-up";

★ ★James McCord's unexpected voluntary confession to Judge John Sirica in an attempt to get his sentence reduced;

★ ★John Dean's refusal to be a "patsy" and take the punishment for the burglary and cover-up;

★ ★A grandfatherly Senator who guided the Senate's Watergate Committee through unmarked shoals, and thereby became a national folk hero;

★ ★The "Saturday Night Massacre" of Special Prosecutor Archibald Cox;

★ ★Speaker Thomas O'Neill's unheralded (save in Jimmy Breslin's book)[10] but successful effort to get the House impeachment inquiry underway;

★ ★A state of complete panic in the White House, beginning in March 1973 with the McCord letter, which led to a series of stupid tactical decisions;[11]

★ ★Most important of all, Alexander Butterfield's completely unexpected revelation that Nixon had bugged his own office and that the tapes still existed.[12]

For anyone to say that such a series of accidents means that the constitutional system worked is to indulge in sheer fantasy. The Watergate Committee, without Butterfield, would have had to close up shop without pinning the tail on the donkey; and the House Judiciary Committee would have never gotten started. The Special Prosecutor, without the tapes, did not have enough evidence to convict anyone, let alone the President. Nixon would have served out his second term, a trifle scarred perhaps, but with all flags flying. The presidency has a mystical significance for the American people, who will not easily turn even a known criminal from office. (Even a Member of Congress, Mr. Charles Diggs, who had been convicted of a felony in 1978, received 80 percent of his district's vote in the November 1978 election.) Crime and corruption, we must believe, are as American as Mom's apple pie, as every politician knows and as many profit from. The history of the nation can be—it has been—written around a theme of crime in public office.[13]

Americans could easily do without the Supreme Court, even in the expanded role it has assumed in recent years, and there would be little difference in the ways that the affairs of most people are ordered. (Not, however, without the trial courts—where most lawsuits begin and end.) Having no enforcement power of its own, the Court must depend on the good faith and willingness of others, mainly in the executive offices of the nation, federal and state, to put its decisions into effect. The effectiveness of any law, whether coming from the legislature or the courts, depends on the executive's good will. The President, as the sole tribune of the people, and the bureaucracy, are the true courts of appeal because they alone have the power to enforce decisions. There is far more discretion in civil servants, high and low, than most people realize. President Eisenhower proved that in 1957 at Little Rock, if, indeed, proof were necessary; and the bureaucracy proves it every day in the myriad administrative decisions routinely made (the Veterans Administration alone, to take only one agency, makes about twelve million decisions a year—each one of importance to an individual). Think what the Supreme Court might have done had Richard Nixon refused to turn over the infamous White House tapes, after the Court said that he must. Surely the Justices would not have sent a marshal to the White House to demand the tapes on penalty of commitment for contempt. For the ordinary person, yes: a judicial order can be enforced through contempt proceedings. But not the President. "The American people," said former Senator Edward Brooke, "have created almost a God-King in the office of the presidency."[14]

As with the courts, so with Congress. That branch, despite specialized and limited powers in some chairman of committees (examples are Senator

Russell Long and Rep. Al Ullman) and despite the power of the Speaker of the House, is an anachronism—a nineteenth century institution. Its powers are small, as compared with the executive (and despite the seemingly explicit words of the Constitution). The target of interest groups, with little self-generative power, it is the prime example of a nineteenth century institution that will not reform itself, and that has outlived its usefulness. Congress staggers along, full of unrequited self-importance and dashed expectations, with some individual members participating in the "sub-governments" of Washington.[15] Most members are simply "there," for personal aggrandizement and to represent those who have actual power in the nation.

Congress, at most, has a power of delay and, at times, of veto. It can postpone programs the President desires and it can block some specifics of other programs. That is so even though the Constitution nowhere gives that power to Congress. It is a self-assumed, but seldom used way to try to keep proliferating bureaucracy in check. The ability to delay is, however, at best a negotiating position, not one of ultimate authority. In sum, Congress—any legislature—has little function today other than that of putting the decisions of experts (mainly in the bureaucracy) and of pressure groups into statutory form.[16] No doubt it will continue to exist; its quaint ceremonies will not cease. The facade will remain, but with little behind it. Bargains will be struck with the executive when sufficient pressure from constituents, local or national, demand them. The twentieth century belongs to the executive. In the future —the immediate future—that will become even more obvious. Congress not only does not govern (in general); it does not want to govern. There is no desire discernible in either House to take responsibility for steering the ship of state through the perilous waters and uncharted seas of the future. The members have no interest in the overall public good, only in their own welfare and the welfare of their most important constituents. These may be "local," but not necessarily so. The important political communities are not districts or even states, but the interest groups of the nation—those with the will and the ability to influence decisions. Congress, in sum, has power to the extent that it represents powerful interest groups of the nation.

The norm for executive-congressional relationships is cooperation rather than conflict. Separation of governmental powers under the Constitution into three branches has been distorted by lawyers, who have concentrated on the abnormal—the conflicts—and managed to confuse it with the normal. Witness Chief Justice Earl Warren in 1965:

The Constitution divides the National Government into three branches—Legislative, Executive and Judicial. The "separation of powers" was obviously not instituted with the idea that it would promote governmental efficiency. It was, on the contrary, looked to as a bulwark against tyranny. For if governmental power is fractionalized, if a given policy can be implemented only by a combination of legislative enactment, judicial application, and executive implementation, no man or group of men will be able to impose its unchecked will.[17]

That, in brief, is lawyers' history—the wisdom, or what passes for wisdom, in the legal profession. Modern scholarship has refuted, at least partially, that view of separated powers.[18] The absence of an independent executive under the Articles of Confederation was a primary reason for calling the convention of 1787 and for creating an executive branch. In other words, efficiency as much as prevention of tyranny motivated those who wrote the Constitution, despite the conventional ignorance to the contrary. Among others, Thomas Jefferson, John Jay, John Adams, Alexander Hamilton, and James Wilson. Said Wilson:

In planning, forming, and arranging laws, deliberation is always becoming, and always useful. But in active scenes of government, there are emergencies, in which the man, as in other cases, the woman, who deliberates is lost. But, can either secrecy or dispatch be expected, when, to every enterprise, mutual communication, mutual consultation, and mutual agreement among men, perhaps of discordant views, of discordant tempers, and of discordant interests, are indispensably necessary? How much time will be consumed! and when it is consumed, how little business will be done! . . . If, on the other hand, the executive power of government is placed in the hands of one person, is there not reason to expect in his plans and conduct, promptitude, activity, firmness, consistency and energy?[19]

Exactly: That *may* be so—but "it ain't necessarily so." The problem is that we have neither prevented despotism (at times) nor achieved efficiency. The inability of government to govern adequately may be traced only in part to a state of guerrilla warfare between President and Congress. There is much more; in essence, the ability of important social groups to control segments of public policy. No one except the President (and then only in theory) is interested in the "common good" or the "public interest." The political system is breaking down; "pluralism" is not working.[20]

Pluralism is the operative ideology of American political scientists, who see politics as the interplay of conflicting interest groups. Public policy has become the resultant of a parallelogram of diverse political forces, each pulling against the others. The problem with this, which is a product both of the dominant pragmatic temper and of the growth of social groups within the nation (groups strong enough to challenge the State), is that no one has any interest beyond his own narrow, parochial interests. Each group pursues its own selfish desires, the theory being that by some magical way the public interest will be furthered. This is Adam Smith's "invisible hand" writ large; it is market economics translated into the political arena. There is no more validity to it in politics than there is in economics. A generation ago, Professor John Kenneth Galbraith, in a burst of myopia, maintained that the "countervailing power"[21] of social groups offset each other and maximized human welfare. He soon saw the error of those notions, gave them up, and has repudiated the invisible hand to the extent that he is now a fervent advocate of wage and price controls. My point now is not to labor the failure of pluralism. Rather, I merely wish to underscore the obvious: that the constitutional division of powers today means neither the absence of despotism nor an efficient government.

Government, as we have seen, is repressive when need be. Further and of more importance, it is the source of largess for millions of Americans—the Earth Mother from whom bounties supposedly magically flow. In brief, it resembles a giant recumbent sow, stretched out on the ground, with hundreds of teats to which millions are coupled. That is obvious enough. On top of the unwieldy mass that is government sits the President—precariously, briefly, but with an increasing ability to command.

What, then, is *the* presidency? Amaury de Riencourt listed nine attributes of "the most powerful single human being in the world today"—although some of those may be questioned. For our purposes, the presidency is a trinity: the President as head of State (the father-figure); the President as head of government (the chief executive); and a bureaucracy. The latter is the entire executive branch of government in theory. What is important, however, is the American version of the Roman Curia—the executive offices of the President (EOP). As for the remainder of the executive branch, the President has a theoretical power of command, but the agencies and departments usually operate as independent fiefdoms with whom the President must negotiate treaties.

Every four years Americans, as Seward said, elect a king—but a king who is also, as Senator Brooke said, "almost a God-King." The presidency is not to be understood until it is seen, as Michael Novak put it, as "the nation's most central religious symbol."[22] Surely Novak is correct. The American people, outwardly traditionally religious, have substituted the nation for religion, and the President for God. The nation, as a social unit, "is not merely an aggregate of individuals; it is an entity in its own right, endowed with a life of its own, a collective life greater and far more lasting than the lives of the separate individuals who belong to it; it is a spiritual organism."[23] Over it rules the high priest of America—the President. That rule may be splintered, and at times may be no rule at all, but he sits in the White House—the American version of the Vatican—slowly taking on the character of a secular Pope.

A close counterpart to the United States in the world today is the Roman Catholic Church. The resemblances between the political organization called the United States and the theological entity called the Catholic Church are more than coincidental. Each is headed by a father-figure, who has, or at least asserts, great authority. The Pope maintains that he is infallible, something no President has yet been able to do, at least publicly; but the statements of some recent Presidents, for example, Lyndon Johnson and Richard Nixon, asked for confidence in "your" President. Surely that is close to assertions of presidential infallibility. Confidence because only he knows all the facts—or so he says. We are asked to trust "your" President on faith alone.

Each, furthermore, operates in mysterious ways his wonders to perform. Secrecy characterizes both. They are twin objects of reverence—not by all, for both must suffer the slings and arrows of disbelief from some. Finally, from each are expected miracles—the Pope as the spokesman for God, the President as symbolic leader of the civil religion: the nation itself; and of the "free" world. Much is expected from both men, by people who find the problems of everyday life too daunting for personal conquest. And much is given, but not everything, for neither has absolute power.

Prayer breakfasts and State dinners in the White House are the American equivalent of the public audiences of the Pope. Those who attend either one gather sustenance and warmth in a cold and harsh world. Each, President and Pope, feels the need, as Lyndon Johnson put it, to "press the flesh"—to mingle with the people, among them but simultaneously above them.

The President is head of State, as well as chief of government, which makes the United States unique among the major powers of the world. No other nation (save perhaps the USSR with its new constitution, and the evidence thus far is too scanty to tell), places in one person both the ceremonial powers and duties of the State and administrative responsibilities of a prime minister. Were Great Britain to abolish the monarchy or the prime ministership, and merge the two functions into one person, a comparable situation would arise. The President as secular Pope derives mainly from his being head of State. That was clearly seen during the 1974 impeachment proceedings against Richard Nixon. Why was it so difficult to remove the man from office? Because impeachment was considered to be akin to regicide. To remove the President meant killing the "king" (or impeaching the American "Pope").

The President as pontiff cannot, and does not, act alone. Neither does the Pope. Each has his "intimate" bureaucracy: the Curia in Rome is paralleled by the executive offices of the President in Washington. The presidency (and the papacy) thus is an organization as well as one man. For the President, some 500 people of greater or lesser power cluster around him in the "inner" presidency; there are another 4000 or so in the "outer" presidency. The immediate White House staff, plus the Director of the Office of Management and Budget, constitute the inner presidency. These are men and women, only a few of whom get public attention, who do the day-to-day work of the White House. The office could not operate without them. They are aided by the outer presidency—anonymous people who are probably the highest quality civil servants in government. Everyone in both presidencies shares two basic characteristics: a penchant for power and an ability to work long and hard. The OEP is no place for dilettantes or time-servers. Within the OEP are hierarchies of importance, the two most important subbureaucracies being the Office of Management and Budget (the basic planning office for the executive branch) and the National Security Council (which exercises effective control over foreign and military policy decisions).

What types of people cluster around the President? The inner presidency is manned by men and women who share a desire for power and a willingness to do almost anything to satisfy it. "The one factor almost all of them have shared is uncommon ambition, a thirst for power and glory, even reflected power and glory, and a willingness to sacrifice friends, family, and personal health, often to suffer personal and political humiliation in order to satisfy their ambitions."[24] That means that the "king's" court is as important as the king himself. He cannot operate without his staff. That is relatively new in American history. Not until the twentieth century did the President get a staff. Cleveland answered his own telephone and Wilson often typed his own letters. A minor furor broke out in the 1930s when President Roosevelt asked for a few assistants, "with a passion for anonymity"—something his successors now have many times over. Not since the days of Louis XIV has anything comparable been seen in the Western world.

The President as high priest, as Pope, must have a church and a religion. The church is the nation—the State. As we noted previously, State and religion are the only human institutions that can give meaning to death; the State —the nation—can because it is a religion. A person can die, at times far from unwillingly, because he is swallowed up in a larger whole. Americans have a mystical attachment to home and country. The American Dream, the American Creed, sustains them when deep down inside they fear that God is truly dead. What is a "civil" or "secular" religion? Says Novak: "It is a public perception of our national experience, in the light of universal and transcendent claims upon human beings, but especially upon Americans; a set of values, symbols, and rituals institutionalized as the cohesive force and center of meaning uniting our many peoples."[25] America, as G. K. Chesterton said, is "a nation with the soul of a church."[26]

The religion of the United States is neither Christianity nor Judaism nor any of the many formal religious sects that speckle the land. Ours is a true *civil* religion. The established church in America is the State, which fills the vacuum left by the death of traditional religious symbols. A "born-again" Baptist resided in the White House; but his message was not so much Christian love as it was patriotism. Patriotism, as Samuel Johnson said, may be the last refuge of a scoundrel; but of more importance, it is the first refuge of America's secular pontiff. The nation is a mystical entity, with its pantheon of heroes and saints. To be patriotic is to be religious—deeply so (and it is also to be irrational, but that is another matter).

President Carter's troubles during 1977-1980 came from being perceived as *not* being sufficiently authoritative, *not* the strong father-figure for whom Americans yearn and for whom they vote each four years. His popularity soared when he became outwardly stronger, when he asserted "strong" leadership, when, in a word, he was not quiescent.[27] Carter's attempts to demystify the presidency went askew when it was slowly realized in the inner presidency that mysticism and symbolism—the strength of a remote father—were precisely what the American people wanted. The people do not want the man in the White House to try to be "small" in power and posture; they want someone they can respect or even revere, someone on a pedestal high above the sweaty mob, a person of compassion with an interest in the people but not of the people. They want, in sum, a father-figure, a secular Pope, and that is precisely what they hope to elect.

Of recent Presidents, Richard Nixon knew that better than anyone. Soon after the 1972 election he stated that the American people are like children, looking for and needing someone to trust and lead them on. Nixon's resignation, at most, proves that even father-figures can err. Since 1974, the gradual resurrection of a disgraced President may be seen. Nixon now has left San Clemente—his island of Elba, where he was exiled—and speaks out on public issues. No longer a candidate for public office, he is an "elder statesman." No clearer evidence of the sanctity that envelops the presidency could be found. Nixon may have fallen from grace, but the deep-felt need of Americans to believe in something enables him to come out of the San Clemente closet and again receive media attention. Something deep and irrational is evident when a known criminal can be rewarded, as Nixon was and is, by public largess and growing public acceptance, even acclaim. Even a fallen and disgraced "secular pontiff" receives accolades. Can there be any doubt that in the eyes and hearts of many, a president is more than just another human being? A person elected to the presidency gains a special status, far beyond that of the often quite ordinary men who gain the White House.

This would be amusing were it not so pathetic, and so portentous. It is pathetic because it reveals that "ordinary" people need to believe in something larger than themselves in order to withstand the trauma that is human existence. That "something" no longer is God; it has become and ever more is becoming our elected "God-King." That alone should be considered to be bad enough; mature people who see life whole and without self-delusion should know that trust in any human being in whatever position is a counsel of ultimate despair.

Worse, however, are the portents of the President as pontiff. Can any person live up to expectations Americans today have of the chief executive? Surely the answer is "no." The demands laid upon the State and upon its apparatus, government, by the people now far exceed not only the capacity of the presidency but the capacity of the government itself. But Presidents will try, and, in trying, will have to resort to measures which under any criterion will be repressive. Not that they will necessarily want to do that. In all likelihood, their desires will be directly contrary. Simply stated, conditions—as we have outlined previously—will require such a response from La Maison Blanche. When it comes, as it will, the people will accept, if for no other reason than that they have been trained to obedience and will see in the

President an authoritative father-figure. That may not be a rational response, as rationality is understood, but it is a quite human and understandable reaction.

Security, economic and psychic, is the need, something that people cannot, for deepset psychological and social reasons, develop for themselves. So they must look elsewhere: to groups, to the State. B. F. Skinner said it well in *Walden Two*: "Most people live from day to day. . . . They look forward to having children, to seeing their children grow up, and so on. The majority of people don't want to plan. They want to be free from the respon-sibility of planning. What they ask is merely some assurance that they will be decently provided for. The rest is day-to-day enjoyment of life. That's the explanation of your Father Divines: people naturally flock to anyone they can trust for the necessities of life."[28] We may not want to believe Skinner, for we are influenced through society's processes of socialization to think otherwise, but certainly the explanation of cult worship now so prevalent in the United States lies in what he says. The Moonies are not exceptions. But even the Moonies and their counterparts cannot provide the assurance so desperately required; the only institution that can is government and, within that institu-tion, the President. The explanation of Senator Brooke's "God-King" is that people trust the President to supply the necessities of life, both economic and psychic. That helps to explain the Nixon resignation: people must be able to trust their father-figure. When trust vanishes, mental security goes with it—that type of personal security being as important as economic. What people emphatically do not want is freedom, the myth to the contrary notwithstand-ing. "The fear of freedom," says Lionel Rubinoff, "is greater than the desire for it."[29] In Erich Fromm's mordant phrase, people want to "escape from free-dom."[30] When any President fails, as fail all will, sooner or later, then the ensuing despair will create the conditions for even more repressive controls.

The President—any President—may be the high priest of America's civil religion, but he is also a "king," a "Caesar." The United States is becoming one man's imperium.

Whatever the saints in America's hagiology—the Founding Fathers—anticipated in 1787, surely they did not foresee permanent crisis government. They made no express provision for emergency action by government, as did, for example, France in Article 16 of its constitution.[31] That part of the 1958 French constitution has been used only once—by President Charles de Gaulle in 1961. As with the United States, however, that does not mean that the French government does not take extraordinary actions when deemed necessary, without invoking Article 16.

The American and French constitutions are really alike in that respect. Their silences permit maximum political maneuvering. Since Americans are on the verge of, or already into and will continue in, crisis government, this becomes vastly significant. The Constitution of the United States is no barrier to whatever the President wishes to do as chief executive, provided only that he get approval of Congress. The limits on presidential power thus are *political* rather than *legal*. Law as interdiction, as a series of "thou-shalt-nots," simply does not exist for the President. He can be as big a man as the political process permits him to be. It is going to permit him to be a very big man indeed.

Modern government cannot operate without a chief executive and a large bureaucracy, save, perhaps, for Switzerland (which, whatever its merits, is far from a major power). The President, despite the Constitution, is the "chief legislator," and has as much to say about general policy as Congress; and the public administration which he heads as chief executive has the everyday details of governance firmly in its grip. Whatever the original conception might have been—and that is lost in the mists of history—the President is "sovereign" within the national government today. He is not only the high priest of America's civil religion; he is truly an elected king. He rules through the American Curia—the executive offices of the President. He is not omnipotent, and surely is far from omniscient, but no one in government is even remotely close to his stature and importance.

No extended discussion is necessary to document the importance of President and staff. As economic planner, he has since the days of the New Deal tried to tune the economy to achieve the goals of maximum employment, no (or slow) inflation, and economic growth. In much of this, the President acts through delegations of power from a Congress quite willing to allow the executive to run the show. Thus President Nixon's imposition of wage and price controls in 1971.[32] Thus also actions taken, or proposed, on fiscal and monetary matters. The economy cannot be "fine tuned," as some politicians and pundits in an excess of zeal maintained in the 1960s; but it can be and is managed to a fairly high degree. Much of that is done through the many agencies and departments of the executive branch, again with cooperation of Congress and full approval of the affected interest groups.

The United States is moving, more rapidly than most think, towards a fully managed economy, one that is directed, even controlled by the federal government.[33] At the moment, the State relies on private groups and the remnants of a market economy to provide the means to satisfy, at least partially, a rising tide of "entitlements." This does not mean that public government is superior. As has been discussed, the State today is *the corporate State*. Private groups, principally giant corporations, influence and benefit from public policies enunciated by government. The President may be America's chief economic planner, but he cannot—he does not—operate without the concurrence of the important interest groups of the nation. These groups, headed by narrowly based and autonomous elites, control governmental policies, whether legislative or executive. They tend to follow their own specialized interests, and do not become involved in the larger issues of statesmanship, unless those issues in some way affect their own interests.

The meaning is all too clear: the President as economic planner is not really "sovereign" in fact. He is neither omnipotent nor infallible. He must strike bargains with the leaders of interest groups in order to govern at all.[34] That means that public policy all too often becomes a crude type of barter economics, rather than the "rule of law." Public policies, to be sure, become law, statutory or otherwise, but only after the bartering—the bargaining process— takes place. The important matter is political clout. Important, too, is the fact that the line between public and private in the United States, which has always been dimmer than the myth would have it, has been all but erased save in theory. No longer is it possible to tell where private ends, and public begins, in the entire range of public policies; those policies are the resultant of close interactions between the leaders of public government and of private governments of the nation.

Economic planning requires, by definition, a "plan," a document designed to get the nation "there" from "here." For the United States that document is not, as in other nations, a "five-year plan" or other long-term engagement; it is issued annually. Each January the President, under the guiding principles of the Empoyment Act of 1946, sends his budget message to Congress. That message is the basic planning document for the American political economy. It sets priorities; it allocates resources; it sets the terms of whatever debate takes place in a given session of Congress on economic policy.

Presidents cannot and do not act alone; they have the indispensable assistance of the nameless and faceless people in the "inner" presidency and the others in the "outer" presidency. For planning purposes, the Council of Economic Advisors in the inner sanctum, and the Office of Management and Budget in the outer area are the President's principal aides. They are the key personnel in economic matters in America's Curia. OMB prepares the annual budget message; and in so doing, has much more to say about specific governmental matters than many people realize. Relatively minor OMB officers pass on budgets of important bureaus and agencies. OMB has not only the task and the power of financial clearance of the many budget requests coming from the agencies, but also has the power of passing on the merits of given programs. OMB, furthermore, is the conduit through which public funds appropriated by Congress must funnel. Here, again, power is exercised. Not everything that Congress says should be spent is in fact spent.

Over the process sits the President as titular head. In his name the decisions are made. Most do not receive his personal attention; he must rely upon subordinates. Broad guidelines are issued and minions in OMB are expected to follow them. When the budget goes to Congress, that body can approve, disapprove, or delay. It spends a great deal of time and energy in doing what everyone expects it to do in the long run: approve the President's recommendations.

That approval comes because the initial decisions within OMB are, in matters considered important to affected interest groups, the product of a system of intense bargaining. There are three parties to the system—the executive, individual members of Congress, and leaders of interest groups. They make up the "subgovernment" structure. There is, for example, a subgovernment of agriculture, consisting of the Farm Bureau (and other representatives of agribusiness), Representative Jaime Whitten and his colleagues in Congress, and the executive (Department of Agriculture plus OMB officials). When bargains are struck, as they are, between those three groups, a budget decision is made. Eventually that decision becomes law through formal congressional action.

If that is the structure and the technique, what are the President's goals? He must at once try to balance productivity against demand, inflation against employment. His tools are few, but when properly employed (particularly with Congressional help), they are powerful. Fiscal controls. Monetary controls (here he must negotiate with the Federal Reserve Board). International trade. Budget deficits. They do not allow him to fully control the economy; but they do permit a certain degree of management. The American system of public planning is still in its primitive stages (private planning is in full bloom). But it will become more sophisticated and more coercive as the demands welling up from people both within and without the nation press ever harder against resources, and against the very capacity of government to fulfill them. When in 1978 Congress enacted the Humphrey-Hawkins bill, a formal structure for economic planning came into existence.

What will happen in the future? Here the principle of political convergence will operate. An ostensibly private enterprise economy will move toward the overtly planned economies of other nations. Not merely the halfway-house of Sweden; but the full planning mechanisms of the USSR and China. All that remains to be settled is: Who controls planning? And in whose benefit? Once those questions are answered, as they will be, then full-scale planning will come into existence. Not the halfhearted measures such as Humphrey-Hawkins, but planning up and down the line. There is no alternative. As political economist Robert Heilbroner observed: "We shall live for a long period, in all likelihood, in the shadow of a crisis of faith. However unforeseeable the outcome of that trial, I think one can predict with a fair degree of assurance that the institutional changes necessary for national planning will come, despite the vociferous opposition that they will raise."[35] Heilbroner is too timid; he should know better. He should know, if not empirically then intuitively, that environmental forces will mean a continuing, perhaps a permanent state of crisis and of centrally imposed, coercive economic controls.

When that comes, as it will, the President will be in the driver's seat. In Riencourt's words, he is the "Guardian of Economic Prosperity."[36]

That does not mean that the controls will be administered well. The capacity of government to govern adequately is dubious at best. What it does mean is that the effort will be made—and that the people will applaud. The further meaning is that economic planning will probably doom the remnants of representative democracy and of personal liberties. Only those liberties inconsequential to the State will be permitted.

The President as chief economic planner is fast becoming so obvious that all know, or should know, it—and most want it. Even so, the process is far from complete. That, however, cannot be said for the President as commander-in-chief and world leader. Throughout American history, the President has employed the armed forces both internally and externally[37]—internally for suppression of rebellion, enforcement of judicial decrees, quelling disorder; externally, in a series of engagements, both minor and large, to further American interests. Not that the use of force has always been justified under either morality, the Judeo-Christian or the pagan. We have already seen that all too often the contrary was the case, that some use of violence simply did not comport with any discernible standard of decency. To repeat Justice Robert H. Jackson's statement, in one of the *Japanese Exclusion Cases*:

Of course the existence of a military power resting on force, so vagrant, so centralized, so necessarily heedless of the individual, is an inherent threat to liberty. But I would not lead the people to rely on this Court for a review that seems to me wholly delusive . . . If the people ever let command of the war power fall into irresponsible and unscrupulous hands, the courts wield no power equal to its restraints. The chief restraint upon those who command the physical forces of the country, in the future as in the past, must be their responsibility to the political judgments of their contemporaries and to the moral judgments of history.[38]

Surely in Vietnam, and also in repression of native Indians, as well as elsewhere, the "moral judgments of history" run strong and deep against presidential unilateral use of violence. The "political judgments" of contemporaries finally turned against the Vietnam fiasco. There is such a thing as decency, something that too many Presidents for too long have forgotten.

Does any President really care about the moral judgments of history? That is highly unlikely. If what he does is politically acceptable, then he will proceed when considered necessary. This makes him "sovereign" in the use of violence—a king with little or no restraint. This has long been known, but little acknowledged by those who write learned treatises. Within a few years of the time the Constitution was drafted, Senator James Hillhouse complained that the President had already acquired "the power, not of declaring war in form, but of adopting a course of measures which will necessarily and inevitably lead to war."[39] No other major nation in the world gives such an awesome power to one person.

If Hillhouse was accurate in 1817, think how much more accurate he would have been today. FDR took the United States into World War II—of that there can be no real doubt. He needed a trigger and got it when the Japanese bombed Pearl Harbor. Before 1941, Americans were already deeply and doubtless irreversibly committed to helping Great Britain and France. So it was in Korea, where President Truman quickly sent armed forces to battle the North Koreans without asking Congress to participate— even though, contrary to Lincoln in the early days of the Civil War, Congress was then in session. It could have acted speedily, one way or the other. The essential point is that Truman saw no need for formal action from the Hill. The same for Vietnam: a gradual build-up to more than 500,000 troops was done on the order of the President alone. Everyone knew about it, of course, but no one did anything until years after the initial commitment.

The lesson is clear. The principle of political convergence may be seen, but much more clearly than in economic matters. Industrial nations tend to produce similar institutions, when external forces bear similarly on each. So the U.S. and the USSR come slowly to resemble each other. The President is an elected king, or sovereign; he knows few restraints in law and even fewer in morals. He does with the armed forces what the political process permits. That may be harsh, but it is a fact. And in the future, it will become even more factual. As internal turmoil erupts, as it seems certain it will, the military forces (regular or national guard) will be employed. The consequence? The "Latin-Americanization" of the United States.[40] Nothing in the Constitution will stop it; nothing the judiciary can do will stop it. Only the political process can, which means that if the President has Congress with him, he will prevail. That is what happened in the past. In this respect, the future will be an extension, an extrapolation, of the past.

Not only are the visible armed forces employed. Perhaps of more importance are the paramilitary forces of the nation, principally in the Central Intelligence Agency. The CIA is the President's "private army," operating under his direction and that of the National Security Council in the White House. The NSC is the principal staff organ for military and foreign policy matters. Only thirty years old, it is the effective center of control over the details of foreign policy management. Its "40 Committee" approves action by the CIA or other agencies. The people in Chile and Guatemala, Brazil and Iran, Vietnam and Angola, to name only a few that have surfaced to public attention, know well what the CIA has done—and continues to do.

Having a private army at his command with untold (at least, unknown to the public) resources gives the President and his close advisers an extraordinary opportunity to intervene in many parts of the world. That opportunity has often been seized. No longer is it necessary to call upon the Marines as a police force. Only when matters get out of hand, as they did in Vietnam, are the armed forces brought in. Short of that, the CIA is a group of "hit men" to carry out presidential orders.

Finally, the President as commander-in-chief has effective control over war-making in the nuclear age. He alone can trigger a nuclear war; and he alone can respond to what appears to be a nuclear attack. We can all hope that petty and unscrupulous men do not get elected to the presidency, and that Presidents choose men of commonsense and probity to advise them. On that score, however, no one should be optimistic. A chief executive who could mount the abortive Bay of Pigs Invasion, or the several Presidents who got us into Vietnam, or Presidents Ford and Carter in their African adventures, to name only some of the better known instances, certainly give little cause for optimism. The American political system does not elect great men to the presidency, great in the sense of having good judgment and solid common sense.

The enormous economic power of the United States was best seen in the 1945-1970 period, of the age of pax Americana. Since 1970 the dollar has been in trouble, but the domestic economy, save for inflation, remains strong. America, through the medium of some 500 billion "Euro-dollars" which float around the world's currency markets but for which there is no hope whatever that they will be redeemed by the United States (which has dropped conversion to gold), has managed to "export" inflation. Those in Europe and other parts of the world which have a much higher inflation rate than the U.S.A. are helping to pay for American prosperity and relatively low inflationary rate. That is one of the great, albeit unheralded, achievements in human history. Whether it will last is by no means certain.

Economics plus military power, nuclear and otherwise, enable the President, in Riencourt's words, to be "World Leader of Western Civilization." Use of paramilitary forces, backed up with the nuclear threat or the use of lesser weapons (as in Korea, Vietnam, and the Dominican Republic), have transformed the non-Sino-Soviet world into one man's imperium. No other single person in the world has such power, actual and latent. People throughout the non-Soviet world look to the White House for guidance. One has only to note the stream of world leaders who pour through the White House, there to meet the President, to realize that 1600 Pennsylvania Avenue in Washington, D.C. is the center of the world for those outside the USSR (and perhaps China). Washington is the Rome of the modern era—headed by a Caesar. And a High Priest.

The United States is moving toward an authoritarian government, with a God-King at its helm. Power has accumulated in the office of the presidency since the beginnings of the republic. That trend has accelerated in recent decades; and the massive challenges now facing the nation will make it become even more evident in the future. Power is a very heady thing. It is also a dangerous thing, a subtle poison to which any man may succumb.

Power, however, is also a very necessary thing. Someone must exercise it. No vacuum in politics now exists or ever has existed. The problem now is how to insure that when power is employed, as it will be, it will be in the interests not of the few but of the many. That question must be deferred for later discussion. Let us now merely ask that if Americans do permit, as they have in the past, Presidents to operate outside legal barriers to meet emergencies, actual or supposed, what is to prevent someone from seizing dictatorial power? Americans have already become inured to crisis, "loath to withhold power demanded by their leaders, reluctant to appear 'men (and women) of little faith'."[41] Americans have been uncommonly lucky thus far. Their emergencies, of whatever type, have been limited, and their Presidents keenly aware of the tenuous nature of their powers. Whether that will continue is by no means self-evident. Is there anything, except the vigilance and courage of the people, to prevent future Presidents from grabbing for authoritarian power? Very little, if anything. For that matter, vigilance and courage in the people, speaking generally, are in very short supply. When to the lack of "guts" is added the techniques of manipulation of opinion and other means of thought control now technologically possible, the future does not augur well for what routinely is called American democracy.

9

Government as "Controlled Anarchy"

Government in the United States may be presidential, but it is in obvious disarray, teetering on the edge of decay. At whatever level—national, state, or local—it is clear that government's reach exceeds its grasp in a wide range of activities. The reason for this is simple: Government is not an independent entity; it is an amalgam of public and private power. Too much, furthermore, is being asked of the apparatus of the State. Too many people demand too many "entitlements."[1] At precisely the time that they cannot be fulfilled, a rising tide of expectations threatens to engulf it: the nation has been brought to the brink of financial disaster, principally because of an all too pervasive factor of "social" bankruptcy. The politics of selfishness has become so widespread that the system will not withstand it. Something will have to give and soon; that "something" is constitutionalism as it has been known in this country. This chapter develops the theme of growing authoritarianism in American government as public officials seek at once to maintain internal order, external security, and satisfy the rising demands of people everywhere. The organizing principle is that the United States is fast moving into government under the Constitution of Control.

It will do little good—probably it will do much harm—for Americans to continue to indulge themselves in the fiction that the governmental system remains about the same as it came to us from the Founding Fathers. It distinctly is not. We have strayed far from the original conceptions—limited government, federalism, separation of powers, prevention of a "democratical despotism."

Some reference to history is desirable. In Number 10 of *The Federalist Papers*, written to help get the Constitution ratified, James Madison long ago saw the political process as the interplay of diverse political groups (which he called "faction"). Consider this well-known passage:

The latent causes of faction are . . . sown in the nature of man; and we see them every-where brought into different degrees of activity, according to the different circum-stances of civil society. A zeal for different opinions concerning religion, concerning government, and many other points, as well as speculation as of practice; an attach-ment to different leaders ambitiously contending for pre-eminence and power; or to persons of other descriptions whose fortunes have been interesting to the human passions, have, in turn, divided mankind into parties, inflamed them with mutual ani-mosity, and rendered them much more disposed to vex and oppress each other, than to cooperate for their common good. . . . But the most common and durable source of factions has been the various and unequal distribution of property. Those who hold and those who are without property have ever formed distinct interests in society. Those who are creditors, and those who are debtors, fall under a like discrimination. A landed interest, a manufacturing interest, with many lesser interests, grow up of neces-sity into civilized nations, and divide them into different classes, actuated by different sentiments and views. *The regulation of these various and interfering interests forms the principal task of modern legislation, and involves the spirit of party and faction in the necessary and ordinary operations of the government.*[2] (Emphasis added.)

Madison wrote in the late eighteenth century, before the rise of political parties. What he called "the principal task of modern legislation" was to reconcile the differing interests within the nation so that they did "cooperate for their common good." He thought the new Constitution filled that prescrip-tion.

Well and good, so far as it goes; the trouble is that it does not go very far, and that it has worked in the past only because of an ever-expanding eco-nomic pie that enabled diverse groups to sup, if not at will, then adequately. When in 1908 Arthur Bentley wrote *The Process of Government*,[3] he saw in the Madisonian process one of pluralistic groups that struggled in the political arena; out of that struggle, he, too, believed that the common good was achieved. The very statement of such a proposition today is its refutation. Interest groups—factions—indeed try to guide the course of public policy, but it is only happenstance, and not by design, that the nation has thus far achieved wealth and prosperity and a large measure of security. "The extra-ordinary affluence of the United States," says Rufus E. Miles, Jr., "has been produced by a set of fortuitous, nonreplicable, and nonsustainable factors."[4]

So it is. And so, too, are the successes thus far of a system of factions or pluralistic social groups that has permitted government to govern adequately in the past. Those "nonreplicable" factors about which Miles spoke have already been discussed. My point here is their political consequences.

Pluralism is failing. Professor Grant McConnell,[5] among others, noted as much in the mid-1960s when he said that much of government was "under the influence or control of narrowly based and largely autonomous elites." These elites, contrary to Madison and Bentley, act separately from each other on many issues. None rules in the sense of dominating the entire nation. On the contrary, each follows a policy of not being involved in the large national issues except in those instances when those issues touch their own interests. The consequence (as we have seen): The distinction between public and private has been compromised far more deeply than we like to acknowledge. Take, for example, the hidden conspiracy between labor and business. Wage increases are won at the bargaining table, often far more easily than outwardly appears, with the corporations immediately passing on (usually with a larger than necessary price increase) to the public the burden of bearing that cost. That could not take place without the cooperation of government, which provides the legal framework for "collective bargaining" and the money to pay for the bigger payrolls and increased prices. Consumers get a larger buying power through easy credit and governmental deficits. Hedonism? Yes. The future has been mortgaged to pay for the present—at the precise time that serious doubt exists about the ability of the future to pay those obligations. Most Americans today are unthinking hedonists, buying present pleasure at the expense of the future. (What they do not realize is that, with the rapid pace of events, *they* are the future.)

As with labor and business, so with others who guide the course of Madison's principal task of modern legislation. Those who so act, as well as those who extol the "system," do so by making one basic assumption—that by some means the common good, the "public interest," results from the process. That "invisible hand" theory was, or could be, true in only a limited period of time, when a special set of unique circumstances permitted America to wax large and strong, and to fulfill, reasonably adequately, the demands of the individuals who make up the pluralistic social groups. With the slowing down, even near cessation, of economic growth (in real economic terms, and also in inflationary dollars), individual and group selfishness or greed no longer will suffice. The "we want it all now" ethic will not do. Pluralism, rather than being adequate to the need, is a type of controlled anarchy.

Controlled anarchy? That is a contradiction in terms. Anarchy, by definition, is the absence of government and of law. Control is the antithesis of anarchy. Can the apparent contradiction be reconciled? The answer is "yes," but to explain it requires further inquiry into the nature of law. This, of necessity, must be brief.

We have already suggested that law is something other than what the laity thinks it is. We now focus on a different matter: two types of law, public and private. Historically, most law was "private law;" it regulated the relationships between individuals. What lawyers call contracts and torts and property were the principal elements of a legal system that gave little place to public law. The 1000-year history of the Anglo-American legal system is largely a history of the development of legal relationships between individuals. Put another way, American law for most of our history had an individualistic basis.

Only when the State commanded something, and that was mainly in the area of criminal law, could there be said to be a system of public law. Public law in recent decades has become dominant, far overshadowing private law. What, then, is public law? It is the set of policies enunciated by Congress and the bureaucracy that deal, not with persons between themselves, but with the person and government. Whatever government touches becomes law. Much of this is routine—for example, the criminal law, tort claims against the government, minor contract matters, claims of various types.

Of a different order of importance are the policies promulgated following the operation of the group struggle outlined above. Once that struggle is completed, statutes are enacted and administrative rules issued. These, too, are law; but of a different type than private law, or even of the run-of-the-mine claims against the government. Here, for example, subsidies for farmers, large and small, are voted into existence; here, the Federal Communications Commission issues radio and television licenses; here the Department of Energy regulates natural gas; here, in short, is the placing into public form of the outcomes of private group struggles. Each group strives to control the thrust of a segment of public policy. Bargains are struck and compromises reached. The final result is law—public law. A primitive type of barter economics is translated into public law. Pluralism is a form of barter economics, as the elites in the groups trade off for mutual advantage. The only rule of the game is that once a bargain is struck and it becomes law, the parties will at least temporarily abide by it. But the law so enunciated is never set in concrete; it is fluid and changing, open-ended and always in a process of "becoming." The struggles among groups continue, fiercely at times, and the law reflects changing configurations of power within the political arena. Government is both a participant in those contests and the object of battle of "private" groups.

One should never believe—one cannot believe—that public law is interdictory. Generally speaking it emphatically is not a set of "thou-shalt-nots;" rather, it is avowedly instrumental. Resources, becoming scarcer as the years go by, are allocated; the economic pie is sliced up and distributed. The important thing to perceive is that discretion is the norm. There is discretion in Congress, in the public administration, and even in the courts. Hence, it is here that the term "controlled anarchy" can be seen as valid, anarchy in the sense that no pre-existing rules determine the conduct of the group struggle, controlled in the sense that once the struggle ends the result is a rule that does set the limits of activity, however temporarily, for the interested parties.

Political pluralism, which as Madison saw was operative in the eighteenth century, and which as Bentley and others saw continues to the present time, is a type of sophisticated jungle warfare. It is jungle warfare, often without quarter, because as George Orwell presciently observed, pluralism is based on some untenable assumptions: that "the truth will prevail and persecution defeats itself;" that "man is naturally good and is only corrupted by his environment;" and further, that "the world is immensely rich and is suffering chiefly from maldistribution."[6]

Pluralism is not working simply because it is anarchic in form and in spirit. No one—no group—thinks of the overall common good. Each group pursues narrow, parochial interests, without regard to others or to the transcendent issues of statesmanship. Pluralism, in short, has become social and political bankruptcy. That is so, even though it has existed for almost two centuries, because the national cupboard is not large or sumptuous enough to permit reasonable realization of the demands being made upon it. The politics of selfishness have taken over at the time when selfishness—always present—no longer will do.

For various reasons, not least of which are the precepts of our secular religion of nationalism, people have been led to believe that hard work and diligence will inevitably lead to greater material rewards. That is the "Protestant Ethic." Materialism is one of the more prominent features of the civil religion. Another reason is the belief that nature's bounty, if not infinite, is surely enough to satisfy the rising expectations of people. Those demands, finally, have been subtly influenced by national advertising and mass higher education, which together breed desires for greater affluence. Not that selfishness— the politics of greed—has not always been present in America. Of course it has. What is different today is the fact that it has been "socialized"; people throughout the land believe they can couple on to the cornucopia of material plenty. The few benefited in the past; the many wish to do so today. They cannot. There is not enough to go around.

Americans, furthermore, have no institutional means of at once satisfying the expectations of people (of making them want what they get, rather than get what they want) and simultaneously making sure that the national interest is served. The Constitution is no such instrument. Outside of the formal document, the political party has grown extraconstitutionally. It is not, however, the sole efficient means of producing union between the executive and legislative branches of the government. Potentially, perhaps, but actually no. Members of Congress owe allegiance, not to the national party, but to local constituencies; their loyalties run the same way. No President can command obedience.

The net result is that pluralism is demonstrably faulty; and that the constitutional system has serious shortcomings.

Pluralism being a controlled anarchy and the political arena being a jungle of competing group interests, there should be little wonder that the constitutional order is in distress. The failure of pluralism is paralleled by a failure in constitutionalism. Presidential government does not mean that government is efficient; it merely means that the chief executive is dominant—quite a different thing. Neither the formal nor the living Constitution permits effective government *at the present time*. The historical system, of both types, is in trauma. It will soon be in extremis unless measures are taken, and quickly.

Great constitutional questions, Professor Henry Steele Commager once observed, are great "not because they are complicated legal or technical questions, but because they embody issues of high policy, or public good, or morality."[7] So it is here: the constitutional questions presented by the climacteric of humankind and by the accompanying politics of greed—which we have called the breakdown of pluralism—are of enormous importance to the American people. They are neither complex, technical, nor even legal; they strike to the root of how a polity that calls itself democratic is ruled.

The questions can be analyzed under traditional rubrics, such as federalism, separation of powers, and the position of the individual in an organized society. It is better, however, to think in terms of a general malaise in government. Something is out of kilter in the way that our official institutions have evolved. In December 1978 *The London Economist* flatly stated: "Across the English-speaking world, the system of government is breaking down. In the lucky countries (the United States? Australia?), government is due to decline in importance, so the breakdown should not matter."[8] The system is in decay: "In the past decade it has become clear that voting democracy cannot work." We have already discussed the demise of liberal democracy, so there is no need for further exposition. The breakdown has become so obvious that even journalists can perceive it.

This is a constitutional crisis of the first dimension. The ancient ways are no longer working. Confidence in government and in the ability of government to fulfill its promises is visibly ebbing away. Americans are, as a consequence, at sea in a rudderless ship, without a compass to steer by. (That cannot last.) The decisional process in America has all but collapsed, as governments at all levels limp from crisis to crisis. No one knows quite what to do.

A national economic system (more, a multinational economic system) sits astraddle a decentralized political order. In economics, both the fifty states and the nation itself are anachronisms. The secular religion of nationalism is making chauvinists of us all, as we draw inward and seek to export both unemployment and inflation. That those policies are self-defeating should be self-evident. But they are not; and they will be followed until something catastrophic occurs—as occur it will, sooner or later. At the very time that we should not do so, Americans are becoming increasingly isolationist. A generation ago, Gunnar Myrdal, the Swedish Nobel Laureate, warned that "Welfare" States—what we have called the positive State—were nationalistic.[9] But no one listened.

Governmental institutions in the United States are for the most part monuments to old problems. Examples are easy to locate. The fifty states: the price that was paid for the Constitution in the federal system. Separation of governmental powers: to achieve efficiency and prevent despotism. (That old problem is still around.) Any number of federal agencies. The Department of Agriculture is a classic example. It is a memorial to nineteenth century farming problems. Those problems have largely been solved, but the Department not only continues—it has expanded. The Department of Labor is another. And does anyone know what the Department of Commerce does—or, better, is supposed to do? The Interstate Commerce Commission should have been abolished long ago.

The bureaucracy proliferates into what *The Economist* termed "public-sector imperialism."[10] Political power is in the hands of those Solzhenytsin called "political bureaucrats" and "official bureaucrats." The White House staff—the inner presidency—plus cabinet and subcabinet officers and members of Congress make up the political bureaucracy; the official bureaucrats are the civil servants. Together they control the highest portion of the gross national economic product of any group. No corporation, whatever its size, can approximate their resources. They have the public treasury at their command. Their aim—their principal morality—is directed toward the survival and, indeed, the expansion of the group. As with business corporations, public bureaucracies believe they must expand or die. Raison de groupe is as important in government as it is in business.

Huge public and private bureaucracies came into existence for certain obvious purposes. Whether they are any longer needed, certainly in the numbers they now have, is by no means certain. The nation—the world—is in the beginning stages of the "third industrial revolution," that of micro-data processing (through silicon chips), which promises to transform the social milieu as much, or more, than the first industrial revolution. The latter came in the nineteenth century; the machine replaced the need for much manual labor—a process that continues to this day. More and more unskilled jobs are being done by machines, as technology is applied throughout the industrial order. The second industrial revolution came as recently as the 1940s and 1950s when many menial tasks were found amenable to technology. Now, the third—the "information"—revolution is markedly decreasing the need for many of the millions who work for the government (directly or indirectly). Says *The Economist* in a blunt, perhaps overly fervid statement: "Anybody who believes that after this information revolution a voter-employed bureaucracy can continue to be the main instrument of government is being as daft as anybody who forecast in 1816 that the number of handloom weavers will continue to grow and grow."[11]

Perhaps that is correct; perhaps not. No one knows yet for certain the actual impact of the third industrial revolution. What is known is that the traditional American constitutional order is not prepared to deal with it. Our institutions were created for problems that have now either disappeared or have been merged with other greater problems. Constitutional change, according to the original document, comes through the amending process only. There are still commentators who assert, sometimes quite fervently, that amendment is the only proper method of updating the Constitution. That it is not has long been known: the living Constitution—of Supreme Court decisions, of presidential and Congressional actions—allows each generation of Americans to write their own Constitution. The time has now arrived, however, to question whether even those extraconstitutional processes are sufficient to the need; or whether there is not a persuasive case to be made for substantial constitutional alteration.

The fundamental law, as written and as interpreted, and whether it be the formal or the living Constitution, is a barrier to desirable change. It cannot keep up with the massive transformations brought by science and technology. During the nineteenth and early twentieth centuries, during the time of the first industrial revolution, it did so through a pretense and a fiction—that the Constitution remained the same, whatever the conditions were. That it did not has already been shown. Those means of constitutional alteration have about run their course. There is little more that they can do. Unless something is done, and soon, to update the fundamental law in certain basic ways, the decay that is all too apparent in government will mean that the Document of 1787 and its amendments will become a mere historical curiosity (at worst) or (at best), even more of a phony facade than it is at present.

The problem, in other words, is that American constitutional institutions show a hardening of the arteries. The ancient words ring hollow in an era of massive social change. Decay has set in at the heart of the flowering tree of American constitutionalism. It still blooms, but its core is dying. Its inability to adapt, when adaptation is so obviously necessary, reflects a social and political order that still adheres to ancient ways at a time when those ways are no longer up to the need.

Consider, for example, the failure of pluralism outlined above. Consider also the tensions between the need for uniformity in human responses and attitudes, if technology is to work (the need, that is, for predictable people), and its polar opposite: the still-lingering values of individualism and of the dignity of man. Technology works toward uniformity. Many would like diversity—or at least a modicum of personal choice. The nation is becoming "standardized." The constitutional order is not now up to the mark in resolving that basic tension.

Think, too, about "structural" unemployment and the problems brought by a leisure society. An odd, even touching, faith that the third industrial revolution is not making man obsolescent may be discerned throughout the land, particularly in the scientific community. A mammal which has spent untold millennia at the hard and grinding task of earning its living is now confronted with an entirely different set of environmental circumstances. The new society that is being built in the electronic age needs neither mass manpower nor a large number of highly trained technicians.[12] In process of creation is an industrial order with a few specialists in new technology at the top, specialists who need a considerable number of people at lower rungs who can follow orders and do certain mechanical tasks. The dignity of man is a disappearing concept. The need of the new social order, based as it is on technology, is for a populace not far from that etched in acid terms by Aldous Huxley in *Brave New World*. And that, unhappily, is what seems to be in process of creation: A large, relatively quiescent group at the bottom, kept docile by various means, ruled over by a small number of technocrats with specialized skills and knowledge.

There is no way under the Constitution as it has been known for problems such as these to be adequately resolved. Neither the political nor the official bureaucrats can do the job; and for the problems to be left to the workings of the "marketplace" is a counsel of despair. The market does not work adequately. When to the malaise of government is added the sure to come (already here) climacteric, then all but the willfully blind should be able to perceive that something is badly awry in the constitutional order. The Constitution in essence establishes a set of *procedures* for dealing with social problems. Procedure alone, as we have already observed, is not enough. Attention must be paid to the content of decisions, as well as to the means for making them. There is, in short, a need for an avowed ideology.

The present governmental system cannot last. It will not last, simply because it is absurd. Nothing so out of phase with the realities of modern life, domestic and planetary, can long survive in anything near its present form.

What, then, will supplant it? It takes no special gift of clairvoyance to be able to predict with a high degree of assurance what the future will bring. If one accepts the view that government has always been relative to circumstances, then government—the constitutional order—will change to reflect the circumstances of the future. And if, as has been postulated, the future is one of the crisis of crises, measures are sure to be taken—sooner or later—to deal with those crises. Slowly at first, but then with a rush, some type of authoritarian government is in the making. It will begin with the economic sphere. Government may be decaying, but it is not going to collapse.

What will collapse are the values inherent in constitutionalism. Says Dr. Lester Brown: "Coming to terms with the political dilemma . . . will not be easy or necessarily pleasant." Historian Arnold Toynbee sees increasingly authoritarian governments emerging as economic growth slows or stops. "In all developed countries," he writes, "a new way of life—a severely regimented way—will have to be imposed by a ruthless authoritarian government."[13] The Constitution of Control is fast emerging.

Part IV

THE FUTURE:
THE EMERGENCE
OF THE CONSTITUTION
OF CONTROL

The past is but prologue. Adherence to the past is not a duty; it is merely a necessity. Americans cannot escape their history; perhaps they should not want to do so. If the transition to an ecology of scarcity is to be effected without massive strains on traditional constitutional values, then humans everywhere should make that attempt. Even if the effort is made, it by no means is certain that authoritarianism will be escaped. Quite the contrary: The major indicators of social change point inexorably to the rise of repression. In part IV, the emergent Constitution of Control is outlined, together with discussions of the end of the American Dream and of the baleful use of technology. The future beckons—and it could be Orwellian in nature.

10

The Future, Yes:
The American Dream Endeth?

Americans face a rude dilemma, as do the people in other relatively affluent, industrialized nations. Worldwide and domestically, two apparent irreconcilables are on a collision course: burgeoning demands for a better life versus the probability that a politically managed, humanistically oriented society (domestic and planetary) seems ever more to be an impossible dream. Not that a reconciliation of sorts will not take place, at some time and in some way; of course it will. The problem is not that, but to make the resolution reasonably satisfactory to people generally. That's a large order, calling for an effort never before known in human history.

To diagnose the human condition is relatively easy. Some may dispute the conclusions or inferences drawn from known facts, but the facts themselves are beyond argument. It is quite another thing to prescribe, to propose policies that are both desirable and feasible. Here, again, it is easy enough to know what is needed; the problem is to develop feasible ways of getting from the present parlous situation to a more satisfactory future. All we have to work with is present knowledge. In constructing scenarios, will the future be a mere unilinear extension of the past and present? No, not necessarily so: Just as the present is a mutational leap from previous (say, pre-1800) human history, there is little reason to believe that science and technology will not continue their dizzy pace of altering the social milieu in which other human institutions must operate.

What, then, are the constants of the future social order? The following seem, if not beyond dispute, at least reasonably sure.

Americans, avowed pragmatists, are in reality prisoners of an ideology, one that is seldom stated but is nonetheless pervasive. The most important thing about forecasting the future is to realize the basic tenet of that mind-frame. Writing in 1936, John Maynard Keynes maintained that "the ideas of economists and political philosophers, both when they are right and when they are wrong, are more powerful than is commonly understood. Indeed the world is ruled by little else. Practical men, who believe themselves to be quite exempt from any intellectual influences, are usually slaves of some defunct economist."[1] The power of ideas may indeed be great, as Keynes said, but more than mere ideas is important. The economists and political philosophers, about whom he spoke, quite often are the intellectuals who tell men of action what they have done and why. Ideas, in the Keynesian sense, do not rule the world; burly sinners do.

Keynes's perspective was too limited. Had he focused, not on economists and political philosophers but on the deeper thinkers on whom they built, his quoted view may well have been correct. The fundamental question is this: Is man a part of nature or superior to it? That has been answered, in Western thought antedating even the birth of the Judeo-Christian religions, by the belief that man is *not*, in his heart, part of the natural process. "We are superior to nature, contemptuous of it."[2] That has had enormous consequences for the nature of human thought and action; and is the base upon which the Keynesian assertion attains a large measure of validity. It is worthwhile, therefore, to sketch its antecedents. Only by understanding that basic concept can the American Dream be understood.

What is that Dream (a dream, it is important to realize, that has now been transferred planetwide)? In brief, it is the faith that nature can be subdued and bent to man's will, the faith that leads Americans to assume there is no puzzle that humans cannot solve, no barrier that cannot be surmounted, no journey that cannot be triumphantly ended. Historian Charles Beard put it well a half-century ago: To him, American history revealed a concept of progress based upon individual freedom and the humane use of science for democratic purposes and human betterment. "If there is anything which history demonstrates," he maintained, "it is this generalization. All legislation, all individual efforts are founded on the assumption that evils can be corrected, blessings multiplied by rational methods, intelligently applied. Essentially by this faith is American civilization justified."[3] With the coming of the "global city" (or "global village") that indigenous American faith has now been spread throughout the world. The Chinese peasant, the Indian Untouchable, the underclass in the nauseous barrios of Latin America dream the same dream.

1. *Is Man the Master?* The beginning of man's attitude of superiority toward nature is often attributed to the Judeo-Christian traditions. God gave

the mission: subdue the earth and earth's creatures, and do so because man himself is separate and apart from other creatures. He is "special": The idea of special creation, long exploded (at least since Darwin wrote in the mid-eighteenth century), still abides.

In pre-Christian Greek philosophy, the universe was anthropocentric—man-centered. Aristotle, to take only one example, wrote in his *Politics* that "plants were created for the sake of animals, and the animals for the sake of man."[4] The book of Genesis bids man to go forth and multiply, and to exercise dominion over every living thing. For centuries this was—and in large part still is—interpreted as a license to dominate the planetary environment, animal and vegetable and mineral, oblivious to the interests of natural things except man himself.

Ultimately, both philosophy and religion were based on a conception of the universe—upon a cosmology. The ancients drew theirs from Claudius Ptolemy, who in the second century A.D. spread the idea (long assumed but, from the records, never before stated) that Earth was the center of the universe. That probably was psychologically necessary; but as we now know, it was astronomically faulty. From that scientific idea came the theological notion of a human-centered universe, the idea that man was superior to all else. Cicero summed it up when he said: "We are absolute masters of what the earth produces."[5] Even animals were made, not for themselves, but for man and man alone. Whereas "primitive" man identified with the environment, Western man sought to dominate and subdue it.

The consequences are all too apparent. We see them all around us. When the Ptolemaic cosmology was shattered by Copernicus 500 years ago, the mind of man was released from a mental strait-jacket. The scientific revolution was born, fathered by Sir Isaac Newton about 300 years ago. As with Ptolemy, so with Newton: his cosmology was assimilated by the dominant philosophers of the age (and since then). The American (the human) Dream cannot be understood without first understanding the impact of the anthropocentric (man-centered) views of Ptolemy, combined with the mechanistic ideas of Newton.

Ptolemy established the pervasive view that man was a being apart from others of nature's creatures, one with a special mission. Newton, of course, built on Copernicus, and thus repudiated the man-centered universe. But he did not reject the idea of special creation or of special mission. He believed that men, acting through their "reason" (often capitalized as Reason), could persuade nature to reveal her secrets, and in revealing them bow to the needs of man. Newton thus complemented Ptolemy. Man was considered to be separate from, rather than a part of, nature. Ptolemy's views were assimilated by the monotheism of the Judeo-Christian religions. For Newton and his followers, God existed and had created the world, but thereafter assumed no control over it or over the lives of people. That is "deism." Reason is all that is necessary to conquer the world. The deism of Newton and his intellectual disciples has now been transformed into "humanism"—a philosophy or religion that asserts the dignity and worth of man and his ability to attain self-realization through reason and the scientific method. Of humanism, more later; the point now is simply to show the unilinear progression of Western thought from the pre-Christians to the present day, to the extent that, as Raymond Aron said in 1967, "modern societies are the first ever to justify themselves by their future, the first in which the motto 'Man is the future of man' appears not so much blasphemous as banal."[6]

Newton's famous "laws of motion" were translated into "laws" of causation in human affairs, particularly his third law: "If two particles interact, the force exerted by the first particle on the second particle is equal in magnitude and opposite in direction to the force exerted by the second particle on the first particle."[7] That seemingly innocuous statement has had enormous consequences. We need not get into the intricacies of Newton's scientific laws to see that. Suffice it to say that in the Newtonian cosmology the universe was likened to a great clock, with interacting parts; pressure applied at one part would have a predictable effect elsewhere. A moment's reflection will readily reveal how that conception, which was the basis of the scientific revolution and which was accepted in toto until very recent times, in turn had an enormous impact on the Western intellect. The scientific law of cause and effect became the social law of cause and effect. All things seemed possible; the natural world could be subdued, through the force of reason, for the purposes of man. That conception underlies the widely accepted modern idea that planning, economic and social, of human affairs is possible by men of good will. The dream set in motion by Sir Isaac Newton was translated into philosophy by Rene Descartes, among others: "I perceived it to be possible," he wrote, "to arrive at knowledge highly useful in life . . . to discover a practical [method] by means of which knowing the force and action of fire, water, air, the stars, the heavens, and all the other bodies that surround us, as distinctly as we know the various crafts of our artisans, we might apply them in the same way to all the uses in which they are adapted, and thus render ourselves the lords and possessors of nature."[8] In brief, the law of causation, of cause and effect, was transferred into human affairs.

The basic inference, particularly by the philosophers of the Enlightenment, was that nature is understandable and subject to iron laws. From that came the idea of "progress" and the American Dream. That the Cartesian perception, and that basic inference, are faulty needs no extended discussion. As is well known, Max Planck, Albert Einstein and Werner Heisenberg have corrected some (not all) of Newtonian mechanics, and shattered the intellectual underpinnings of the Enlightenment and its American disciples. Harvard physicist Percy Bridgman (an insightful student of human affairs) succinctly stated the consequences as long ago as 1929: The discoveries of Heisenberg and others, he wrote, can only mean

that our conviction that nature is understandable and subject to law arose from the narrowness of our horizons, and that if we would sufficiently extend our range we shall find that nature is intrinsically and in its elements neither understandable nor subject to law. . . . The precise reason that the law of cause-and-effect fails can be paradoxically stated; it is not that the future is not determined in terms of a complete description of the present, but that in the nature of things the present cannot be completely described. . . . The world is not a world of reason, understandable by the intellect of man, but as we penetrate ever deeper, the very law of cause-and-effect, to which we had thought to be a formula we could force God Himself to subscribe, ceases to have a meaning.[9]

Nature, in sum, is not a machine, however much man with an arrogance that surpasses all understanding, so believes (and in believing, acts). A classic example of that mind-frame came in 1810 when Justice William Johnson of the Supreme Court could hold a Georgia statute unconstitutional using these words: "I do not hesitate to declare, that a state does not possess the power of revoking its own grants. But I do it, on a general principle, on the reason and nature of things; a principle which will impose laws even on the Deity."[10] No more hubristic assertion ever came from the Supreme Court—a group of men never known for modesty. Less then two centuries later that intellectual world lay in ruins, and with it the American Dream.

Not that people do not continue to act as if the Dream were possible; of course they do. Many, including much of academia, assert a confident, unthinking belief in "progress" as *the* natural condition of free men acting in open environments, and in the capacity of the human intellect to perceive and effectively deal with social problems. Old ideas die hard, particularly when the alternative is so dark. But the environmental factors that made the Dream possible will not be repeated; and there is a dawning realization that Newton's law of cause-and-effect, repudiated in the laboratory, cannot be applied in the social arena. The effort will be made, however, to manage the future, and, paradoxically, it will succeed in small part.

We have become accustomed in recent decades to massive social changes caused by scientific and technological developments, changes that have so altered the environment in which human institutions operate that it bears little resemblance to that of even one hundred years ago. Alvin Toffler's term for that, future shock, has now passed into the common lexicon. A crucial question is whether that accelerative development can continue. By no means is that a certainty; quite probably, the contrary is or will be true. Certainly, economic growth cannot go on as it has in the past. As Rufus Miles, drawing on economist Kenneth Boulding, put it: "Anyone who believes that exponential growth can go on forever is either a madman or an economist."[11]

An even more crucial question is this: "Can the future be 'engineered'?" It must be if even an adequate, let alone completely satisfactory, resolution of the problems attendant to the human condition is to occur. My conclusion is that even more radical social changes will have to take place for social engineering to be successful; required are alterations in human values, in human ethics, in human governance. That is indeed a large order. No valid reason exists that they will happen.

Everyone would like to believe that he is indeed in control of his own destiny. We like to think that we are the masters and that all things can be bent to our needs. Having given up the belief in a benevolent hereafter, man has seized upon the present and seeks to plan it. Planning involves the establishment of public policies through law—purposive or instrumental law. In this respect, law is considered to be like Newton's clock, a seamless web of mutually interacting principles, logically consistent internally. A few decades ago, Dean Roscoe Pound of the Harvard Law School, and others, wrote glowingly of the possibility of social engineering through law (presumably accomplished by lawyers trained for that purpose).[12] The clock could be tinkered with and adjusted to suit the purposes of man. Pound's views still infect the academic world, in law and elsewhere. Lawyers and economists, political scientists and even natural scientists, have at least a tacit faith in the power of reason to control the human condition in beneficent ways.

That belief-system is faulty, but only partially. The universe, contrary to Newton, is not a great clock. It is, as Charles Darwin has told us, a "process" rather than a closed system. Open-ended and always changing, human affairs are a stream. One cannot step twice into the same stream. Planning will come, nevertheless.

Heretofore, humans have drifted from generation to generation, the object of forces and conditions external to themselves, over which they had no control. Change in social life came slowly; torpidity characterized the species for hundreds of thousands, even millions, of years. Suddenly, however, we are entering into a new age of planning, of trying to invent or control the future, of attempting to exercise dominion over those external forces. Even though it is, when viewed historically, a wholly new experience, it is certain to succeed (barring nuclear war) in small part. In net, though, the results will not be palatable to most people.

Civilization is such a recent phenomenon for humans that they do not know how to deal with it. Before recorded history began a few thousand years ago—and then only in small segments of the planet (the Mediterranean basin; China)—the lot of man was neither civilization nor civility. (When speaking of civilization I refer to the concept adhered to by people in the Western

World, even though insights of such people as Claude Lévi-Strauss[13] now reveal that what Western man called uncivilized or primitive in, say, Africa, often was quite the contrary.) In all except a minute number of the millions of years that Homo sapiens has roamed the planet, he was little different from other brutes in the forest. No one knows (or can know) why civilization as we know it dawned little more than three millennia ago. All that is known is that prehistory suddenly became history.

Even then, the records tell only a smidgen of what occurred during the beginnings of Western civilization. Before then, all is blackness, a void of anything more than fragments of knowledge (many of which are disputed). Were it possible to know definitively why civilization blossomed when and where it did, there might be greater hope that the future could be planned adequately. Be that as it may, the perspective of history must always be remembered— both the history that is known and that which is unknown. How much and in what respect people today are the creatures of—are influenced by—the unknown and unknowable as well as the known past is itself not known. Controversy, for example, still rages about the relative importance of heredity and environment on human behavior, a controversy that is not likely to be settled definitively.

A person is rash indeed to attempt to forecast the future. "What happens happens, and follows from antecedent states, but whether necessarily or unnecessarily we have no dispensation to know."[14] As in the physicists' subatomic world of "particles," so it is in human endeavor: a principle of indeterminacy operates. Even so, some idea of future conditions and attitudes is indispensable as the age of planning begins.

Man, however, is *not* the master. The future may be unknowable, and no doubt there will be many attempts to transform the "thou-shalt-nots" of the historical Constitution into a set of obligations (of "thou-musts"), but we delude ourselves if we think that man is not a part of nature and must not be reconciled with it. We live today in man-made, synthetic ecosystems; and we have not yet learned to "respect and preserve the stability of natural ecosystems and . . . to learn the secret of stability."[15] A few halting beginnings have been made, as Lord Ashby of Brandon has pointed out;[16] but they are as yet insufficient. Nor do they take into consideration other adaptations which affluent industrial societies must make: coming to terms with the growing scarcity of resources and the demands of an exploding population upon them; and, in Ashby's words, "the reconciliation of man with members of his own species who live by different ideologies."[17]

Successes achieved in the past 300 years to alter the status of humans may in large part be attributed to the great discoveries of the new world. There is a rough correlation in time between Newton and his disciples in the Enlightenment, and the flow of material wealth from America and other parts of the world to Europe. How much that had to do with the belief in progress and in social engineering cannot be proved. One can only speculate about it. Is it more than a coincidence that ideas of the perfectability of man grew and flourished at precisely the time that, and in precisely the places where, the immense wealth of the great discoveries poured into Western Europe? One would be foolish to think that there was no relationship between those phenomena (physical and intellectual). Such a relationship is not empirically verifiable; but surely it is at least arguably accurate. Turn the question around: As with the demise of the idea of liberal democracy, is there any better explanation of a belief-system that is limited in time and in space—unique in human history?

   2. Reductionism—narrow-minded specialists knowing more and more about less and less—will continue to characterize the intellectual world. At the very time that a holistic view of the world and the world's peoples has become indispensable, intellectual currents run strong and deep the other way. Holism, in sum, maintains that a part cannot be understood in isolation from the whole; and that the parts of an organic whole are dynamically interrelated and interdependent.
   The climacteric of mankind is an interconnected web, no part of which can be understood without reference to all of the others. The intellectual need is for "generalists"—precisely what the education system is not producing. Knowledge is becoming more and more specialized; specialties exist within specialties. One need not go to the natural sciences to see that: Look, for example, at the medical and legal professions. No one can be expert in all of the aspects of either medicine or law. Historically, lawyers were the principal generalists of American society. A legal education, whether in a law office or in law school, enabled some lawyers to take the larger view and thus to confront and grapple with the problems of yesteryear. That is no longer true. Legal education, as it is taught today, is really a form of brain damage. Narrow-minded technicians are being produced at the exact time when society needs broad-minded generalists. No other discipline or profession fills the gap, certainly not those poor deluded economists who repair to mathematics (econometrics) and try to produce useful proposals for public policy.
   The need is for seeing the climacteric of mankind in its entirety and for perceiving human problems holistically. Problems (and solutions, if solutions there are) can be split only for purposes of convenience. At some time, someone or some group of people must put the parts together. Whether the necessary generalists can or will be produced, and if so, whether they will be heeded, is by no means self-evident. Human affairs and human knowledge are far too complex for any person to comprehend even their outlines, let alone their intricacies. There are no Renaissance men today; nor can there

be. The explosion in knowledge has made that type of mind a manifest impossibility. Generalists will not be produced. Reductionism will continue to characterize the intellectual scene.

3. That means something quite important in politics (in constitutionalism): There will also be a continuation of *incrementalism* in policy-making. Rather than following an ideology, crisis-to-crisis decision-making will take place. Under this conception nothing is a problem until there is a crisis—until it is too late to do more than try to patch it. As a nation, we do not know what we want, other than a vague hedonism as individuals and a rather less vague *Pax Americana* in world affairs. The first cannot last; the latter has already ended. Americans will continue to limp along, hoping for the best (and even expecting it), at a time when giant strides are necessary.

Incrementalism—what Yale Professor Charles Lindblom with a straight face termed the "science of 'muddling through'"[18]—is one result of American pluralism. It is also an application of the scientific method, as espoused by Isaac Newton, in the realm of public affairs. Scientists attempt only the tasks that appear "do-able"; the impossible or even the improbable are set aside. So it is in government.

The process is demonstrably faulty. Hit-and-miss improvisation no longer will suffice. Take, as an example, a now-dated discussion of America's arms control efforts, Bernhard Bechhoefer's *Postwar Negotiations for Arms Control* (1961). Bechhoefer relates how the efforts, if that they were, to control arms proceeded without any long-range planning. He concluded:

In the summer of 1956, apparently there was no broad over-all American policy that comprehended within itself both the unity of the West and a negotiable position toward armaments regulation. Rather, the American policy in all areas had emerged as a series of brilliantly conceived tactics to meet specific situations, to extinguish specific bonfires. . . .

By the summer of 1957, the Secretary of State had reached the situation where as a result of brilliantly executed tactical maneuvers to meet specific situations, *United States foreign policy had become the sum of the tactics and the Secretary of State was imprisoned by it.*[19] (Emphasis added.)

That is precisely what happened in Vietnam: A series of tactical judgments became in time a strategic commitment, and policy-makers found themselves imprisoned by their own tactics. There is a name for this: pragmatism or empiricism—terms used with pride in Washington, by deluded men who should but do not know better.

Under that approach a policy issue becomes a search for empirical data, and consensus becomes the test for validity. American policy-makers believe

that the "facts" of foreign (or other) policy are all that matter. Facts are supposed to "speak for themselves." Pragmatism or empiricism are employed as
though being pragmatic and empirical when faced with a political problem is
to be rational by definition. Problems are called "headaches" and dealt with in
the same manner as actual headaches—with the quick "fix," the aspirin
tablet, that will enable that problem to be "solved" and permit attention to be
devoted to the next one.[20] (This may be called the "aspirin theory" of public
policy-making.) Since policy-making is a quest for the common denominator,
the search is more concerned with method than with judgment. Judgment
(similar to due process decisions in legal matters) is reduced to methodology.
It is, in legal terms, procedural rather than substantive. The result, as Henry
Kissinger said before he became a mover and shaker of events, is a vicious
circle: "As long as our high officials lack a framework of purpose, each problem becomes a special case. But the more fragmented the approach to policy
becomes, the more difficult it is to act consistently and purposefully. The
typical pattern of our governmental process is therefore endless debate over
whether a given set of circumstances is in fact a problem, until a crisis removes
all doubts and also the possibility of effective action."[21]

Surely this type of policy-making is faulty beyond measure. Facts do not
speak for themselves; they do not exist apart from a theory, however buried
in one's subconscious mind that may be. Incrementalism will not do. In public
policymaking, and elsewhere, a holistic approach is needed. There is little
evidence that this will be done until the coalescing crises facing humankind
become so obvious and so enormous that few, perhaps no one, will disagree
that a different approach to ordering the affairs of humankind is required. By
then, it will be too late.

4. *Micawberism* will continue. People fervently want to believe—they do
believe—that something will turn up, sooner or later, to rescue them from
their follies and their tribulations. It is a touching belief. Drawing on history as
taught in America's schools, they see the nation as something different from
the rest of humankind; and they think that the system, however defined,
works. The "system" is never defined; it seems to consist of a vague adherence to a private-enterprise economy and its analogue, a legal system based
on contract rather than status to settle the roles that people play in life. American society, however, is more and more one of status, of a new type of
feudalism, in which a person's rights and obligations depend upon the group
or groups to which he belongs.

Micawberism is a wistful dream, part and parcel of the American Dream.
Anything seems possible: we may not (yet) have the best of all possible
worlds, but given time that, too, will come about. Dickens's Mr. Micawber has
his literary counterpart in Voltaire's Pangloss, he who travelled the earth
repeating that all is for the best in this best of all possible worlds. There are

modern counterparts to Dickens and Voltaire, people who see the explosion of scientific knowledge about control of the environment and spin fantasies about the future. Two examples must suffice. First is Adrian Berry, who in *The Next Ten Thousand Years* maintains:

Contrary to the Club of Rome's belief there are no "limits to growth'. . . . Even if the Earth's resources prove ultimately to be finite, those of the solar system and the great galaxy beyond are, for all practical purposes, infinite. . . .

A permanent or semipermanent colony of Lunarians, numbering some hundreds of thousands, is likely to exist on the moon by the middle of the twenty-first century. . . .

Living on Venus will have its inconveniences. . . .

Unfortunately, Venus is the only planet in the solar system whose size and proximity to the sun makes it suitable for comparatively cheap terra-forming. . . . As for the big planetary masses in the solar system, it will take many centuries and great expense before they can be exploited for the actual building of new Earth-size worlds close to the sun. . . . It will be necessary in the meantime to migrate to the planets in orbit around other stars.[22]

Berry is serious. He really believes that. Nor is he alone. Many, possibly most, accept if not the details then the general pattern. Deep down inside, they believe, consciously or subconsciously, that something will turn up, even if that "something" is building new planets close to the sun. Berry is pathetic, of course, but he is far from a lone voice crying in the wilderness. There is light at the end of the tunnel, say these observers; humankind need not be prey to the caprices of fortune and nature. Listen now to Murray Bookchin:

After thousands of years of tortuous development, the countries of the Western world (and potentially all countries) are confronted by the possibility of a materially abundant, almost workless era in which most of the means of life can be provided by machines. . . . For the first time in history, technology has reached an open end. The potential for technological development. . . . is virtually unlimited. . . . From the moment toil is reduced to the barest possible minimum or disappears entirely, the problems of life, and technology itself passes from being the servant of man's immediate needs to being the partner of his creativity. . . . We can only ask one thing of the free men and women of the future: to forgive us that it took so long and was such a hard pull.[23]

What is one to make of that? Were we to believe Bookchin, human destiny is no longer God's will nor even the will of an oft-times capricious nature: Man's destiny is in his own hands.

That is Micawberism run wild. That is the American Dream brought to its ultimate. That is latter-day Newtonianism at a time when his concepts have been invalidated. Technology, Berry and Bookchin tell us, will rescue us from our mistakes and our sins, and provide for everyone, everywhere, the good life. It is based on faith and the assumption that technology can and will be harnessed, and used for socially beneficial ends. That is hubris, pure and simple, to the highest degree ever known. No doubt it is possible to build a colony on the moon, but it would be immensely expensive. Taking Berry's proposal seriously, is there a case to be made for giving space exploration and colonization priority? The question answers itself, if for no other reason than that colonizing the moon or even Venus will do nothing to solve the pressing problems of the antheap civilization on earth. Furthermore, with silicon chips and other technical developments in the minute, no doubt it is possible, as has been said, to eliminate the need for much of human work. Here, again, basic problems are "handled" by being ignored.

5. *The "information society,"* sparked by a communications revolution, will dominate the Age of Technology. An IBM vice president who is also its chief scientist believes that information is the "ultimate frontier," the means by which a pattern of societal interdependence can be made "more flexible, practical, and rewarding for all of us."[24] (That is still another example of Micawberism.)

There can be little doubt, however, about the coming information society. What is in doubt is its meaning. The computer is the perfect tool for the bureaucrat, enabling government officials to manipulate information, for good or bad purposes, against our interests. Consider Solzhenitsyn's vivid description in *Cancer Ward* about the ways that an information bureaucracy operates: "As every man goes through life he fills in a number of forms for the record. . . . There are hundreds of little threads radiating from every man, millions of threads in all. If all these threads were suddenly to become visible the whole sky would look like a spider's web and if they materialized as rubber bands, buses, trams and people would lose their ability to move." Those who control the threads in that cobweb control society itself. The information society is the controlled society.

No doubt much of that control, when it comes, will be done for outwardly benevolent purposes. Benevolent or not, the information network made possible by the electronics revolution means that personal privacy is a thing of the past. Data banks, both public and private, make it possible for a person's record to follow him throughout life. In recent years, one's social security number has become a substitute for his name. It must be used, for example, on federal tax forms, and is routinely used elsewhere even though a federal statute attempts to prohibit it. The District of Columbia puts it on a driver's license. In Gian Carlo Menotti's opera, *The Consul*, which vividly relates the frustrations of persons dealing with nameless and faceless bureaucrats, there is a line that goes: "Your name is a number. . . ." When Menotti wrote that in the early 1950s, he presciently foresaw the information society of the future. A person's name today is indeed a number—the ultimate submergence of individuality into the collectivity called society. The key to the spider's web or rubber bands in *Cancer Ward* is the number which, although not given at birth, follows one wherever he goes. All that remains is for it to be assigned at birth and tattooed on each person's arm.

Not that there is no need for this; of course there is. An antheap society dominated by technology is highly complex, intricately interrelated. Without information processing, it could not operate. It would fall of its own weight. We have the antheap society now, and will be even more so in the future. The cost, however, comes high: the very notion of freedom is ebbing away as technologists make it ever more possible to control the lives and even the habits and perhaps the thoughts of those caught up in Solzhenitsyn's spider webs. It will not do, in this respect, to take a roseate view of the probabilities that emanate from the information revolution. That is the position of Dr. Lewis Branscomb, IBM's chief scientist. For some unexplained reason, he thinks that Solzhenitsyn's cobwebs "give us the basis for a democratic society. Without informational linkages of this kind we could not have developed the infrastructure that guards our liberty and security, while we seek to share the world's opportunities and resources."[25] Branscomb believes that the cobweb system can be managed, but he doesn't tell us how. Who will do the managing? In whose interests? And how? Those questions are not asked.

His message, however, is clear: the future can be managed, in some way, by someone with the wit and will and wherewithal to handle the threads in the cobweb of American society. Only a fool or an IBM scientist could view that future with equanimity.

6. The age of *scarcity* is upon us. Wherever one looks, shortages are becoming the norm—in energy, food production, water supplies, topsoil, forests, grasslands and croplands, capital, in everything except that most dispensable being: the human animal. All of this is familiar enough, and has already been discussed. An abundant life dawned and flourished in a relatively small part of the world (mainly, the Western world) for a brief time. That time, although not completely over, is rapidly drawing to a close. The economic pie is shrinking; the politics of scarcity are upon us; ecological crisis spawns the absolute need for crisis government.

The obvious reaction, in the short as well as the long run, should be some means of population control. The earth cannot support the masses that now throng almost its every corner. Population control can come, in all probability, only by a change in values—which is not likely—or by coercion. (The only place now overtly applying coercion is Singapore; and there it seems to be working rather well.) Both in the underdeveloped countries, where the pressure of numbers on resources is so blatant, and also in the industrialized

West, which has through technology made mass man obsolete, a requirement for drastic population control is the indispensable prerequisite necessary
to stave off impending disaster.

A change in values shows little likelihood of occurring; and coercion—even
of the economic, and thus bland, type employed in Singapore—so runs
against the grain that no political leader would dare to suggest it—unless the
leader or leaders are in a nation that was under a tight, even rigid, system of
authoritarian government. (That happens to be so in Singapore.) The utter
hopelessness of adequate population control leads sober and thoughtful and
humane observers, such as Professor Warren Johnson, to extreme conclusions:

> As heartless as it may sound, the merciful thing may be for some catastrophe to
> come quickly in the half dozen or so countries that are hopelessly overpopulated, a
> catastrophe that will drop population below where it is at present, ease the pressure on
> the surviving population, and provide undeniable evidence to encourage changed
> attitudes toward large families. Even that might not be adequate, and it could take
> several generations of unremitting population pressure before the necessity of popula-
> tion control is integrated into the culture.[26]

Is there no way out other than catastrophe? Are humans on the way to breeding themselves into extinction? Johnson's "remedy" is a counsel of ultimate
despair.

Scarcity is relative to population and to the expectations of people. Both
must diminish, and soon, if even greater shortages are to be avoided. Professor Johnson believes that we can "muddle toward frugality"—toward a different life-style in the age of scarcity. As with Mr. Micawber, he thinks that "a
new social logic will assert itself," and that sharing and cooperation will characterize the new age of frugality. One can hope that he is accurate. But he
leaves unanalyzed the crucial problem of how to get there from here, how,
that is, to navigate the white water and shoals that are dead ahead. Johnson
admits that violence may characterize the immediate future, but asserts that it
can be avoided.

7. *Social turmoil:* On any list of probabilities, this must certainly rank at or
near the top. We already see the evidence all around us, both in the United
States and elsewhere. The needy are squaring off against the greedy in what
may well be one final apocalyptic struggle.

There not being enough to go around (in the sense of fulfilling in a reasonably satisfactory manner the demands or expectations of people), only three
alternative courses are foreseeable: (a) The human race immediately accepts
an ethic of frugality by taking on a new set of values; (b) a time of continuing
tensions, even violence, as the deprived—whether economically or psychi-
cally or both—of the earth battle for more; (c) an increasingly repressive

governmental system, accompanied by an overt attempt to keep the masses quiescent. Each merits brief discussion, although the first can be summarily dismissed as being so improbable that it is not worth contemplating.

The values of the Western world, which we have attributed to the Judeo-Christian religion but which have an even earlier history, have now been transmitted the world over. Blacks in Soweto, Hispanics in the slums of Rio or Caracas, even the Untouchables in overpopulated India, dare to hope, and in hoping to strive, for something better. But those with the wealth of the world in their hands have every reason to hang on to what they have and not to diminish their present share of the world's resources. Whether within the United States or any other nation, or whether on a worldwide basis, the "lifeboat ethic" is taking over. Not altruism; not sharing; not frugality. But triage.

What is triage? It is a term taken from the French army's experience in World War I. The wounded were divided into three categories—those who would get well either without aid or with only minimal medical attention, those who with medical attention could be made whole (and to fight again), and the hopelessly wounded. The latter might be kept alive, but if so, at a great cost; and they would serve no socially useful purpose. Hence, they would be left to die.

The world today is on the verge of an international system of triage. According to Robert McNamara, president of the World Bank, at least 600 million people are in absolute poverty, for whom there is no hope of extrication.[27] That figure is probably low; it is more likely on the order of 1 billion—about 25 percent of the human race. These teeming millions will be left in poverty, without any sustained effort to lift them out of it. The consequence will be social turmoil on a scale not before known in history.

On a lesser scale, the same may be perceived within the United States. An underclass made up of most blacks, many Hispanics, and many whites is being developed. A caste system is being built, based not on legal commands but on the fate that puts children (and eventually adults) in a status out of which they will find it increasingly difficult, even impossible, to climb. Much of that can be traced to technological unemployment. The result? Not that of the Luddites, they who smashed the machines that took their livelihoods in the early days of the Industrial Revolution. But turmoil. The unwashed and the unfed, the poorly clothed and housed members of American society are not long going to tolerate a system that at once holds out the promise of betterment and simultaneously dashes it. An educated lumpenproletariat is being created. Young people, men and women, with degrees from higher educational institutions cannot find the jobs that they think should be available.

Discontent will grow; and unless it is siphoned off in some way will eventually explode. That a massive attempt to siphon it off is already under way, and will expand in the future, will be discussed below, in connection with an exposition of technology as a means of human domination.

8. Social and economic planning, comprehensive and permanent, is as sure to come as anything that may be forecast. The question is not whether planning will come, but in whose interests and by whom? Suffice it now to say that technology is creating not only the need for planning but also makes it theoretically possible.

Given that set of intellectual and social circumstances, there should be no disagreement over the prognosis for the human future: It is grim, even more so than the present. We are proceeding pellmell into that future, at a pace rapid beyond measure and surely beyond individual human comprehension. But as we do, our heritage from the past—the intellectual garbage (and wisdom) that has accumulated for millennia—move with us. We cannot escape history; we are as much the prisoners of the past as we are of a technology that is out of control. Scenarios can and will be constructed of the future, with the principal focus on the desirable. Too few pay attention to the feasible—to the question of how to get there from here. The American Dream has ended, and we should face up to that harsh fact. It has had, and will continue to have, major constitutional consequences.

11

The Future, Yes:
The Tyranny of Technology

Is there a way out? Some think not. Others believe in the saving grace of technology. Most do not consciously think about the question of survival. But think they all will, and soon, as the imperatives of the ecology of scarcity become more evident. This chapter inquires into the impact of technology on the constitutional order. Its main theme is simply stated: *Society is becoming like a giant computer, programmed as such by technicians who are the servants of real political power.* And the human being is a small computer: The question is not whether a computer can be made to act like a man, but whether man can be conditioned to act like a computer. Technology is a tool of tyrants, "benevolent" perhaps, but tyrants nonetheless. Man, in sum, is a machine, manipulable as such; and those who will not or cannot be manipulated will be dealt with in other ways. From Plato in ancient Greece to Thomas Hobbes in the seventeenth century to B. F. Skinner today, a straight line runs—man is to be manipulated for his own good. That grim assertion is not so much a forecast as a statement of fact. Like it or not—both society and man himself are becoming "robotized."

As the great German sociologist, Max Weber, foresaw, society is becoming more rationalized and more bureaucratized. This is spiritual death: "Specialists without spirit, sensualists without heart; this nullity [society] imagines that it has attained a level of civilization never before attained."[1] Man, by making a Faustian bargain with technology sold his soul in an attempt to subdue and transcend nature. Economic growth is still the preeminent value. But it is a pact with the Devil. Ecological self-restraint must come. It *will* come, either by

war, pestilence, and famine, as the forces of nature crowd the antheap civilization, or by ruthless, authoritarian governments—or by a final human effort
to transcend age-old limitations.

No one should be sanguine about what will happen. Governmental officers,
seeing growing social unrest and turmoil and faced with increasing shortages,
will impose repressive rule. In sum, nature plus technology can mean permanent repression. The ecology of scarcity coupled with the technology of
control can mean that those who move the levers of power will try rigid
control measures. Is there a way out? "The collectivizing trend of society
under machine production, whether the society calls itself democratic, Fascist,
or socialist, is irrevocable,"[2] Waldo Frank maintained a generation ago. Will
collectivism mean authoritarianism? The question asks much.

That technology is both boon and bane admits of no doubt. However
defined, technology has brought untold benefits to human beings. Whether
the price is too high has been often questioned, mainly by intellectuals.
"Men," said Thoreau, "have become the tools of their tools."[3] Says Professor
John McDermott: "If religion was formerly the opiate of the masses, then
surely technology is the opiate of the educated public today, or at least of its
favorite authors. No other single subject is so universally invested with high
hopes for the improvement of mankind generally and of Americans in particular."[4] My purpose is not to evaluate the merits of technology versus no, or
little, technology. The arguments have been going on since the early days of
the Industrial Revolution, when Luddites smashed the machines that took
away their jobs. Rather, I ask whether new technologies can extricate
humankind from the dismal swamp in which it finds itself.

The basic inquiry is into the nature of the technological "fix": the delibera-
tive contrivance of mechanical means to meet the challenges of the climacteric of mankind. Some, mainly scientists, believe that the future can be
invented, that man has it within his power to produce whatever type of future
he desires. Possibly that is so, but it leaves unanswered the costs involved in
the process. No doubt it is true, as Alfred North Whitehead once remarked,
that the most important invention of all was the invention of the art of invention—but that leaves unanswered two vital questions: (a) Is technological
development a "neutral" force? Can, that is, scientific and technological
change proceed unregulated and uncontrolled, in a counterpart of the economic theory of laissez faire? Does technological innovation work, as by an
"invisible hand," toward the general welfare? (b) What is the role of "politics"
in the process? Can politics be eliminated, replaced with government by
technicians?

The theory of the technological fix is based on one simple assumption: that
technology can produce shortcuts to ameliorate the human condition, and
this can be done much more easily than by employment of political or

economic solutions. For example, Sir Peter Medawar of Great Britain said in 1969: "The deterioration of the environment produced by technology is a technological problem for which technology has found, is finding, and will continue to find solutions."[5] But the very use of the term, "technological fix," poses interesting questions. (Can it be derived from the drug culture?) Shortcuts do, of course, achieve short-range goals. But nature fights back. Examples are legion: a type of "superbug" is produced that can survive DDT and other insecticides; rats have adapted to, and now flourish on, poison that once killed rodents. Add to that the unanticipated second-order consequences of new technologies—for example, the pollution the automobile brings to cities, the tendency for everything to become more like everything else, the problem of disposal of chemical and nuclear wastes that are poisoning vast areas, the side effects of new drugs (can anyone forget the tragedy of thalidomide babies?), the malign use of drugs produced for benign purposes (morphine, heroin, and Darvon were created as painkillers, but each has become addictive).

Nonetheless, many fervently believe in the technological fix—not only some scientists but many among the unthinking masses. The billions of dollars poured into cancer research provide a ready example; that effort is based on the assumption that cancer is a disease and curable as such. Technological optimism, pure and simple. The hope—indeed, the expectation—is that the research will produce a cure. Whether it will eventually triumph is beside the present point; of equal or more importance is the latent question of whether the cure, when (if) it comes, will carry with it other unanticipated social consequences. Technology does not exist in a vacuum, although many believe it is essentially neutral in character. Consider, for example, an outspoken proponent of the technological fix, Dr. Alvin Weinberg, who for many years was director of the Oak Ridge National Laboratory of the Atomic Energy Commission. He belabors environmentalists and others for proposing "social fixes" for ecological problems, maintaining that technology can produce "more humane" solutions because they "do not disrupt the economy and . . . cause the human suffering that such disruption would entail."[6] But he concedes that a technological solution may have accompanying enormous social consequences. Speaking specifically of nuclear waste—Weinberg is an avid proponent of nuclear power—he admits that those wastes will have to be kept under perpetual surveillance. Their "half life" is on the order of 500,000 years! This will create immense challenges for the political order. Says Weinberg:

We nuclear people have made a Faustian bargain with society. On the one hand, we offer . . . an inexhaustible source of energy [in breeder reaction]. . . . But the price we demand of society for this magical energy is both a vigilance and a longevity of our social institutions that we are quite unaccustomed to.[7]

When one remembers that human history is not known for more than about 3000 years—and much that is known is sketchy at best—and that no government in that history has lasted more than a few hundred years, the political demands of such technological fixes seem insurmountable. That alone, is bad enough, but consider a further statement by Weinberg:

In a sense, what started out as a technological fix for the energy-environment impasse —clean, inexhaustible, and fairly cheap nuclear power—involves social fixes as well: the creation of a permanent cadre or priesthood of responsible technologists who will guard the reactors and the wastes so as to insure their continued safety over millennia.[8]

Note the term: "priesthood." The technicians are to take over. The political end is clear: technocratic government, run on principles of efficiency. Aldous Huxley had a label for that: *Brave New World*. And so did George Orwell: *1984.*

Whether technological fixes will do the necessary job is by no means certain. It is "the arrogance of humanism"[9] to believe that all problems are solvable by exercises of human reason. Or, as Daniel Boorstin, historian and Librarian of Congress, has said: "The Machine is the great witness to man's power. The land was there at the Creation. But every machine is the work of man. The power of the Machine is man's power to remake his world, to master it to his own ends."[10] But, as Boorstin correctly notes, "Every inventor is a Pandora." We know not the consequences of the nuclear power that Weinberg (and the United States government) have so avidly been advocating and producing; nor do we know many other consequences of technology. We do not, in sum, really know whether a technological fix will be boon or bane. The Faustian bargain with technology may turn out to be a true pact with the Devil: "The danger in the Faustian bargain lies . . . in the mounting complexity of technology along with the staggering problems of managing the response to ecological scarcity, for these will require us to depend on a special class of experts in charge of our survival and well-being—a 'priesthood of responsible technologists'."[11]

Responsibility to whom? The question is not even asked, let alone answered. Technology is viewed by the Weinbergs of the nation as a neutral force. It is considered to be a self-correcting system, akin to the market in the economic theories of Adam Smith. That sort of guileless optimism most assuredly is not valid. It creates immense problems of its own (laissez innover is no better as a technological theory than is laissez faire as an economic theory). Politics cannot be eliminated. The "priesthood"—it already exists—consists of technocrats who, in final analysis, are the servants rather than the true exponents of power. They are apparatchiks. As Zbigniew Brzezinski put it in 1968,

in the technetronic society the trend would seem to be towards the aggregation of the individual support of millions of uncoordinated citizens, easily within the reach of magnetic and attractive personalities effectively exploiting the latest communication techniques to manipulate emotions and control reason. . . . The largely humanist-oriented, occasionally ideologically-minded intellectual dissenter. . . . is rapidly being displaced either by experts and specialists . . . or by the generalists-integrators, who become in effect house-ideologues for those in power, providing overall intellectual integration for disparate actions.[12]

The onrushing future is not really terra incognita. Society is becoming dehumanized, as Brzezinski says. The central phenomenon of the present day, the one that connects us with the past, is what Lewis Mumford has termed "the megamachine."[13] The megamachine is akin to a huge computer, a social system that ever more functions like a machine; the people who make up that system are parts of the machine. Modern technology is leading toward "organization by total coordination, by 'the constant increase of order, power, predictability, and above all control'."[14] Consider, as an example, Soviet Russia and mainland China. Both are megamachines, in which coordination is achieved and maintained by a combination of force, indoctrination, and the subtle use of technology; both are rationalized bureaucracies.

The United States is fast going down that route. Not communism. Not really fascism whether "friendly" or not. But a technologically dominated society, one in which people will be programmed and predictable. "We become what we hate."[15] Liken America to a giant computer, programmed by experts, and you will see the future. People, as tiny parts of that computer, will themselves be miniature computers, programmed again by experts.

In political terms, this is authoritarianism—even totalitarianism. We cannot escape politics. The technicians who act as a priesthood in the emergent technological State are not neutral; they are the servants of power—as Brzezinski said. Brain power, D. N. Chorafas tells us, is "the key to the future."[16] But those who have it wield it not for themselves nor for the common good, but for those who are in positions of real political power in the nation. Those with intellectual skills—the "experts"—are replacing those with political skills.

The experts are servants of power. Behind them lurk those in whose interests they act, and will continue to act. American educational institutions are service stations for the emergent constitutional order; they are designed to produce, through a system of intellectual reductionism, experts and brilliant but narrow-minded technicians endowed with what Thorstein Veblen called a "trained incapacity" to see beyond the narrow scope of their profession.[17] Lawyers are the obvious example; the law schools turn out men and women with keenly honed "legal" minds, but minds that do not have the ability (or, indeed, the interest) to see beyond a strictly "legal" analysis of human problems. They know more and more about less and less—in other words, they are products—really, victims—of reductionist training. (Lawyers are important, because historically they made up the only body of generalists Americans had.) To paraphrase President John F. Kennedy, the lawyer says this: "Ask not what your country needs; ask rather what your client wants—and strive to get it." As with other technicians, this too is based on a false assumption—that resolution of the myriad disputes lawyers handle for clients will somehow and in some way—as by an invisible hand—inure to fulfillment of the overall common good.

Lawyers are technicians; not as obvious, perhaps, as those who toil in the laboratories or who program computers, but technicians nonetheless. They and their counterparts in science and technology, are distinctly not a separate power group of guilds. They operate the giant societal computer in the interests of those who make up the ruling class of the nation, those increasingly apparent American aristocrats of family and wealth.

They will seek technological "solutions" to human problems—and will succeed in part. But not for long. The capacity of the species to engineer the future "benevolently" is the arrogance of humanism. It cannot—it will not—be done. Even so, it will be tried; and in trying, those in power will of necessity have to act in a repressive manner. In the emergent society, the individual counts for nothing—and he will be treated as such.

Man has conquered nature, is conquering space, and is well on the way toward conquest of the human mind. The prophet is B. F. Skinner: "What is being abolished is autonomous man—the inner man, the homunculus, the possessing demon, the man defended by the literatures of freedom and dignity. His abolition is long overdue. . . . A scientific view of man offers exciting possibilities. We have not yet seen what man can make of man."[18]

One would like to believe that Professor Skinner is joking or speaking in hyperbole—but that is precisely what he is not doing. He believes in the abolition of "autonomous man." He wants man to make something else of man. That cold view of Homo sapiens—the quotations come from *Beyond Freedom and Dignity*,[19] but a fictionalized account may be found in *Walden Two*[20]—is the deadly serious view of a person whose books, like Hitler's *Mein Kampf*, should be studied to perceive the shape of things to come. Not that Skinner will do the actual work; he himself is harmless, and no doubt has a firm belief that his work is furthering the cause of humanity. But others will seize upon his ideas and apply them. Already, this has been done—and in the United States. As William Irwin Thompson has said, "Gobineau was a harmless intellectual crank, but out of his harmless theory of the intellectual superiority of the Aryan race came National Socialism. As Keynes noted: 'The political fanatic who is hearing voices in the air has distilled his frenzy from the work of some academic scribbler of a few years back'."[21]

Until recent times, only three types of mind control were possible: persuasion through propaganda, torture, and "co-optation" by buying the loyalties of men. As we have previously noted, propaganda is pervasive in all nations. But it is expensive and slow and too often not successful. By itself, it is not sufficient to the need of producing compliant human beings required by the modern State. Torture is effective, as Orwell showed in *Nineteen Eighty-Four*, but is essentially a one-on-one procedure. It can "convert" one person, but at too high a price. Co-optation is better, and is often employed. It is, for example, the way in which upwardly mobile young people are drawn into the outer circles of the governing class in America and richly rewarded for contributing their brain power to service for that class. Lawyers are the classic example.

In the past, propaganda and co-optation were adequate. That no longer is true. A growing disparity between classes, the growth of a large underclass, the absence of any economic need for many people—all of these occurring when population is rapidly increasing—create the pressing need (as seen by the technocrats and their leaders) for some greater and more efficient means of control. As Machiavelli knew, a kingdom might be captured by force of arms, but it could be held in the long run only by loyalty. The problem now becoming apparent is how to insure the undeviating loyalty of the citizenry.

Some rudimentary techniques have already been employed in the United States. During the Truman administration, loyalty oaths and security clearances were instituted—a practice still followed by government, federal and state. Secret police tactics, such as infiltration into, and surveillance of, groups thought to present at least potential harm, have become a familiar part of the national constabulary. (Americans pretend that they do not have a national police force, but the FBI has long been one in fact.) Agents provocateurs ferret out other dissidents. In the past, violence was used, as in the suppression of the early forms of labor unions, a practice that came from private industry but which had the force of the State behind it. These methods however, no longer are up to the task. The perceived need now is for mind manipulation, as Aldous Huxley knew:

We have had religious revolutions, we have had political, industrial, economic, and nationalistic revolutions. All of them, as our descendants will discover, were but ripples in an ocean of conservatism—trivial by comparison with the psychological revolution toward which we are so rapidly moving. *That* will really be a revolution. When it is over, the human race will give no further trouble.[22]

Huxley's revolution has already begun, but not in a dark and conspiratorial way. As more and more controls are placed upon human activity, a subtle "trade-off" is taking place. The beginnings of "popular dictatorship with freedom of expression" (Auguste Comte's phrase) are apparent everywhere. Consider the following: a permissive society, changes in lifestyles, widespread use of marijuana and other drugs, growing consumption of alcohol, blatant obscenity and pornography, freedom of expression—all of these, and more, constitute a way of keeping the masses quiescent. People, in brief, are allowed to do anything they wish, so long as their activities do not harm the

State. More, those "innocuous" activities are encouraged, at times not so subtly, by the mass media and national advertising. The price for increasing State controls is that permissiveness. When added to the other techniques—propaganda, co-optation, repression—the process has been successful thus far. Whether it will continue to suffice is the question.

Aldous Huxley brilliantly forecast this development in *Brave New World*. The differences between his ideas of soma pills, the "feelies," test-tube babies, Bumblepuppy, free love, etc., and the situation today, are but two: Huxley projected his 1931 fable far into the future—500 years A. F. (After Ford)—and controls were consciously and overtly imposed or permitted by a world dictator. The problem today's governments ever increasingly face is, as Huxley said in a 1946 version of his book, that "of making people love their servitude."[23] (As of now, not enough do.) That is essentially what Skinner advocates: people loving repression.

Technology provides the best means for producing that attitude. When it is added to the Grand Inquisitor's trilogy of human wants—miracle, mystery, and authority—there is little reason to suppose that it will not be effective, at least for a time. Rulers since at least the Romans have known that bread and circuses are enough to eliminate social discontent. The circuses we have in television, in mass sports, in other similar activities—and the problem remaining is for the rulers to produce the "bread" segment of that social equation. The cry of "give me liberty or give me death" has been replaced in the United States by the cry of "give me junk food and television, but don't bother me with the responsibilities of liberty." Americans do not want the responsibilities of citizenship, a status that puts great demands on individuals, particularly in a nation that is at least nominally democratic.

Revolution, in sum, can be, and is being, staved off by sensual pleasures and by relative affluence. Rulers in the immediate and distant future will, however, have to continue producing that flow of consumer goods that many now think is their brithright—either that or manipulate the minds of people so that they will be induced to want less. In the long run, after what will no doubt be a strife-ridden transition period, stability will come. The price will be great —human freedom itself—but it will be paid, in one way or another, as adjustments are made in time-honored ways of doing things. Huxley said it well in *Brave New World Revisited*:

The older dictators fell because they could never supply their subjects with enough bread, enough circuses, enough miracles and mysteries. Nor did they possess a really effective system of mind-manipulation. In the past free-thinkers and revolutionaries were often the products of the most piously orthodox education. This is not surprising. The methods employed by orthodox educators were and still are extremely inefficient. Under a scientific dictator education will really work—with the result that most men and women will grow up to love their servitude and will never dream of revolution. There seems to be no good reason why a thoroughly scientific dictatorship should ever be overthrown.[24]

The familiar old institutions will remain—legislatures, courts, elections, and the like. Underneath the facade will be a form of technological tyranny—nonviolent and imposed in the name of the people. Tradition will be honored; the same slogans will be repeated on Independence Day: Democracy and freedom, but only as a surface coloration. Meanwhile a ruling oligarchy, with its technocratic elite of policemen and mind-manipulators, will quietly control affairs as they see it.

The basic problem for the ruling class will be to navigate the treacherous waters of the transition period. When that is done, through fair means or foul, then the imposition of "benign" controls advocated by Skinnerites will be possible. And will be imposed. For one of the guiding principles of the Technological Age is that something *should* be done because it is possible to do it. In other words, invention is the mother of necessity. If it is possible to produce an atomic bomb, then it must be used. If it is possible to land a man on the moon or send space craft far into the ether, then these must be done even if there are many unfulfilled needs on earth. As Hasan Ozbekhan has said, "feasibility, which is a strategic concept, becomes elevated into a normative concept, with the result that whatever technological reality indicates we *can* do is taken as implying that we *must* do it.[25]

Add to that the principle of efficiency, which implies the need for predictable man, and the result is easily foreseeable. The individual will become like a machine, a small computer, programmed by stimuli externally imposed. "There is no reason to suppose," writes Marvin L. Minsky, an authority on computers, "machines have any limitations not shared by man."[26] The problem now is not to construct such a computer—indeed, they are already here—but to mold man to make him like a computer.

The meaning of this is clear: A principle of political convergence exists. The American "megamachine" ever increasingly resembles that of Soviet Russia. The pretense of representative government and voluntary participation is kept. Older traditions of "localism" still endure. But the pluralism of decentralized power is tending to be a pluralism that is not local but national in scope. An economy dominated by supercorporations cannot and will not brook the diversity of local autonomy. The industrial system is becoming a huge, sprawling single conglomerate system, closely intermeshed with the federal government.

Two rival nation-states are locked in mortal combat, each striving to dominate the earth: the "free world" of capitalism and the controlled world of communism. There is no common meeting ground for them, although their institutions, economic and political, begin to resemble each other. One or the other will triumph—or perhaps both—and the world, along with them, will be vaporized in nuclear war. They are like two scorpions in a bottle, each trying to sting the other. Each probably *will* sting the other, and in so doing will bring down what we now call civilization. If so, it will tumble into ruins, not unlike Mayan artifacts in Mexico. To see this we must refer, not so much to scientists as to artists and novelists. Nevil Shute's *On the Beach* graphically portrayed the final, apocalyptic struggle. Huxley, writing before the atomic bomb was exploded, without full knowledge of nuclear power, saw continuing struggles between two systems.

Were man the rational being he assumes that he is, and thus capable of deliberate choice, he would find a way out. Reason, however, is applied only to technical problems, those which readily lend themselves to solution. Landing a man on the moon provides the classic illustration. For social and political affairs, ours is the age of "unreason."[27] We do not do the things that should be done, comforting ourselves that the problems are not as great as some say or that something will turn up to alleviate them. Man's rationality extends only to technical questions. Man Thinking—Emerson's term—does not transcend the laboratory. Thus it is that man finds it necessary, even desirable, to try to turn man into a machine—so that the supreme artifact of man is man himself. As Skinner insists, the autonomous person has no role in this scheme of things. Franz Alexander noted in 1960 that the "inevitable social process was relentlessly progressing toward a mass civilization producing a new species— the communal man. It came to its strongest expression in the United States, where its development was not interrupted by dramatic ideological warfares and social revolutions. It is in process of producing the organization man, the other-directed person, the conformist, the man with a social role but without a well defined and subjectively perceived ego-identity. . . . In its deepest meaning all this is a growing trend toward an impersonal, rational, planful organization of life which threatens the particular, the irrational, the instinctual in man."[28] The unique and particular among humans increasingly confront a rational, mechanized social order. In that organization, each individual has a role, one in which "only categories count and not individual differences." Those differences will be eliminated, sooner or later, so that a "rational" social order will be produced.

The trade-off, to summarize, for increased State control over human beings will be more permissiveness in behavior—but only so long as an individual's activities do not conflict with those of the State. Autonomous man is disappearing. Freedom is becoming Hegelian—one is free to do what he ought to do. Professor Skinner asserts that the views that a person is free and has dignity or worth "are particularly troublesome"; his call for a "technology of behavior" is one that, when followed (I do not say "if"), will eliminate the inner-directed, autonomous person. Governments will prevent defection "by providing bread and circuses and by encouraging sports, gambling, the use of alcohol and other drugs, and various kinds of sexual behavior."[29] The total effect will be to keep people within reach of "aversive" sanctions—what Skinner calls "negative reinforcers"[30]: things that organisms, including humans, turn away from. One does not have to look very far to find ample evidence to buttress the assertion that Skinnerism is already here.

That analysis cuts against the grain of traditional American humanistic thought. Writing almost a century ago, Henry Adams perceived the psychological malaise that accompanied the accelerating use of energy from the twelfth to the twentieth century: "Prosperity never before imagined, power never wielded by man, speed never reached by anything but a meteor, had made the world nervous, querulous, unreasonable, afraid."[31] Adams did not foresee that exponential growth in energy would soon lead to imminent shortages, and with those shortages, impending social chaos. He did not think of the climacteric that humankind is now entering. Not that he didn't come close, so close that words of his written in 1910 could be taken as the text for the present volume:

The assumption of unity, which was the mark of human thought in the Middle Ages, has yielded very slowly to the proofs of complexity. The stupor of science before radium is a proof of it. Yet it is quite sure, according to my score of ratios and curves that, at the accelerated rate of progression since 1600, it will not need another century or half century to turn thought upside down. Law in that case would disappear as theory or *a priori* principle and give place to force. Morality would become police. Explosives would reach cosmic violence. Disintegration would overcome integration.[32]

But no one listened. At least, no one heeded. Technological "progress" became an end in itself. No one in positions of political authority wanted to believe that technology was not neutral or that second-order consequences would result from new technologies. Americans gave the world something never before known in human history—the unquestioning faith that man was omnipotent, that he could indeed invent whatever future he wished.

History as we know it, as Roderick Seidenberg has said in his important though neglected *Posthistoric Man*, is only an interlude between two fixed states: the prehistoric period when instincts prevailed and life was about the same through centuries; and the posthistoric period, when life is completely organized and solidified. The conflict between instinct and reason, Seidenberg says, is now almost over. A glacial chill is setting in, as reason triumphs. "The shedding of these inestimable illusions may be merely stages in [man's] diminishing stature before he himself vanishes from the scene—lost in the icy fixity of his final state in a posthistoric age."[33] That's the nub of it: intelligence prevails over instinct and emotion. Rationality—cold rationality—is applied to the social process. Efficiency is the central criterion of organization, which is the most prominent characteristic of modern societies. Throughout the world, the process is the same: organization prevails—oligarchically controlled groups with lives of their own.

Technology is worshipped, openly or subconsciously. It has been for three centuries, since 1687 when Isaac Newton published his *Principia*. The historian Herbert Butterfield has said, "Because of the repercussions that Newton's

Principia had on many aspects of human thought, we must regard the year 1687 as a most important date in the history of civilization."[34] But technology is becoming a force of its own; and as such, is a tyrant. All people are prey to its insidious blandishments and to its terrible capacity to reduce man to a mere cypher. "Technological power does not free man," Paul N. Goldstene tells us, "but transforms his bondage into the tense comfort of the organization man, in interchangeable part, accorded the dignity and self-respect due all cogs equally in the vast complexity of the postindustrial machine."[35] A cog in a great machine called society: That is the ultimate tyranny of technology.

12

The Future, Yes:
The Constitution of Control

The bony finger beckons. The drumming hooves of the Four Horsemen of the Apocalypse grow louder: Pestilence, War, Famine, and Death stalk the earth, edging ever closer as the climacteric of humankind threatens to engulf the billions of people who throng the planet. The Fifth Horseman—Dictatorship—rides with the others. Uneasiness and uncertainty, deep-felt and inchoate, are widespread. There is growing realization that Micawberism is not enough. Hope may spring eternal, but increasingly those hopes are based only on blind faith and numbing despair; they are the last remnants of the Age of Enlightenment. Political officers try to respond; but their responses, because of external factors over which they have less and less control, are feeble and unavailing. They lash out, futilely following long-exploded political and economic theories.

Their reactions, thus far at least, border on the absurd. In the West they are based upon repudiated ideas—of the universe as a Newtonian clock, of the Enlightenment, of rationalism, of the perfectability of man, of humanism—which endure even though their scientific foundation has crumbled. The situation cannot—it will not—last. "Mere anarchy is loosed upon the world."[1] A major constitutional crisis looms—is already upon us—both internally (in both the written and unwritten Constitutions) and externally (in the system of understandings that make up the unwritten constitution of the world). This chapter develops the emergent American Constitution—the Constitution of Control.

Emergency government, in the United States and elsewhere, is becoming the norm.[2] The age of liberal democracy being over, and factors both external to and internal in the nation reaching a boiling point, Americans are drifting toward authoritarian (and perhaps totalitarian) government. No one should be confident that the movement can be halted—or even stayed for a time, though it might be slowed depending upon the rapidity with which those external factors develop. The principle of the acceleration of time in the technological age is still operative. Thus far, the drift is more than glacial, but it has not yet reached a climax. Whether that shattering climax can be prevented is the basic underlying question. If it cannot—and at present there is little evidence to the contrary—then the principal questions that remain are these: How soon will repressive government come? What form will it take? And in whose interests will it rule?

Technology works toward the consolidation of power; politically, it is centripetal, not centrifugal. Or, as Franz Neumann phrased it, "The higher the state of technological development, the greater the concentration of political power."[3] The constitutional history of the United States is testimony to the validity of that generalization. Americans have gone through three constitutions, and are now entering a fourth, in the two centuries since 1776. Each one in turn evidences a trend toward the consolidation of power.

Little thought is given to the first constitution, the Articles of Confederation, which lasted a dozen years—from 1776 to 1787 (fourteen years, perhaps, because the First Congress of the new Constitution did not convene until 1789). The Confederation was exactly that—a confederacy of thirteen states which, as the Second Continental Congress unanimously voted on July 2, 1776, were, "and of right ought to be, free and independent States." Political power, in a word, was decentralized. The national government was weak unto impotence. A legislative government, without a separate executive or a national judiciary, it had to depend on the good will of the states for its very livelihood. "Each State retains its sovereignty, freedom and independence, and every power, jurisdiction, and right, which is not by this confederation expressly delegated to the United States, in Congress assembled." In retrospect, it seems to be a brave document, somewhat similar to the way that Switzerland is governed today. No strong central government; power residing in the thirteen states (just as it does in the Swiss cantons). Perhaps it might be called an early form of what today is called participatory democracy, although government was in fact oligarchic.[4]

Government under the Articles was soon subverted by a group of citizens, the Founding Fathers, who drafted, contrary to their assigned mission, the Constitution of the United States of America. When ratified, the second Constitution was born; a structural revolution soon took place. Localism began to become nationalism; the presidency was created and, with George Washington, the trip to executive hegemony began. The beginnings of a superstate emerged, a political giant that could and eventually did override the wishes of any single state. The 1787 Constitution has been called a "counterrevolutionary" document,[5] and indeed it was. No longer did the states retain their "sovereignty, freedom and independence"; that became utterly clear three generations later when the South was crushed in the Civil War. No attempt to create a new formal government has since been mounted. Lost in the view that the South was fighting, at least in part, for a morally bankrupt system of slavery is the fact that the right of self-determination—"the touchstone of the American Revolution"[6]—was shattered. (Lincoln was more interested in saving the Union than in smashing the unholy institution of human slavery.)

The second Constitution (of 1787) has often been called one of *limitations* (or of *rights*)—and that is what it was, and still is, in part. (The most influential text on constitutional law in the nineteenth century was Thomas Cooley's *Constitutional Limitations*.) But only in part. A sea change from the Confederacy of 1776-1789, it is noteworthy for the manner in which it permitted the powers of the federal government and of the presidency to wax large and strong and dominant. The process began in the Document itself which fudged the problem of sovereignty—and of ultimate power—by ignoring it.

John Locke and Adam Smith were the intellectual prophets of what should more accurately be called the second Constitution of Quasi-Limitations, for government has always been relative to circumstances, summed up in the motto that "that government is best that governs least." "Least" government never prevented aid to business (and other groups). Political principles of ostensibly limited, balanced government had a counterpart in economic principles of laissez-faire—but again, only in part. Alexander Hamilton, truly *the* father of the second Constitution, stated in his 1793 *Report on Manufactures*[7] the guiding principles under which the new government operated: To him, the prosperity of the State was identical with the prosperity of business, and government could be used to dispense aid to the business community. The resulting economic benefits, he maintained, would percolate down to other segments of society. Even earlier, Hamilton had written in 1787: "In matters of industry, human enterprise ought, doubtless, to be left free in the main: not fettered by too much regulation; but practical politicians know that it may be beneficially stimulated by prudent aids and encouragements on the part of the government."[8] That neatly sums up the dominant thread of American economic history, as witness Herbert Hoover's statement in 1931: "The sole function of government is to bring about a condition of affairs favorable to the beneficial development of private enterprise";[9] and as witness all Presidents, including Jimmy Carter, wooing industry.

The Constitution of Quasi-Limitations, in not preventing government aid to business, had a positive side that was seldom litigated; it thus was hidden from those who saw (and still see) only the formal Constitution, even though positive government far outweighed the idea of limited powers. Specific limitations, added in the Bill of Rights in 1791, were seldom enforced against the federal government, and not at all against state governments (not until 1925 did the Supreme Court apply a segment of the Bill of Rights to the states).[10] Of much more importance, clever interpretation of Congressional powers by the Supreme Court led to enormous expansion of what had in 1787 been thought to be limited, delegated powers of the federal government. Chief Justice John Marshall wrote the principle of "implied" powers into the Constitution in 1819,[11] significantly increasing Congressional authority. Simultaneously, the Court successfully asserted a power to review final decisions of state courts in both civil and criminal matters, when the Constitution was at issue.[12] The resulting principle of federal supremacy—of one nation, not a Balkanized group of states—was born a lusty infant. Its importance was summed up many years later by Justice Oliver Wendell Holmes: "I do not think the United States would come to an end if we [the Supreme Court] lost our power to declare an Act of Congress void. I do think the Union would be imperiled if we could not make that declaration as to the laws of the several States. For one in my place sees how often a local policy prevails with those who are not trained to national views and how often action is taken that embodies what the Commerce Clause was meant to end."[13] Limitations under the second Constitution came, as Holmes said, from judicial interpretation of the power of Congress to regulate interstate commerce. In a neat bit of judicial legerdemain, the Court in 1851[14] took to itself the power to say what an appropriate regulation of commerce was—thus simultaneously being able to strike down state regulation considered too destructive of commerce and enabling the Court to second-guess Congress when later in the nineteenth century the national legislature began to regulate.

Limitations came also from the Bill of Rights and the Fourteenth Amendment, principally in the "due process of law" clauses.[15] The Court invented "substantive" due process about 1890, and then read laissez-faire economics into the Constitution[16]—not, however, to prevent aid to business, but to outlaw regulation (in minimum wages and maximum hours) of business. The Justices became a group of Platonic "philosopher-kings," ready and willing to rule on the wisdom of what legislatures, state and national, did. The character of judicial review was changed from a rather innocuous tool to a powerful instrument of governance.

At the same time, political power became consolidated, a development that took a large leap forward with the enactment of the Sixteenth Amendment, permitting a national income tax. That tax meant that the states would soon become economic vassals of Washington—precisely the opposite of the situation under the Articles of Confederation. And business corporations waxed large and strong, both by a favorable legal climate (the corporation became a constitutional person in 1886)[17] and by what Galbraith has called "imperatives of technology,"[18] and took over much of the substance of sovereignty. "Private" governments were created, operating in symbiosis with public government.[19]

The powers of public government, however, were not sufficient to social needs. By the turn of the twentieth century, it became obvious that too many people were imprisoned in a class system out of which there was no apparent exit. Legal and political institutions, even so, have a way of enduring when the social conditions that made them possible have inalterably changed. Historical forms lasted until the Great Depression—a social disaster of the first magnitude. When it came in the 1930s, the third *Constitution of Powers* was born—without fanfare and without amendment of the second Constitution. John Maynard Keynes was the intellectual prophet. Keynesian economics— the affirmative intervention of government into the economy—was "constitutionalized" by the Supreme Court's validation, after a few years of nay-saying, of New Deal economic legislation. The second Constitution has lasted, although not to negative economic policies. These have been politicized— turned over to Congress and the President and the private governments of the nation.

Simultaneously, the Supreme Court sought and found a new role in enforcing for the first time the personal protections of the second Constitution —civil rights and liberties. The development began about 1940, although a few precursors came in the early 1930s. Seventeen decades after the Bill of Rights was added to the Constitution, and more than seven decades after the Civil War amendments, the Court began to rule that they meant what they said. For the first time in American history, ordinary men and women were able to invoke the Constitution.[20] That had important secondary consequences: The Court lost its main historical supporter, the business community; and the Justices changed their role to that of an authoritative faculty of social ethics. It has immersed the Court in continuing controversy.

A golden age of plenty, or seeming plenty, came in the 1945-1970 period. All things seemed possible in the "economy of abundance" and the political principles of affirmative governmental intervention into economic matters. The slogan became, tacitly at least: "That government is best that governs best." A primitive type of economic planning came into existence.[21]

The economic constitutional revolution of the 1930s, and the libertarian revolution of the 1940-1970 period, came at precisely the time that economic growth peaked and the United States became *the* superpower in the world. Since 1970, another sea change in social affairs has occurred—again, with little fanfare. The economy of abundance is rapidly being replaced by the "ecology of scarcity," raising major ethical, political, economic, and social problems.[22] Scarcity is eliminating the social—the material—basis for the comparatively individualistic politics characteristic of American history.

"Ecological scarcity . . . seems to engender overwhelming pressures toward political systems that are frankly authoritarian by current standards."[23] There is no other way to deal with growing material shortages, overpopulation, and the burgeoning need for planning a complex society's affairs. William Ophuls believes that "Leviathan may be mitigated, but not evaded"[24] (although he does not go into detail). In other words, a fourth *Constitution*—that of *Control*—has become a necessity. It is slowly coming into view. Its major prophet is Thomas Hobbes, who wrote *Leviathan* in 1651. Those who would understand America under its fourth Constitution should read Hobbes, who advocated complete domination by the State to prevent internal disorder and stave off external threats.

The Constitution, thus, is a palimpsest—an ancient parchment written in 1787 which has two overlays upon it. Ostensible limitations, which in fact were partial at most, in the original document have, first, powers and, now, control as layers. All three constitutions exist today.

Any important document that endures through time and is still considered to be authoritative takes on such a gloss of interpretation, custom, and usage that its modern version has only a tenuous relationship to the original. Exegesis is not confined to theological documents, such as the Bible. The Christian religion has been able to absorb the insights of Copernicus, Darwin, and Freud without outward alteration of the ancient language—but with considerable change in its application. In law and politics, even Soviet theoreticians have had to apply a concept of "living Marxism" to be able to explain and justify new doctrine.[25] There should be little wonder, then, that the second Constitution of 1787 has undergone immense alterations. Justice Holmes said it well: The Constitution is an experiment as "all life is an experiment. Every year if not every day we have to wager our salvation upon some prophecy based upon imperfect knowledge."[26]

The formal (second) Constitution of 1787 is obsolescent. So much gloss has been added to the original words—by judicial decisions, by amendments, by custom and usage, by certain congressional and presidential actions—that it is only tenuously connected with the fundamental law of the present day. Americans should have long known, although a form of social myopia has prevented its acknowledgment, that a wide difference exists between the formal and the living constitutions. The Constitution of Quasi-Limitations should be seen as a facade, a false front, a legal Potemkin Village. Its language remains, but serves to clutter rather than illuminate thought; its "thou-shalt-nots" have been subtly replaced by a set of "thou-cans" (if the zeitgeist permits). The seeming absolute limitations of the Document of 1787 (plus the Bill of Rights) have become mere hortatory pronouncements. Far from being enforceable commands not to do something, they are mere suggestions of proper behavior, suggestions that are honored only when convenient to the State. They serve the purpose of the appearance of the rule of law, while cloaking the reality of the rule of men.

Nevertheless, those ancient admonitions endure; the second Constitution overlaps with the third—and now with a fourth. Institutions two centuries old, although decayed, do not crumble. The result is a hodge-podge of constitutional norms, some real and some spurious, that outwardly appear to be conflicting. In fact, they are not. The steely consistency of the three constitutions is the relativity of seeming absolutes. Dean Don K. Price put the matter well in his 1965 volume, *The Scientific Estate*:

Science, by helping technology to increase prosperity, has weakened the kind of radicalism that comes from a lack of economic security. But science has helped to produce other kinds of insecurity: the fear of the new kind of war that science has made possible, the fear of rapid social and economic change, and the fear that we no longer have a fixed and stable constitutional system by which to cope with our political problems. And these fears are breeding a new type of radicalism.

The new radicalism is ostensibly conservative. It springs in part from the resentment men feel when their basic view of life is unsettled—as medieval man must have felt when he was asked to think of a universe that did not revolve around the earth, or as some physicists felt a generation or two ago when their colleagues began to talk about relativity and indeterminacy. The new conservative radicalism has a fundamentalist faith in the written Constitution, and the high priests of that faith seem to have desecrated it. The Supreme Court has applied relative policy standards in place of fixed rules of precedent; but worse still it has admitted into its system of thinking not only the moral law as revealed in tradition, but arguments from the sciences, even the behavioral sciences.[27]

In that statement, Price implies that the Supreme Court's use of "relative policy standards" is something new. Quite the contrary: The Court, in developing part of the living Constitution, has never followed "fixed rules of precedent," save when the Justices so wished. Price is correct in his view of the new radicalism; but its perturbation stems not from a new posture of the Court, but from decisions in the past three decades when the Justices sought a new role and found it in widespread protection of civil rights and liberties. That time lasted from 1938 to 1969—1938 being the date of the first school segregation case and 1969 the end of Earl Warren's tenure as Chief Justice. Even during that time, however, the core principle of constitutional law was protection of the State.[28]

Under both the second and third Constitutions, crisis government was possible and was employed. But it was limited in time and in space. The movement of American society now is into an era when crisis is routine, requiring that emergency (or crisis) government also become routine. The extraordinary of the past is becoming the ordinary—not only of the present but surely of the future. That there should be *formal* constitutional changes cannot be doubted; the third Constitution, overlaid with the second, is demonstrably faulty. Its powers are not sufficient to the obvious need. Not only is it a barrier to needed change because of an inability to adapt adequately to external stimuli (to the ecology of scarcity), the government it established is not efficient and it is thoroughly capable of despotism.

Government is changing rapidly, a process that doubtless will continue and perhaps will accelerate. Political responses must be sufficient to the need. The need is manifest. However, ancient institutions of the second and third Constitutions will doubtless remain; their applications will change. When governments decay, they resemble religions: the forms tend to outlast the substance. Ritual continues to be followed even when it is no longer believed. The Constitution of Control is being "democratically" imposed, even though it has an Orwellian future at its center. Of the 137 scientific and political predictions in Orwell's nightmarish *Nineteen Eighty-Four*, all of the former have already occurred or could soon occur, and many of the social and political trends attest to his prescience.[29] "Fascism" may be coming to America; but if so, it will be in the name of freedom. In Bertram Gross' terminology, it will be "friendly fascism"[30] (how friendly it will actually be remains to be seen). Circumstances could—in my judgment, likely will—alter even that dismal forecast. Even "friendliness" can be repressive, at least under traditional standards.

Americans consider themselves to be individualists, and indeed a few are. It is, however, individualism in a collective society—a corporate society. That contradiction in terms means that Americans are able to hold two inconsistent ideas in mind at the same time and believe both of them. They can believe in individualism and also in the public and private collectivism of the modern age. No doubt many Americans feel, and are, freer than most others now alive, and more so than those who lived in the dark and feudal past. But they are faced with powerful forces over which they have no control—technological change and the economic marketplace—and thus, in fact, are far from free. As individuals, they do not have control over their own destinies; the American Dream has indeed ended. Only by engaging in Orwellian "newspeak" can they believe that bureaucratic control is freedom.[31]

The greatest good in the emergent society is neither human dignity nor individualism, however defined. It is simply this: the survival of the collectivity known as the United States of America. Niccolò Machiavelli would probably have approved, the Old Nick of *The Prince* rather than the republican-statesman of *the Discourses*. "Many," he says in *The Prince*, "have dreamed up republics and principalities which have never in truth been known to exist; the gulf between how one should live and how one does live is so wide that a man who neglects what is actually done for what should be done learns the way to self-destruction rather than self-preservation. The fact is that a man who wants to act virtuously in every way necessarily comes to grief among so many who are not virtuous. *Therefore if a prince wants to maintain his rule he must learn how not to be virtuous, and to make use of this or that according to need.*"[32] Substitute the term the State for Machiavelli's prince, and much of American constitutional history unfolds. That history provides the intellectual basis for the Constitution of Control. However repellent the pagan morality of *The Prince* may be in theory, the teachings of that slim volume are those that most men, including all politicians, follow in practice.

Machiavelli frankly admitted that in practice those who govern (formally or tacitly) are always willing to act ruthlessly to achieve their ends. He knew that a ruler should be both loved and feared; but also saw that if it proved to be too difficult to have both, then "it is far better to be feared than loved."[33] But, the Florentine cautioned, a ruler should escape being hated—not because of moral scruples but because it is in his best interests. As long as a ruler "does not rob the great majority of their property or their honor, they remain content. He then has to contend only with the restlessness of a few, and that can be dealt with easily and in a variety of ways."[34] A moment's reflection, following perusal of, say, President Jimmy Carter's budget messages and State of the Union addresses will quickly reveal that, wittingly or unwittingly, he follows Machiavellian principles. Carter is no exception; it has always been so.

Love is one thing; hatred another; and still another is contempt. On contempt, Machiavelli is silent. Contempt for authority is typical of the modern era—whether it be the authority of the State or of any other group that seeks to control, at least in part, the lives of people.[35] Those who govern today have to reckon with that too prevalent attitude. Corrosive and destructive, it presents a greater threat to established values than either hatred or fear. The future, however, may be different. As the nation and the world move into the ecology of scarcity, contempt may be a luxury that people can ill afford. It is easy to be contemptuous of authority when one is not beholden to it. When, however, one owes close allegiance to the State, as people in the future increasingly will, that luxury will likely be one of the first to disappear. If so, we are then left with the Machiavellian trilogy of love, fear, and hatred. Winston Smith, in Orwell's novel, ended by being forced to love Big Brother. His is a "conditioned" love and is not the love about which the Florentine spoke. After going through fear and hatred, Smith was finally broken; the "love" he felt was forced upon him.[36] Man is indeed a machine, manipulable as such.

In any event, the highest good in America today is the survival of the State —the nation itself, the collective entity rather than its individual components. It is, the Supreme Court said in 1951, "the ultimate value."[37] The aim of public policy, however and by whomever stated, is to further that goal. All else is expected to give way. That, at the moment, everything does not give way bespeaks the inability of the political order (the system of pluralism) to achieve the goal. Overmighty "private" groups today challenge the authority of the State. The future will be different. The theory, already present, of the Constitution of Control has as its basic tenet the glorification of the State. The primary value is "security," both national and personal. Private groups are merging with public government into a corporatist State,[38] one in which pluralism as a political system should be seen for what it is—a temporary luxury, a luxury that cannot be afforded and will not be tolerated under the emergent Constitution.[39]

Despite outward appearances to the contrary, there has been a decline of interdictory constitutional law. When the third Constitution of Powers edged aside and overlapped with the second Constitution of Quasi-Limitations, a process began whereby the actions of government are limited less by prohibitory rules of law than by technical considerations and the political system. The question for policy-makers today is not: Do the rules permit the proposed action? Rather, it is this: Is the action physically and politically possible?[40] The limitations stated in 1787, 1791, and 1868 still exist, but are applied only in situations when the State has no overriding interest.[41] Nothing important to the State is proscribed by the Constitution. Neither the fundamental law nor the Supreme Court will stay the drift of public policy in whatever direction political officers wish to go.

The preceding paragraph requires documentation, for it runs against the grain of popular wisdom about the Constitution and the Court. For whatever reason—and no doubt the reasons are multiple—the pretense still is that Americans have a Constitution of Limitations. (Study of the Constitution, in law school and college, does not even recognize that the second Constitution was one of both limitations and powers. Academia prefers to see the surface, rather than to probe the depths.) Reality, however, is to the contrary. Governmental actions, national and state and by all the branches, reveal not only a Constitution of Powers but one of Control.

The Constitution of Powers needs no present development. Suffice it only to say that President Hoover's statement about government's function no longer reflected political reality when his successor entered the White House —and particularly after the Supreme Court "constitutionalized" Keynesian economics in 1937 and thereafter. The Constitution of Quasi-Limitations remained. The Court's new role as guardian of civil rights and civil liberties posed, however, the critical question: When do the liberties of individuals prevail over those of the group—the State or, as it is usually put, of "society."

But what does "society" mean, when the Justices of the Supreme Court say that in cases involving human liberties the rights of "society" are to be balanced against those of the individual? It may surprise those not privy to the mysteries of constitutional law that at no time has the Court ever defined the term. When used, in such cases as *Dennis* v. *United States* (discussed in chapter 6), it applies a "balancing test."[42] The trouble there is that no one really knows what that means—not the Justices, not lawyers, not students of the Court. In their opinions (which are the main and usually only source of information about the Justices), the Justices never state how interests are identified, for either the person or society, or how weights are assigned to them, or why one interest prevails over the other. The failure of judges, lawyers, and political scientists to probe the intricacies of either the term "society," or the "balancing test," means that much of what the Court does is an enigma. When leaving his position in 1969, Chief Justice Earl Warren said: "We, of course, venerate the past, but our focus is on the problems of the day and of the future as far as we can foresee it." He went on to say that in one sense the Court was similar to the President, for it had the awesome responsibility of at times speaking the last word "in great governmental affairs" and of speaking for the public generally. "It is a responsibility that is made more difficult in this Court because we have no constituency. We serve no majority. We serve no minority. We serve only the public interest as we see it, guided only by the Constitution and our own consciences."[43]

Since no one has ever been able to define "the public interest"—either generally or in specific contexts—we may infer from the Chief Justice's statement that the public interest is what the Court says it is; and in determining that, the Justices are guided only by their own consciences. The Constitution, accordingly, is little more than a point of departure, a bucket into which the nine men can pour almost anything they wish.

How, then, should the Court's decisions on individual liberties be analyzed? The popular wisdom is that, as a spokesman of social ethics, the Court has greatly advanced the cause of liberty. In part, that is correct—but only in part. Certainly, much has been done to help further the cause of decency for black Americans, to aid those caught in the toils of criminal-law administration, to eliminate the "rotten boroughs" of state legislatures, to further freedoms of speech and of the press.[44] In these and other matters, gains have indeed been made. But a nagging question persists: Were those gains in any area considered crucial or even important by those who speak for the State? I think not. Another question: Was the increased protection of human liberties a reflection of the "golden age of plenty" (the period of 1945-1970)? The likely answer is "yes."

The rudiments of the Constitution of Control may be seen in a series of decisions during the past forty years that came down on the side of "society." It is obvious, but never asserted, that the Supreme Court considers society and the State (and, for that matter, government) to be synonymous terms for the same phenomenon. That phenomenon is the "super-group-person" we have called the corporate State. The Court has never ruled against the State in any matter of consequence. An example is the question of privacy. Not mentioned in the Constitution, but read into the "liberty" part of the due process clauses (and other parts of the Bill of Rights), privacy receives protection, not as an absolute but only when the vital interests of the State are not involved.[45] So it is with other judicial decisions which *seem* to protect individual liberty: they, too, are examples of the Supreme Court's willingness to place society (the State) as the highest good in the nation. The American Constitution is only ostensibly one of the protection of individual freedoms.

So much for background. No special gift of prescience is required to be able to detect and outline the main contours of the emerging Constitution of Control. They include the following (no doubt other characteristics could be listed, but these will suffice). And it is not as yet a steady, unilinear progression. Human affairs are too complex for that. Nevertheless, there can be little doubt that a new constitutional era is developing.

1. The State — the Corporate State — is the over-arching social reality. It is a "group-person" — *the* group-person — as the German legal philosopher Otto von Gierke used the term. To Gierke, "groups were real persons — real 'unitary' persons, existing over and above the multiple individual persons of which they were composed." He went on to say: "Properly understood, the analogy [to real persons] only suggests that we find in the social body a unity of life, belonging to a whole composed of different parts, such as otherwise we can only perceive in natural organisms. We do not forget that the inner structure of a whole whose parts are men must be of a character for which the natural whole affords no analogy; that here there is a spiritual connection, which is created and developed, actuated and dissolved, by action that proceeds from psychological motives; that here the realm of natural science ends and the realm of the science of the mind begins."[46] His view, in sum, is that of "a real corporeal and spiritual unity in human groups." Gierke wrote, not about the nation as such, but about human groups that make up nations. But his analysis surely is applicable to viewing the modern State that is the United States of America. Whether realized or not, those vested with the authority and responsibility to make constitutional decisions espouse notions of a mystical entity called "society" which has been reified into a group-person for purposes of litigation.

The danger here has been well stated by Gierke's chief translator, Ernest Barker, who observed in 1933: "If we make groups real persons, we shall make the national State a real person. If we make the State a real person, with a real will, we make it indeed a Leviathan — a Leviathan which is not an automaton, like the Leviathan of Hobbes, but a living reality. When its will collides with other wills, it may claim that, being the greatest, it must and shall carry the day; and its supreme will may thus become a supreme force. If and when that happens, not only may the State become the one real person and the one true group, which eliminates and assimilates others; it may also become a mere personal power which eliminates its own true purpose directed to Law or Right."[47] So the United States is becoming. One need not look far to recognize the validity of Barker's fears. Once the Supreme Court had made the business corporation a constitutional person (in 1886),[48] then the development of the State as a "real person" became inevitable.

2. The State, being corporatist (the merger of political and economic power), means not only that Americans are governed by both public and private governments; it also means that a new form of feudalism is emerging.

Feudalism historically meant both a theory of society, one in which rights and duties derived from a person's position or status, and a legal concept—a body of institutions creating and regulating the obligations of obdience and service—mainly military service—between a free man (the vassal) and another free man (the lord), and the obligations of protection and maintenance by the lord to his vassal. Those terms—vassal and lord—should not be construed broadly. The only persons who counted, both socially and legally, were king (or duke)—the lord—and those who held "fiefs" (the heads of decentralized groups)—plus the clergy—at least the leaders of the Church. "Ordinary" people—the masses—were neither lords nor vassals. They were serfs rather than free men. They served but did not rule; without them the system could not exist, but they did not count. The system, such as it was during the heyday of feudalism, in the twelfth, thirteenth, and fourteenth centuries, was one where one's duties (and whatever rights he may have had before and after Magna Carta) derived from his status in society—a status, speaking generally, into which he was born and lived and died without being able to escape.

That changed with the Protestant Reformation and the emergence of a capitalist economic order. But it was not until 1861 that Sir Henry Maine could utter his oft-quoted aphorism that the movement of "progressive societies" was from "status to contract"—from a society in which rights and duties were determined by one's "station" to a society in which those rights and duties were determined by "contract."[49] Maine's assertion had some validity, but not much. For most people, it was as untrue then as it had been in the past and as it is now. Contract, however, was and is the legal instrument for a private enterprise economy. In that sense, the movement from "mercantilism" (pervasive state intervention in economic matters) to capitalism had freedom of contract as its basic legal tenet.

Freedom of contract, whatever it may have meant in the past, has now been largely replaced by new forms of consensual agreements—"contracts of adhesion." Most of the agreements into which people enter are not the product of arms-length bargaining—the theory of free contract—but of one party adhering to the terms and conditions of the other. Ready examples may be found: Insurance contracts are perhaps the best known, but there are many others. A moment's reflection soon leads one to conclude that there is little bargaining as such in most transactions he enters. A person takes a given product or service, or leaves it; but dickering over the terms of the contract is little known. If he does leave it, to go to another, he will increasingly find that, in an economy dominated by giant corporations, the next firm proceeds under a similar set of ground rules.[50] Most industries of any consequence in the United States are dominated by what economists call oligopolies—three or four companies.

The net result in that a new concept of "status" may be perceived in the emergent constitutional order.[51] It is a core principle of the new feudalism—a "feudal" order that consists of decentralized groups more or less separate in theory from the State (but which in fact are closely intertwined with it). More and more the rights and duties, the identifications and loyalties, of natural persons run to those groups as much as the nation-State. The individual—the natural person—has become politically and economically insignificant. (Indeed, that probably was always true, save in the myth.) He achieves whatever significance he has as a member of a group—by having "status."

Status comes in two types—*ascribed* or *achieved*. Ascribed status is one which is based on personal characteristics over which the individual has no control. Ready examples include race or sex or national origin. On the other hand, achieved status is based upon voluntary personal performance. Examples are easily found: military personnel, corporate officers—for that matter, anyone who works for a corporation—and membership in other groups.

The point here is that a person's "freedoms"—his position in the constitutional order and his relationship to government (both public and private)—depend ever increasingly upon his status (whether ascribed or achieved). That may be but another way of stating that Americans live in the "bureaucratic State."[52] The new feudalism is characterized by status-type relationships between individuals, between individuals and groups, and between individuals and the State.

A major difference between the new and the old feudalism lies in the extent to which obligations of the "lord"—in modern terms, the State—run not only to the barons and others of the landed aristocracy but to people generally. Duties of the ordinary person have not changed. He owes fealty to the State, as well as to the new "feudal lords"—those who rule over the groups of the nation. But they in turn often, but not always, owe some type of obligation to him—a pension, for example—to provide for his economic security.[53] (Security, as we will note below, is the all-pervasive characteristic of the Constitution of Control—both personal and national security.)

Corporatism, in sum, means neo-feudalism. The legal analogue of the system of political pluralism is a set of rights and duties that individuals owe to, or derive from, the social groups to which they belong. The system increasingly is one of status rather than of individualism.[54] Historically, feudalism predated the rise of the nation-state as the characteristic form of political order; its period lasted from roughly the eleventh through the fifteenth centuries. Later, in the eighteenth century, the term meant such social realities as the political dominance of a landholding aristocracy and the exploitation of the small and weak by the powerful. It also came to mean a political system where the power of the State was weakened, even paralyzed by the privileges of a few and rendered inefficient by the splintering of political power, or by the opposition of powerful political or economic aristocratic factions.[55] (Power was based on ownership and control of land—of property.)

That's where we are now—with one exception: Power is based, not on property, but on ownership of new forms of wealth—such as stocks, bonds, and other "promises." We have, as A. A. Berle said, a system of "power without property."[56] Political power has been fractionated because powerful social groups exercise a segment of sovereignty. A difference between historical and present-day feudalism is in the fact that today the State encompasses the "factions"—the centers of decentralized power, such as corporations and unions. The feudal units make up part of the State. A new political system has been created. The United States is not yet the Leviathan of Hobbes, who argued for an absolute sovereign. But sovereignty then (circa 1650) meant the rule of one man—a Cromwell or a Charles II. Men, he said, constructed a commonwealth, *Leviathan*, to enforce social rules and to provide for security against sudden death. To prevent civil war and relapse into a state of nature it is necessary, said Hobbes, to have an absolute monarch to keep the peace with a rule of iron: "For covenants without the sword are but words and no strength to secure a man at all."[57]

Pluralize the "monarch," and what may be seen? A shifting number of groups interlocking with public government into the group-person called the State. The "barons" of the new feudal order are the members of the elites which control the groups. Their power, to repeat, derives from a new form of property—that of "promises," of intangibles, rather than land. The "serfs," who of course are not called that, are the rank-and-file members of the groups—employees, for example, of large corporations.[58]

In neo-feudalism, the aristocracy is not hereditary in a formal legal sense; it is one of wealth and family (and thus aristocratic in the social sense), for today's "aristocracy" as well as for the "serfs," their rights and duties, privileges and responsibilities, identifications with and loyalties to, run as much to the group as they do to the nation-state (the United States of America). A new form of citizenship is being created: corporate citizenship.[59] It is not the same as the traditional view of citizenship, which ran to the outwardly political orders. People have a multiplicity of loyalties, at times conflicting loyalties, rather than a single loyalty. The Supreme Court said in 1913 that "citizenship is membership in a political society and implies a duty of allegiance on the part of the member and a duty of protection on the part of society. These are reciprocal obligations, one being the compensation for the other."[60]

I do not suggest that corporate citizenship is full blown. More emergent than actual, it is a tendency or trend rather than a settled matter. Duality in citizenship, however, is "an idea whose time has come"—and provides additional evidence of the emergence of corporatism in the United States. The "reciprocal obligations" about which the Supreme Court spoke are owed to and by corporations (and other groups) as much as public government. They are, in short, owed by the super-group-person we have previously called the corporate State, American style. In this situation, since the fundamental constitutional concept is one of status, of membership in a group or groups, rather than that of "free" contract, the movement of modern industrial societies, including the United States, is away from contract and toward a new form of feudal status. Who says (modern) society says organization. And organization means oligarchy: in a word, feudalism. In the past century, an "organizational revolution"—Kenneth Boulding's label—has occurred: "There has been a worldwide increase in the number, size, and the power of organizations. . . . whose activity is directed toward the economic betterment of their members."[61] "The modern corporation, the juristic person formed for specific purposes by its members, is now, and its presence has created societies with different structural foundations than those which existed in the past."[62] The label for that is feudalism.

3. Elitism. The third characteristic of the Constitution of Control is acknowledged government by elite. Since C. Wright Mills wrote *The Power Elite* in 1956, it has been widely debated but generally conceded that an elite structure governs the nation. The most individuals can do is collectively to elect the elite(s) who govern—and often, as with the private governments of corporations and other social groups, they cannot do even that. Robert Michels, a German sociologist writing in 1911,[63] has placed the apt label on the phenomenon: "the iron law of oligarchy." Said Michels: "It is organization which gives birth to the dominion of the elected over the electors, of the mandataries over the mandators, of the delegates over the delegators. *Who says organization says oligarchy.*"

So it is. No useful purpose is served in modern America to talk about sovereignty of the people or even about representation. Lawmakers do not

represent people; they represent groups. That is so whatever the size or composition of the group: From the nation-state itself, down through subordinate
groups such as giant corporations to the smallest of human organizations, the
operation of Michels' iron law may be seen. Oligarchy is an essential, an
intrinsic part of any bureaucracy (public or private), or any large-scale organization. The result is that people today are faced with a dilemma that cannot
be resolved: there cannot be large organizations—such as nation-states,
corporations, unions, political parties, churches, universities, or whatever—
without effective power in them being wielded by the few who are at the
summits of these institutions. Not that those who make up the oligarchy
necessarily are highly visible; they may not hold office at all. But their power is
there and those who do hold high office reflect their influences. The basic
question to ask is this: *Who in fact governs?*—not whether a major institution
is "democratically" governed. For that simply cannot be. Consider this statement by three prominent sociologists:

The experience of most people as well as the studies of social scientists concerned with
the problem of organization would tend to confirm Michels' generalization. In their
trade unions, professional societies, business associations, and cooperatives—in the
myriad nominally democratic voluntary organizations—men have learned, and learn
again every day, that the clauses in the constitution which set forth the machinery for
translating membership interests and sentiments into organizational purpose and action
bear little relationship to the actual political processes which determine what their organizations do. At the head of most private oganizations stands a small group of men
most of whom have held high office in the organization's government for a long time,
and whose tenure and control is rarely threatened by a serious organized internal
opposition. In such organizations, regardless of whether the membership has a
nominal right to control through regular elections or conventions, the real and often
permanent power rests with the men who hold the highest positions.[64]

As with private entities, so with public government. In both, however, while
the formal oligarchy controls, an informal group of people may wield effective
control over those decisions.

4. *Marasmic representative government.* A nation of the size and complexity of the United States can be "democratic" only in the myth. Even the idea
of representation, as in "representative democracy," is faulty. To mention
only the federal government, that hydra-headed entity that speaks for the
State, it requires only a moment's reflection to realize that Congress only
ostensibly represents the people.

If government in the United States is an exchange of views, opinions, and
pressures between the organs of government and different social groups, then
the primary factor for study is influence—who exercises it, in what degree,
and for what purposes? Or, as Professor Seymour Martin Lipset phrased it,

representation is a system of actions which have "to facilitate interchange between authority and the spontaneous groupings of society"; a system which includes "most major attempts to influence authoritative decisions.[65] The interaction, to emphasize, is between various social groups and government; the individual—the natural person—counts for nothing unless he is a member of some group. Members of Congress react to the pressures brought to bear against them by groups which are "issue-oriented"; that is, the groups pursue narrow goals and care little or nothing for the overall common good.[66] (That system we have previously labeled as a type of "controlled anarchy.") There is, then, no escape from the truth of Professor Marek Sobolewski's statement: "In the political process of the modern State, the relation between electors and their individual representatives . . . is of minor importance."[67] Whether the representative (the Member of Congress) is to follow the wishes of his constituency (which most people apparently believe should be so) or is to have a free mandate to legislate "in the national interest," the elector as such is of only trivial significance. Of equal or perhaps greater importance is the fact that there is no such thing as "the" public—even for a relatively small electoral district. Rather, there is a congeries of publics—of social groups— each one of which may have an interest in part, but not all, of a representative's work.

The notion that the citizens should control the State is based upon untenable assumptions—mainly that, within the State, Congress is effective in controlling the public administration and the bureaucrats who work there. That, as Jacques Ellul once said, "is a plain illusion."[68] The further illusion is that the citizen as such can control Congress. Representative democracy, if that term can usefully be used (which I doubt), means little more than a way of organizing the masses, not as a means of controlling State power.[69] The lesson to be derived from the increasingly lengthy quadrennial presidential election campaigns is that they are a device, culminating in the party conventions, whereby the machinery of the State is employed to organize the citizenry.

If Congress at best only ostensibly represents the citizenry, the other branches do not even have a spurious constitutional theory of representation. The President, although the only officer other than the Vice-President who is elected by the entire country, and even then the election is through the anachronistic Electoral College, is not now, was not in the past, nor will be in the future, representative of the wishes of "the" people. And that is so for reasons in addition to the fact that "the" people as such does not exist. By practice, if not by express constitutional language, the President is the one person who has the national interest (sometimes called the public interest) uppermost in mind. But he, too, is prey to the blandishments of interest groups. We may live in an era of executive dominance in government, but that does not mean that the President can do much more than negotiate treaties with leaders of the important interest groups of the nation. For that matter, he has only theoretical control over the bureaucracy.[70] In any event, if the President represents anyone in the nation (whatever the theory may be) it likely is what has been called the ruling or governing class. His values and theirs coincide; no one gets elected to the presidency in the United States who does not have the support of that amorphous but nonetheless dominant class.[71]

So, too, with the judiciary. Professor J. A. G. Griffith's conclusions, based on a study of the British judiciary, are surely applicable to the United States: ". . . . the judiciary in any modern industrial society, however composed, under whatever economic system, is an essential part of the system of government and . . . its function may be described as underpinning the stability of that system and as protecting that system from attack by resisting attempts to change it."[72] Judges, thus, are simply not representative of the people generally; and it is idle to argue, as many have,[73] that the practice of judicial review by the Supreme Court of other acts of government (federal and state) comports with any theory of democracy. Federal judges serve for life (more precisely, they serve during "good behavior"—a never-defined term) and are removable only by impeachment. When interpreting the Constitution they seek, as Chief Justice Earl Warren said, to serve "the public interest" and in doing so are guided by the Constitution (which is no guide at all) and "our own consciences."[74] Justices of the Supreme Court, certainly, and other federal judges as well, are an independent power force in the nation, restrained in the main by intuitive ideas of what is politically possible and their own sense of self-restraint.

Myths do not die easily. One of the most enduring is the view that the United States is not only a "democracy" but a "representative democracy." Few other than some largely unread and unheeded scholars ever trouble themselves to define what is meant by those words.[75] The suggestion here is that if one takes them to mean that the "people" are in fact represented in government and that, furthermore, ours is a government with popular sovereignty, that simply is not true. As Walter Lippmann said more than a half-century ago, ours is a "phantom public."[76] The most that can be said for the idea of popular sovereignty is that voters *in theory* can turn officials out of office. The facts, however, differ greatly from the theory, for in practice incumbents have a way of perpetuating themselves—not always, to be sure, but often enough.

5. *"Structural" constitutional changes.* The Constitution of Control exhibits at least four important alterations in the formal allocations of political power under the Document of 1787—in the separation of powers of the national government, where we have already seen that there has been a flow of power toward the executive branch in general and the presidency in particular;[77] in

the system of federalism, where the states ever increasingly are becoming mere administrative districts for federal (or national) policies; in the merger of what historically was called foreign policy with domestic policy, and vice versa; and in the progressive erasure of the line between public and private in governmental institutions and the way that public policy is enunciated.

Each merits discussion, however brief. First, federalism—the price that had to be paid to ratify the (second) Constitution of 1787. Established at that time was a system of "dual" federalism, with the states and the federal government being approximately equal in dignity and power. If anything, the original conception, derived from the first constitution, the Articles of Confederation, made the states the dominant member of the duo.[78] But if so, that did not last long; the question of "state sovereignty" was settled when Lee laid down his sword at Appomattox. Since the Civil War, the states have become weaker and weaker vis-à-vis the federal government. Dual federalism has long been moribund. It did not survive the coming of the federal income tax in 1913. A nation with a central income tax cannot be truly federal, in the sense of dual powers between central and local governments. Economic planning, even in its primitive stages that came in with Keynesian economics and the New Deal of President Franklin D. Roosevelt, is, to speak sententiously, the DDT of the original conception of federalism, whether that planning is by public government itself or the private governments of the "first economy"[79] of the giant corporations. Planning, as will be shown below, is fast becoming a necessity —systematic economic planning, that is, not the half-way measures heretofore employed. The net result is that the allegedly sovereign states are more a source of Senators and of presidential candidates than they are repositories of actual governing power. Problems ever increasingly tend to be *national*, even *planetary*, in scope. This is not to say that the states are mere empty shells; but it is to say that they are overwhelmed both by the national government and by the giant corporations.

Not only are socioeconomic programs, whether emanating from public or private governments, national in scope; they have the consequence of changing the states from "sovereign" entities to administrative conveniences. The further meaning is clear (but not likely to get any serious attention at this time) —there is no need whatsoever for fifty-one political districts (the states plus the District of Columbia). That decentralized political order makes no sense when laid against the realities of the economic power of giant corporations and the burgeoning power of the federal government. The problems of economics and the imperatives of modern technology are simply too much for, say, Rhode Island or South Dakota to exercise anything remotely approaching the attributes of sovereignty. They are even too much for the nation itself.

As population increases, as economic growth declines, as the United States becomes ever more deeply intertwined with others, the trend toward centralization will accelerate—as will the parallel trend toward the internationalization of public policy matters. Nothing in the Constitution will stop them; and nothing the Supreme Court will do will stop or even substantially alter them. We are superstitious and venerate the written word of the fundamental law. That, however, is constitutional fetishism. Some, as has been seen, also venerate the past and the saints—the Founding Fathers—in America's hagiology. The First Amendment protects such beliefs and the expression of them. There is nothing unconstitutional about being an intellectual antiquarian. Those views merely do not comport with reality, now or in the future. In thinking about the Constitution, it must be recognized that neither the present nor the future are mere extensions of the past.

"It has seldom been more important," *The Economist* (London) said in April 1978, "to gear national policies to fit international goals, rather than the other way around."[80] Precisely. The problem posed for American constitutionalism is the further adaptation of an essentially domestic fundamental law to the realities of life on a shrinking planet. Science and technology have diminished time and distance. The United States has an interest in happenings anywhere in the world—and, indeed, far out into space. This is something new under the constitutional sun.

Can the demands of planetary interdependence be met with necessary accommodations in the Constitution—alterations, that is, without amendment? Professor Paul Freund, peering into the future in 1956, maintained that "any really thoroughgoing commitment to supranational authority [by the United States] would be brought about by constitutional amendment, necessarily so if the measures of the world union were to be established as the supreme law of the land secured against change brought about by subsequent national legislation."[81] No doubt that is accurate if, but only if, the change is indeed "thoroughgoing"; the likelihood of such a revolutionary event occurring is remote. Rather, barring catastrophe, constitutional changes will come in this area as they usually have come in other areas in the development through time of the Constitution—incrementally. American adherence to supranationalism will be built—*is* being built—bit by bit, rather like the slow growth of a coral reef instead of a mighty volcanic explosion. If so, then the Constitution as now written can accommodate an accretive commitment to larger than national resolutions of public policy problems. In time, those accretions will become a thoroughgoing commitment.

The development has already begun, and surely will continue—absent a catastrophe such as nuclear war. The little known but greatly important International Monetary Fund is one example. (In early 1980 *The Economist* raised for the first time the question of whether IMF's "special drawing rights" [SDRs] should be substituted for the dollar in international exchange.)[82] NATO (the North Atlantic Treaty Organization) is another. International commodity agreements others.[83] The list is not long, but it is significant: There is a steady trend toward less than planetary but more than national confrontation and resolution of common problems. No constitutional problems of any importance are posed thereby. Bit by bit, sovereignty—that ostensibly indissoluble attribute of nation-states—is being chipped away; slowly, the coral reef of multinationalism grows. The Constitution of Control has multinationalism as a prominent feature.

The political development parallels, of course, the actions of businessmen. No American corporation of any consequence is purely domestic in its operations. The multinational corporation has become a familiar, perhaps dominant, participant in the world arena.[84] With the businessman goes the lawyer; many American law firms now have branches in other countries, sometimes many branches. And with the businessman goes the flag. The late Stephen Hymer said in 1972: "We seem to be in the midst of a major revolution in international relationships as modern science establishes the technological basis for a major advance in the conquest of the material world and the beginnings of truly cosmopolitan production. Multinational corporations are in the vanguard of this revolution, because of their great financial and administrative strength and their close contact with the new technology."[85] Hymer should have added distribution to production, for the giant transnational firms now have worldwide distribution systems.

Corporations often can shape the environment in which the problems of American external relations operate, and can also define the "axiomatic" in public policy. An axiomatic decision is one that is almost automatic—actions, for example, by government which are rarely accompanied by debate and which do not require any means-end (or cost-benefit) calculation. It is axiomatic, for instance, to protect American property abroad. Where economics goes, politics follows—and the Constitution is not far behind. The question is not whether the Constitution follows the flag, but whether the decisions by government officers, indubitably valid under the living Constitution, serve to chip away the foundations of American sovereignty. The answer can only be yes—today and even more so in the future.

In net, then, there has been and will continue to be a merger of foreign with domestic policy. No policy of any consequence to the American government does not have international implications. We don't have both "foreign" policy *and* "domestic" policy. We just have policy—and it cuts both ways: into the nation itself and outside (into other nations). Some sort of a superstructure is being created, not by design, but incrementally. To speak aphoristically, the nation-state as the characteristic form of political order is obsolescent. And that, oddly enough, at precisely the moment in history when there are more such entities than ever before. The imperatives of economics and of technology will not brook the nation-state, any more than they will the fifty states of the United States of America. What will emerge cannot be forecast with precision. Surely, however, it will bear little resemblance to the status quo circa 1980.

One other structural constitutional change merits attention: the rise of private governance, which ultimately means that the line between public and private is being erased in the United States. Here, as in many places, pretense and reality differ. The pretense is that America has a private enterprise economy; but in fact the economy is dominated by corporate giants that make that label absurd.

The nation has been transformed from an agricultural and small shop economy to one in which the corporation—by Supreme Court fiat a constitutional person—controls and rules. Even though corporations, since they were first formed, were a means of doing the public's business in a particular way—they always are created for a public purpose, as Justice Louis Brandeis[86] and others have shown—they have by some sort of mental gymnastics been considered to be private. Perhaps the old ideology of the early days of the republic was transformed to the corporate behemoths. Nothing, however, is less accurate than saying the giant firm is a *private* enterprise. It is plain delusion to consider General Motors or Exxon or AT&T, or any other of the several hundred largest firms (industrial, financial, service), a private enterprise. Those firms are as much *public* enterprises as the U. S. Postal Service. Professor Robert Dahl put the point in appropriate language in 1970: "With gross receipts approximately equal to Sweden's Gross National Product; with employees and their families about as large as the total population of New Zealand; with outstanding outlays larger than those of the central government of France or West Germany, wholly dependent for its survival on a vast network of laws, protection, services, inducements, constraints and coercions provided by innumerable governments, federal, state, local, foreign, General Motors is de facto the public's business. . . . In the circumstances, to think of General Motors as *private* instead of *public* is an absurdity."[87] So, too, with other corporate goliaths, which exercise economic sovereignty in cooperation with (public) government exercising political sovereignty. That really means the fusion of the two types of sovereignty into an indigenous form of corporatism.

More than a generation ago Alexander Pekelis forecast that the next generation of constitutional lawyers would have to grapple with the problem of private governments, by which he meant mainly the giant corporations.[88] Others have echoed that theme.[89] Even so, Pekelis was only partially correct. Constitutional scholars have not been quick to perceive the need for probing the connection between public and private governance and the accompanying fact that the line between public and private has largely been erased. They choose to believe with the Supreme Court that the corporation is a person— AT&T with assets of more than $100 billion is as equal before the law as any natural person—and by concentrating on public government ignore many of the significant facts of American constitutionalism.

In hard fact, however, the corporation is more equal than the natural person—and not only in comparative assets. Corporations as constitutional persons have rights (as, for example, that of the First Amendment[90]), but do not have concomitant duties. A man can be forced, against his will, to fight and perhaps to die in war. But corporations, while they might be forced to engage in military production, nonetheless have built-in profits; they never die for their country.[91] I do not suggest that they should; the point is the lesser, but nonetheless significant, one of saying that corporations are part of the governing order and should be recognized as such. They should be brought into the constitutional order and their actions made subject to those that, theoretically at least, apply against public government.[92] They should be held to constitutional duties.

In sum, the Constitution of Control carries forward structural alterations in governmental powers that began under the second and third constitutions. The division of powers in the national government itself has been changed, as has that between the states and the federal government. Foreign and domestic policy are closely interlocked; and the privateness of enterprise should be seen as public.

6. Security as the most important value. Government under the Constitution of Control has, as do all governments, two basic aims—internal order and external security. Internal order has been achieved at times in the past by repressive measures (as we have seen). During the Golden Age (1945-1970), it came by purchase—through programs designed to provide a minimum amount of economic well-being. Welfare programs of the New Deal, and after, may have been enacted for many reasons; but one clear motivation shines through—that they were a means of buying off social discontent.[93] The "Welfare State" is the "Social-Service State"—at least it has been, although the diminution of economic growth, coupled with other crises of the climacteric of humankind, suggests that the goal of providing economic and psychic security to Americans may be on a collision course with the other security goal —national security. Hard choices will have to be made—are being made, as this is written (early 1980)—between satisfaction by the State of at least minimal security demands of people generally and the more abstract, yet ever-present drive for security of the nation-state called the United States of America. The modern State, to employ Harold Lasswell's apt label, is the Garrison State—one "in which the specialists on violence are the most powerful group in society."[94] Those specialists may be in military or police uniforms, but need not be: civilians, as the Vietnam disaster evidenced, can be as bellicose as (or more than) military officers.

This has also been called the "National Security State."[95] It came into formal being in 1947 with the adoption of the National Security Act, under which a National Security Council was created in the office of the presidency to integrate "domestic, foreign and military policies relating to the national security so as to enable the military services and the other departments and agencies of the government to cooperate more effectively in matters involving national security."[96] Since then, a state of "cold war" has existed between the United States and the Soviet Union.

Under the National Security Act, three major structural changes occurred (in addition to the National Security Council). One was the creation of the Central Intelligence Agency, which legitimated secrecy and intelligence (including covert or clandestine actions) as a necessary form of government. A second was the reorganization of the theretofore independent armed forces into the Department of Defense under a Secretary of Defense, with a Joint Chief of Staffs system. (What had been the Secretary of War became the Secretary of the Army; which, with the cognomen of Defense, subtly changed in the public eye the nature of the security apparatus.) Third, were provisions to ensure that the domestic economy would make sufficient matériel for defense and national security purposes.

With that one statute, Congress did more to undermine the Rule of Law[97] than in any other enactment in its history. A "State within a State" was created in the CIA, which by the 1970s was seen to act as "rogue elephant" throughout the world.[98] Attempts to curb the CIA and other intelligence agencies have proved to be abortive, because of a perception that the world is dangerous and an unfettered capability is needed to protect American interests. Perhaps, however, most Americans, or at least most members of the elite structure, want American hegemony in the world and see in the CIA a way of helping to attain and retain it. Whether that belief is accurate is not the point; it is so considered.

The National Security State is dominated, as has been shown, by the executive branch and the President. That branch is more than primus inter pares (first among equals); it is primus. Period. Congress quite willingly goes along, the membership not at all desirous of shouldering the burdens of governance in the modern age. And the courts acquiesce.[99] The net result is that security is the overriding and controlling desideratum for American policy. The personal security of Americans—individual Americans—is protected, but only insofar as those protections also further national security.

Security as the primary value of the modern State means that the individual is ever more bound to the State (public and private governments) through invisible chains, such as pension plans and other techniques to ensure minimal economic welfare.[100] Of more importance, perhaps, is the diminution of human freedoms by excessive, or at least incessant, attention being paid to national security. Professor Harold D. Lasswell said it well thirty years ago: "An insidious outcome of continuing crisis is the tendency to slide into a new conception of normality that takes vastly extended controls for granted, and thinks of freedom in smaller and smaller dimensions."[101] There can be little doubt that Lasswell was correct. Freedom is being redefined in the modern age to mean freedom in a social organization. In Hegelian terms, freedom means doing what one is supposed to do.[102]

7. *Economic planning.* Controls are coming in two directions: first (as has been previously shown), in the ways in which dissidents are curbed or guided into activities not considered to be inimical to the interests of the State. Enough has been learned in recent decades about political trials[103] and well-publicized techniques of the law-enforcement community[104] to realize that repression of dissidence is as American as apple pie. In addition, the permissive society that has arisen in America in recent decades serves a sociological function not dissimilar to Aldous Huxley's soma pills in *Brave New World*. Certain human freedoms have been extended, but only when they do not cut acainst the interests of the State. National security as the primary value includes use of means by police and intelligence officers to quell discontent.[105] In short, marijuana is the equivalent of soma pills.

Another dimension exists: the use of technology to control humans through ostensibly benign measures. All know about the practice of the Soviet Union to incarcerate certain dissidents in mental hospitals. What is not as well known, although publicized, is that the United States is, at times, doing the same—in yet another example of "we become what we hate." Said Peter Schrag in 1978:

In the past generation, there has been a fundamental shift in the way government and other organizations control the lives and behavior of individuals. No single method and no single phrase adequately describe it—it is both too subtle and too pervasive—but it represents a radical change in the way people are treated and in the relationship between the citizen, his employer, the state, and the state's institutions. In general, it is a shift from direct to indirect methods of control, from the punitive to the therapeutic, from the moralistic to the mechanistic, from the hortatory to the manipulative. More specifically, it is reflected in the replacement of overt and sometimes crude techniques —threat, punishment, or incarceration—with relatively "smooth" methods: psychotropic drugs; Skinnerian behavior modification; aversive conditioning; electronic surveillance; and the collection, processing, and use of personal information to institutionalize people outside the walls of institutions.[106]

The ideologist for this development is B. F. Skinner.[107] The goal is "predictable" man—a person who conceives of freedom in Hegelian terms. Americans are moving into a Skinnerian world, one in which they "will no longer know, or care, whether they are being served or controlled, treated or punished, or whether they are volunteers or conscripts. The distinctions will have vanished."[108]

That, as Schrag suggests, is a "subtle" process. Not so subtle, in fact entirely evident, is the second means of control—in the economic area. It requires neither extensive discussion nor documentation to assert, without fear of contradiction, that the system loosely called capitalism is in deep trouble. Robert Heilbroner, one of the more astute economists, noted in 1978 that a shift to economic planning was taking place in the United States; this was, he thought, "the only institutional transformation that can . . . give a new measure of life, albeit a limited one, to the capitalist system."[109]

Surely that is accurate; surely we are now well into an era of "planned capitalism."[110] That term is a contradiction: Capitalism, by definition, has not been and cannot be planned. Heilbroner is wrong on that score. What is emerging, and much quicker than anyone would have thought, is a system of State socialism governed by the apparatus of the corporate State. That "socialism" is not for the poor, except insofar as it is necessary to buy off discontent. Rather, it tends to be a socialism for the rich or the affluent. Planning, in sum, is coming—and fast—and the only questions remaining are these: Who will control the system? By what criteria? And, for whose benefit?

Some type of economic planning has always existed in the United States.[111] But until recent times it was hit-and-miss, happenstance, and without conscious design. The emerging planning system will not be that. It will be systematic and comprehensive, in accordance with an ideology (stated or unstated). Economic planning involves a close "partnership" between government and business. Until recent years it was probably true, as John Kenneth Galbraith maintains,[112] that the "basic planning unit" of the American political economy is the giant corporation. But the planning of corporate managers, even so, has always been conducted in close cooperation with all branches of government (even including the judiciary);[113] the difference between today and yesteryear is that planning is now much more open, and it has taken on new characteristics. The present "system" may be summarized in these terms: it is not a system as such but a series of ad hoc measures taken to deal with specific problems as they arise. Planning, as Professor Neil W. Chamberlain has defined the term, is "the systematic management of assets."[114] Management there is—but systematic? No. That it cannot so remain is as safe a prediction as one can make. Government under the Constitution of Control will ever increasingly seek to impose "system" on "management of assets."

A holistic view will be—is being—taken of the entire economy, including its international aspects. In the past, except in times of all-out emergency such as World War II, economic controls were noncoercive. That, however, will

change as emergency ever more becomes the norm. Inability to stifle inflationary pressures, accompanied by high and rising unemployment rates,
ultimately means that something similar to State socialism will come into
effect. Not that it will be called by that name; socialism in so many words is
banned. That socialistic programs can and will come seems sure, probably
because they cannot be avoided and even more probably because a number
of them already exist. Those who benefit under State socialism, however, are
not so much the "have-nots" of the nation as those who already are affluent.

Planning, American-style, has thus far not been "redistributive"; the goal is
to create a larger economic pie through economic growth so that more people
can benefit. The emphasis is on growth, not a different deal of the same
cards. The rich stay rich, both relatively and absolutely, but there are more
people with higher levels of living. With, however, the probable cessation, or
at least the sharp decline, in growth rates, accompanied by a rising population
who believe in more and more "entitlements,"[115] the economic pie will not get
larger and those who share in it will increasingly battle over shares.

In net, the idea of socialism has been co-opted by the already rich—by
those in positions of wealth and power. They use it—government programs
of intervention in the economy—to their benefit. Controls that have been
imposed, and that seem sure to be increasingly imposed, are by and large for
their benefit. "Them as has, gits," in the old frontier slogan; or in the words of
the Bible: "For whosoever hath, to him shall be given and he shall have more
abundance; but whosoever hath not, from him shall be taken away even that
he hath."[116] (The answers to the questions of who controls and for whose
benefit are easy. But will the situation remain?)

8. Secrecy. In the United States and elsewhere there is a tendency to
engage in what Professor Christian Bay has called "the democratic make-
believe";[117] by that he meant the notion that every citizen has a chance to
influence public policy and that, consequently, elections determine the
majority's will and mandate. This renders enacted laws legitimate and entitled
to obedience. The further assumption is that the citizenry can hold the feet of
government officers to the fire of public opinion for what they do and can
expel them for their derelictions.[118] Secrecy, however, prevents that type of
accountability from operating. "Where secrecy reigns, government officials
are in a position to rule at virtually their own discretion."[119]

Secrecy is fundamental to the operations of government under the Constitution of Control. The discussion that follows aims mainly at the use of
"executive privilege"—a constitutional "doctrine" of confidentiality by which
Presidents and their subordinates have been able to keep matters internal to
the executive branch secret even from Congress. First, however, it should be
noted that any comprehensive discussion of secrecy in government should

include the system whereby documents are classified and kept from public scrutiny; that is beyond the scope of this book. The point can be made by showing the present status of executive privilege.[120] Other matters of importance are the so-called "state secrets" privilege in lawsuits and the government's success in censoring *The Progressive* magazine's article showing that there is no secret in how to construct a hydrogen bomb. These merit brief comment.

Any study of American constitutional law should always distinguish between the *formal* and the *living* fundamental laws. To repeat Woodrow Wilson's observation: "The Constitution in operation is manifestly a very different thing from the Constitution of the books."[121] So it is—both generally and specifically. The "doctrine" of executive privilege is a classic example. Not mentioned in the Constitution, the convention of 1787, statute, or procedural rules of court, the privilege nonetheless exists as an exemplar of the living Constitution. It is no more a doctrine than is the concept of separation of powers; rather than a definite rule of conduct, to the extent that it exists it is a political accommodation.

That may well explain the paucity of cases decided by federal courts concerning the privilege. They began with *Aaron Burr's Case*[122] (the precedential value of which is nil) and run through *Reynolds* v. *United States*[123] to the two cases involving the improbable Richard Nixon—*Nixon-I* being the 1974 decision commanding surrender of the tapes by which he "bugged" his White House office[124] and *Nixon-II* being the 1977 decision by which the disgraced ex-chief executive could not keep "his" presidential papers secret.[125] Few others exist, and none in the Supreme Court, although another Nixon case— by the Senate's Watergate Committee—was decided in favor of the President in 1974.

That gaggle of judicial decisions make up the formal law of executive privilege. They add up to so little that it may fairly be said that, as with international law, more gibberish has been written about the privilege based on fewer formal statements of doctrine than almost any other area of constitutional law. Save in high level abstraction—at a level that is next to meaningless —there is no law of executive privilege in the sense of positive law. As such, it illustrates once again that Americans have a government of men, not of laws.

It is only when one scrutinizes the living law—the actual practices of government officers in all branches—that one can construct the beginnings of a theory of that part of the executive's secrecy syndrome that travels under the banner of executive privilege. (In law, the word "privilege" is one of multiple meanings; as used here, it fits into a category of situations which are called evidentiary privileges—attorney-client, doctor-patient, etc.—and to the exent that it reaches the plan of constitutional law it is similar to the privilege against self-incrimination.) The practice of Presidents (and other executives) keeping some matters from both Congress and the public runs back to George Washington. He first tested the waters in 1792 when Congress asked for data concerning the Army's defeat by Indians; Washington capitulated at that time, but reluctantly. A few years later he refused to give the House information about the Jay Treaty (although he did inform the Senate). His 1796 success was the first (known) use of what is now (but not then) called executive privilege.[126]

Data do not exist on how many times, in what types of situations, and with what results the "doctrine" has been invoked by Washington's successors. Enough, however, is known that it is an integral segment of that bundle of rights and powers that constitute the corpus of actual presidential authority.[127] And that is so even though it is not known, save in impressionistic form, how the privilege compares with other techniques by which executive officers refuse, neglect, or delay to give information desired by Congress or the courts. In this, be it said, they seem to have pliant allies in most judges and most members of Congress, who are usually quite ready to kowtow when the executive cries privilege.

Those data, when available, would go far to make up a body of living law that would reify Max Weber's astute observation: "Every bureaucracy seeks to increase the superiority of the professionally informed by keeping their knowledge and intentions secret."[128] Secrecy, and thus the aggrandizement of actual power, is accomplished by the executive through a number of techniques, only one of which is executive privilege. Although it has received the greatest—almost sole—attention from commentators, the privilege is one of the least used means of evasion of Congressional (or judicial) requests for data. In the "information society," information (and expertise) is power. Despite the Freedom of Information Act and various demands for openness in government, the organizations of a corporate society attain and retain power by hoarding information. Those organizations are both public and private (or as with weapons manufacturers, a combination of both) and they are legislative and judicial as well as executive.

What follows are a few comments on the theory and practice of executive privilege. This is a mere adumbration, not a full-blown analysis. Raoul Berger has contended, with characteristic hyperbole, that the privilege is "a constitutional myth"[129]—a piece of intelligence that would have amused, perhaps bemused, almost every President and every scholar who has studied the question. Berger's assertion was made just before the unanimous decision of the Supreme Court in Nixon-I; with characteristic chutzpah, Berger maintains that the decision confirms his position.[130] Executive privilege is emphatically not a myth. It is an indubitable part of the living American Constitution.

What may be said about the privilege that has not been said ad nauseam before? I am not so temerarious as to suggest that the following propositions, which taken together may serve to show the present status of the "doctrine," have any flashing new insights. The purpose here is to set out a way of thinking about executive privilege in the context of the secrecy syndrome of government. The propositions are listed in no particular order.

a. Increased employment of the privilege coincides in time with aggrandizement of power in the executive branch—a constitutional development that shows no signs of abating. As the United States has become deeply immersed in world affairs and as the President and the bureaucracy have been delegated large chunks of actual governing power—or have assumed it without delegation—a penchant for secrecy, always present, has flowered. The term "executive privilege" is a latter-day neologism, dating only from the 1950s. It put a convenient label on a long-established practice of doing the public's business in private.

Every political action tends to have a reaction, not necessarily in accordance with Newtonian principles; and it was not long after emergence of the "privilege" in American law that a counter-movement began to open the corridors of government to greater scrutiny. The success of the counterattack has been, and likely will continue to be, minimal. Despite the willingness of some judges to comply with the Freedom of Information Act, and thus to force the bureaucracy to crack its doors of secrecy, and despite the forays of some "investigative" reporters into the bowels of the bureaucracy there to uncover a few derelictions, it may be said with some confidence that the very complexity of government, the staggering amount of information, and the ingenuity of bureaucrats either to hide or destroy evidence will protect government from any thoroughgoing or comprehensive revelation of the innermost secrets of the organizations of our corporate society. That is particularly true for the "private" bureaucracies (corporations, unions, foundations, etc.) and for the courts (despite *The Brethren*)[131] and Congress; but it is also true for that congeries of agencies, bureaus, departments, commissions, and offices that make up the executive branch.

b. The doctrine of executive privilege is not a doctrine at all, in the sense of positive law. However labeled, it is not, despite Chief Justice Burger's opinion in *Nixon-I*, a logical derivation from the constitutional text. An instrument of politics, it is invoked only as a last resort—after all other tactics of evasion have been exhausted. Only by an intellectually indefensible fiction can it be said to be rooted in the Constitution, as Burger maintained. (Whether that was Burger's language may be doubted; if Woodward and Armstrong are correct,[132] the opinion was a collegial effort.)

The Court made up the law in *Nixon-I*, just as they have in divers other decisions rendered since 1789. That makes nonsense out of Chief Justice

Marshall's oft-quoted assertion in 1824 that judicial power "is never exercised for the purpose of giving effect to the will of the judge; always for the purpose of giving effect to the will of the legislature; or, in other words, to the will of the law."[133] The "law" did not exist until that July day in 1974 when the decision was announced, which lends credence to Professor Ray Forrester's call for "truth in judging"—by which he meant that it should be openly acknowledged that judges are legislators (and Constitution-amenders). Forrester's plea is not likely to be followed, simply because there is a wellnigh infinite capacity of the human mind for self-delusion; and there is a cadre of specialists (lawyers and others) with a vested interest in the orthodoxy (as stated by Marshall). Those specialists are the greatest barrier to change in methods and institutions honored only by time; the man in the street is much more willing to accept change.

Americans, however, seem to want to believe that theirs is a government of laws, not of men. They believe in the myth that a set of known external standards called law may be drawn upon when any government officer is alleged to have strayed beyond the pale of constitutional propriety. Not that executive privilege differs from other constitutional decisions. Quite the contrary: Any Supreme Court decision on the merits is law-creative. In constitutional decisions law is made, not found; and insofar as the Court makes law, we have a government of lawyers, not of men.

The point is relevant to prediction of future results in executive privilege cases. When (and if) made, they will be based on political accommodation rather than on interdictory principles of law. The Supreme Court is a political organ, pure and simple, speaking in the language of law but uttering juristic theories of politics. Whether a President or executive officer will succeed when invoking executive privilege will turn on considerations of high policy at the time a controversy arises. (Whether Congress can enact standards of greater specificity in the "doctrine" is discussed below.)

c. Richard Nixon found it politically necessary to surrender recordings made in the Oval Office. He did so only reluctantly, not being able to face a unanimous Court backed by a House of Representatives on the verge of voting out articles of impeachment. To some, *Nixon-I* was a victory for the rule of law; but if so, it was only minor as compared with the major gain the presidency won. Richard Nixon lost but the office prevailed. A presumptive privilege for presidential confidentiality was found lurking somewhere in the murky depths of the Constitution's Article II by the American "legiscourt."[134] The Justices, as usual, did not inform us how they reached that conclusion. It should thus be called an "immaculate conception" of a legal concept—*presidential* privilege, however, not that of the entire executive branch (as Attorney General Richard Kleindienst in a flight of fancy once asserted).[135]

If one may infer a general principle from one particular—which is logically impossible but nonetheless often done by lawyers—then *Nixon-I* established the rule that there is a quantum of data that Presidents need not disclose, however undefined and immeasurable that amount may be. Furthermore, the Court managed to do other things that merit separate attention: (a) It asserted, drawing on *Marbury's Case*,[136] that it is "emphatically the province and function of the judicial department to say what the law is," and thereby nailed another wall to the edifice of judicial supremacy in constitutional interpretation; and (b) the writ of the Supreme Court, for the first time in American history, ran against the President as President.

Worthy of note also is the fact that the Court in *Nixon-I* capitulated to arguments of "inherent" presidential power. That is by no means novel; the practice runs at least as far back as the *Prize Cases*,[137] which upheld President Lincoln's exercise of the prerogative. Since the beginnings of the republic, arguments over executive power have been waged. Only on rare occasions, as in the *Steel Seizure Case* of 1952, has the Court not agreed with what the President wanted. Lincoln in the *Prize Cases*, and the Court in *In re Neagle*, *In re Debs*, *Midwest Oil*, and *Myers* v. *United States*[138] are all testimony of judicial deference to presidential will. I do not suggest that the Court is an arm of the executive. But I do say that the Justices are cowardly lions at best when it comes to eyeball-to-eyeball confrontations with chief executives. Other than in such exceptions as the *Steel* decision, *Humphrey's Case* (on removal of a Federal Trade Commissioner contrary to statute), and perhaps the *Pentagon Papers Case* (aborting a governmental attempt to censor the press), what the President wants the President gets when the Court enters the fray. Nixon's surrender paradoxically aggrandized the office's power and constitutional stature. Nothing in *Nixon-II* dilutes that conclusion. The Presidential Recordings and Materials Preservation Act was essentially a one-shot statute, aimed only at the disgraced Richard Nixon, and is not likely to have lasting significance.

Nixon v. *Administrator of General Services* (*Nixon-II*) is noteworthy mainly for an abortive attempt of the ex-President to control disposition of "his" documents. Congress stepped in and created a category of one—Richard Nixon—to which the Act applied. That, opined Justice Brennan, made Nixon a "legitimate class of one"—a remarkable conclusion that could, but will not, add a new dimension to equal protection and class-action law.[139] The case would be confined to a legitimate class of oblivion were it not for the fact that the decision seems to signify, but does not flatly say so, that Congress has the upper hand in the disposition of presidential papers. Perhaps the most that should be concluded is that when a President resigns in the face of certain impeachment, "his" papers come under the control of Congress. Since only one chief executive has slunk out of the White House by that route, one should not read much into the decision, particularly since the Court was badly splintered.

Two other comments are apposite. First, executive privilege is akin to the "state secrets" privilege; as such, it may be invoked for the benefit of the nation, not the individual.[140] It is not something behind which a President's peccadilloes or other derelictions can be hidden. Second, it is difficult to see why, despite long-standing practice otherwise, papers accumulated by government officers in the course of their duties are not by definition the property of the United States government. If that is accepted, then it is clearly Congress's prerogative under Article IV to dispose of them.

d. "Human experience teaches," Chief Justice Burger asserted in *Nixon-I*, "that those who expect public dissemination of their remarks may well temper candor with a concern for appearances and for their own interests to the detriment of the decisionmaking process." That is the ultimate argument for secrecy, which, in Professor Carl J. Friedrich's view, serves a useful purpose. Says Friedrich in *The Pathology of Politics:*"Secrecy is eminently functional in many governmental operations."[141] He cites jury deliberations among other examples and then goes on to dispute Woodrow Wilson's flight of hyperbole in *Congressional Government* that "there is not any legitimate privacy about matters of government. Government must, if it is to be pure and correct in its processes, be absolutely public in everything that affects it."[142] (It is worth noting that Wilson as President a generation later saw matters differently.)[143]

Whether Burger was correct about "human experience" may well be doubted. He cited no authority for the statement, apparently believing it to be self-evident. But is it? Who knows? When the contrary has not been tried in government—in any branch—can it be definitively said that the teaching of human experience is so clear? Hardly. Surely there are other reasons, even if Burger were correct, for tempering candor than the possibility, even probability, that disclosure will subsequently occur. For example, Irving Janis in his insightful *Victims of Groupthink*[144] has related psychological factors why advisers to Presidents tend to say what they think the President wants to hear. Americans do not have, although they probably need, an *advocatus diaboli* in their governmental structure.[145] Furthermore, there is more to fear from deliberate "leaks" from the White House, issued in efforts to manipulate public opinion, or from executive officers "stroking" members of the press and co-opting them (thus getting a favorable press), than there is in eventual disclosure.[146] No one other than a Special Prosecutor, operating in a unique situation, has ever been able to crack the secrecy syndrome of the Oval Office. That means, finally, that no one would have the requisite status—in legal jargon, "standing"—to hale the President into Court and force disclosure of what Burger quaintly called "the decisionmaking process." The writ of the Supreme Court did run against a sitting President, but, as will be shown below, that is a principle that should not be carried very far. Senator Barry Goldwater's suit against President Carter on abrogation of the Taiwan treaties failed in 1979 on the grounds that it involved a "political question" and was not justiciable. The Justices have numerous techniques for avoiding ruling on a case, and will likely find one of them should some other litigant try to penetrate the Oval Office.

Moreover, as the Grand Inquisitor and Charles de Gaulle, among others, have maintained, mystery—that is, secrecy—may be necessary for prestige and power.[147] As an organ of government with a legitimate political function to perform, the Supreme Court is not at all likely to dilute presidential power in any substantial way. Only when the political order is in turmoil (as in the 1952 *Steel* case) or perhaps in extremis, as in 1974, will the Justices enter the battle. During times of crisis, such as World War II, they have in the past come perilously close, as Professor Alpheus T. Mason put it, to becoming part of the "executive juggernaut."[148]

e. Whether documents are kept is basically a matter of presidential provenience. No internal memo written and circulated within the White House need be retained. Presidents like to keep records, as the several presidential libraries attest, but that seems to be more a matter of ego than of need. And certainly Nixon was under no compulsion to "bug" his office or to keep the recordings. (His promise to the Senate's Watergate Committee not to destroy them may have obligated him morally but surely did not legally bind him; had he destroyed them he would have suffered a major political loss.) Records, furthermore, are kept for multiple purposes. After all, some continuity in government is desirable. And situations do arise when it is necessary to refer to records of what was done in the past.

The latter point has some dangers. By no means should one believe that any documentation, no matter how massive, can reveal the full account of what occurred at a given time and place. Successors in office know only what their predecessors wanted them to know. Records are simply not kept of some decisions. Nixon and his tapes aside, how likely is it that anything adverse to a President will appear in "his" documents? With paper shredders readily available, anything that reflects on a chief executive or his office will almost certainly find its way to the incinerator. Arthur Schlesinger is on record as saying that his stint in the White House with President Kennedy taught him how impossible it is for historians to reconstruct, often far after the event, what actually took place in the past. For that matter, it should never be forgotten that each generation writes its own history. There are few certainties in descriptions of the past.[149]

f. The President as President is amenable to judicial process. He is not above the law. In *Nixon-I*, the Supreme Court's writ ran against a sitting chief executive for the first time in history. Althugh it was not the first time a federal court had held a President subject to a court order—in January 1974 the Court of Appeals in the District of Columbia did so on a personnel question in *National Treasury Employees Union* v. *Nixon*[150]—the Court put an effective quietus on the notion, bruited since *Mississippi* v. *Johnson* (1867)[151] that something akin to a royal prerogative attaches to the presidency.

For present purposes, the meaning is clear: It is the judiciary, and of it the Supreme Court, that claims to have the last word on assertions of privilege. One may ask how the Court can enforce a ruling against the President; and, indeed, there is no way that coercion can be judicially applied. Under no circumstances would a recalcitrant President be held in contempt and transmitted to durance vile to purge his contumacy. Reliance is placed upon "our constitutional tradition [that] rightly relies," avers Archibald Cox, "upon the moral and political force of law."[152] Cox, however, assumes the answer by calling a Court decree "law." Were a chief executive to defy a court—as, for example, President Lincoln did after *Ex parte Merryman* (1861)[153] was decided—there is little that judges can do. (Chief Justice Taney's order in *Merryman*, on habeas corpus, remained unenforced—vivid testimony to judicial impotence.) Nixon capitulated because the political order—the imminence of impeachment—forced him to do so. He could not withstand the political force of a unanimous Supreme Court decision. Only by equating morality with obedience to law, however promulgated, can *Nixon-I* be said to have a moral force, as Cox maintains. The Supreme Court prevails when the zeitgeist is favorable to its rulings. The moral force of law, to put it bluntly, is whatever the political process tolerates. And it will tolerate a great deal, as everyone knows, and as Watergate showed.

The larger meaning of *Nixon-I* is that it paved the way for a number of lawsuits to be filed against the President as President. Senator Barry Goldwater's 1979 action on President Carter's abrogation of the Taiwan treaties is only one example among a growing number.[154] Congress—more precisely, individual members thereof—has begun to use the courts in efforts to bend the executive to its will. This makes for more work for judges in areas clearly unsuited to general judicial action—exactly what the Court held in the *Goldwater* suit. When the political branches cannot agree, too much is asked of the Supreme Court to umpire those disputes. Questions of separation of powers are questions of political theory and cannot be answered by reference to the constitutional text. It will not do to say, with Archibald Cox, that the moral and political force of law will prevail, when he not only assumes that the decision is law but also fails to acknowledge the obvious: that if it is law, it is newly created for the purpose of that very lawsuit. That means that Chief Justice Marshall's assertion in *Marbury's Case* that it is "emphatically the province and duty of the judicial department to say what the law is," a statement repeated by Burger in *Nixon-I*, is a partial truth only. It is the "province" of the other branches to say what the law is, even to the extent of making decisions that are of constitutional dimension. The Supreme Court, furthermore, has no way of enforcing its decrees against either the President or Congress. The uneasy balance of the three departments does not permit "government by judiciary."[155]

An appreciation of their impotence may be one of the reasons why judges are reluctant to intrude into the thorny thickets of executive privilege; or when they do, why they tend—as in the *Reynolds* case[156]—to uphold the claims of the executive. In final analysis, *Nixon-I* is a sport, an aberration noteworthy less for bringing Nixon to heel than for writing a notion of presidential confidentiality into one of the silences of the Constitution. To the extent that the presidential interest in confidentiality "relates to the effective discharge of a President's powers," it is a constitutionally based, said Chief Justice Burger in a notable example of creating law out of the whole cloth. President Nixon's criminality, furthermore, had the result of permitting the Court in theory to be the final arbiter of claims of privilege by his successors.

   g. *Nixon-I* raises more questions than it answers. How much confidentiality does the President have? In what circumstances? What are those powers Burger mentioned when he called the privilege "constitutionally based"? Are they solely those of Article II? Do they include powers delegated by Congress? And, finally, what of the constitutional power of Congress to demand presidential papers?

The latter question is the only one that has received judicial scrutiny. In *Senate Select Committee on Presidential Campaign Activities v. Nixon*[157] the Court of Appeals for the District of Columbia concluded that the Senate's Watergate Committee's subpoena against Nixon would not be enforced, mainly because on balance the judges determined that the Committee had no need for the Nixon tapes. (No appeal was taken to the Supreme Court.)

The decision is far from definitive. By the time the court ruled, the House of Representatives was well toward impeachment. Nixon's culpability was obvious to all save the willfully blind. Furthermore, one Senator on the Committee had blithely announced on nationwide television that the Committee really did not need the recordings, thus making it easy for the judges to rule against the Committee. The Committee had not shown, said the court, that the desired data were "demonstrably critical to the responsible fulfillment of the Committee's functions"—a bit of judicial hocus-pocus that says judges are capable of telling Congress what data it needs and how it can act responsibly. That reasoning, if that it be, is as full of holes as a block of Swiss cheese.

What the Supreme Court will hold when and if a case involving a congressional subpoena of a sitting President reaches it is difficult to predict. Quite possibly, the Justices will flee into the swamp of political questions and tell the two branches to settle their own differences. *Nixon-I*, after all, involved allegations of criminality. The Supreme Court eschewed any reference to state secrets or national security information. One need not be a clairvoyant to be able to predict that an argument of national security will probably prevail against even a congressional subpoena. That would not be true for a subordinate executive officer, unless that person is able to get the President to invoke the privilege in his own name. But for the subordinates, there are several other ways of evasion, most of which have been efficacious in the past.

h. Those other ways have been called a form of executive privilege, but at this time the term has become sufficiently precise to say that they do not fit within its ambit. One listing of other techniques includes the following: (1) Invocation of executive privilege by a subordinate. At times, a pusillanimous Congressional committee or administrative law judge will allow the bureaucrat to prevail, thus lending some credence to Kleindienst's extravagant assertion that the privilege extended throughout the executive branch. (2) Sometimes White House officials claim that certain internal documents are insulated from Congressional scrutiny by the separation of powers concept. (3) Finally, on numerous occasions executive officers have refused to testify or produce documents, citing various reasons not one of which is executive privilege.

In none of the other ways has the question been litigated. An appropriate label is "congressional cowardice" or at least a marked reluctance to pursue lines of inquiry to their ultimate, the reasons for which may go beyond pusillanimity to a tacit recognition that pushing too far would deeply immerse Congress in the details of government. That, speaking generally, is precisely what the membership does not want. Should, however, Congress screw up its courage and hale the executive officer into court, it is difficult to see why it should not prevail. (Not even a special statute giving jurisdiction to federal courts is needed, as in the Senate Watergate's Committee's abortive lawsuit; initially the Committee was told that it did not show the requisite jurisdictional amount for federal court jurisdiction, an obvious error by the learned Judge John Sirica.) The spirit of the Constitution, and perhaps the letter, suggests that Congress should be able to win. Surely it involves a justiciable question (no one should be judge and jury in his own cause), although judges, never known for courage, may want to retreat into the "political question" cop-out. Assuming a court willing to participate, one may forecast with confidence that subordinate executive officers would be forced to comply with judicial decrees. That is so, even though it is probable that no high-level officer will be summoned before a court. The President in all likelihood would step in and invoke "his" privilege.

Ultimately, to be sure, Congress need not rely on the courts. If the judiciary proves to be too timid, Congress can punish contumacious witnesses itself. Since *Anderson v. Dunn* (1821),[158] it has been recognized that either House can punish a person for contempt of its authority—a principle that got later approval in *McGrain v. Daugherty*[159] and *Marshall v. Dillon*.[160] *Jurney v. MacCracken*[161] was a direct holding to that effect. Recalcitrant witnesses may be imprisoned, but under *Anderson*, not beyond adjournment of the body that ordered it. Again, however, the possibility of such Congressional action is remote at best.

No attempt has ever been made by the executive to enjoin a Congressional Comittee from inquiring into executive actions. *Gravel v. United States*[162] however, held a Senator and his aide immune under the Speech and Debate Clause of Article I from questioning by a grand jury concerning their investigations preparatory to a subcommittee hearing, except insofar as those acts were criminal or related to third-party crime. Although *Gravel* narrowed the Speech and Debate immunity, it merely is an admonition to members of Congress to stick to their "legislative" duties, and thus is no precedent at all for halting an investigation. That conclusion draws ample support from *Eastland v. United States Servicemen's Fund*[163] in which the Supreme Court held that federal courts cannot bar an ongoing Congressional investigation. True, that involved a private litigant, not the executive, but there is nothing in the amorphous contours of separation of powers "doctrine" that would suggest a contrary result.

It is of some interest to iterate that judicial action is, speaking generally, a one-way street. Members of Congress can as individuals and as Members (and, presumably therefore, Congress itself) bring suit and not only get the courts to accept jurisdiction, they can prevail. Although there is no Supreme Court decision on the matter, other than Senator Goldwater's suit dismissed because it was a political question, *Kennedy v. Sampson*[164] (on the validity of a pocket veto) and *Nader v. Bork*[165] (on the improper discharge of special prosecutor Archibald Cox; Nader was dismissed for lack of standing, but co-plaintiffs, members of Congress were not) show that much. Of course the Senate Watergate Committee lost, as has been said, in its litigation on executive privilege, but that decision emphatically does not mean that in a subsequent suit, particularly if it were to be better prepared and argued by counsel for Congress, the court would hold even for a sitting President.

i. That leads to the question of whether Congress could by statute enter the field and impose definite limits on the exercise of the privilege by either the President or his subordinates. As for the latter, since all of the bureaucracy except the President and Vice-President are creatures of Congress, surely Congress can condition its powers to make failure to testify or produce documents a punishable offense. The question is more difficult for the chief executive, not only for himself but when he seeks to cast his mantle of constitutionally protected immunity over subordinate officers.

Such a statute was once proposed by Senator Sam Ervin, but it remained in committee. The Mutual Security Act of 1959 had a provision that records were to be available to Congress; but no court test was ever made. President Eisenhower, furthermore, expressed his discontent over the proviso, even though he signed the bill into law.[166] Whether Congress can enact a valid statute controlling use of executive privilege remains an unanswered constitutional question. The arguments pro and con are reduced to the executive maintaining that the term "the executive power" in Article II of the Constitution has some undefined content that insulates not only the President but his subordinates from Congress (once Congress has delegated power to the other end of the avenue); and Congress asserting that the elastic clause's "horizontal" effect[167] is express constitutional warrant for such a statute. These arguments have been posed in testimony before Congress and also may be found in litigation, not yet definitive, over the validity of the congressional veto and the provision in the Impoundment Control Act of 1974 giving the Comptroller General authority to challenge failures to spend appropriated funds.[168]

In final analysis the decision, when and if made by the Supreme Court, would seem to turn on what effect the Justices would give the plain meaning of Article I, Section 8, Clause 18 (the elastic clause): "The Congress shall have power. . . . to make all laws which shall be necessary and proper for carrying into execution the foregoing powers [in Article I, Section 8] and *all other powers vested by this Constitution in the government of the United States, or in any department or officer thereof.*" (Emphasis added.) Does that clause have a "horizontal" effect? We have known since *McCulloch's Case* (1819)[169] that it has a "vertical" dimension (Congress has "implied" as well as "express" powers). Its precise horizontal effect—that is, to control the President and the courts—is unknown, although a few Supreme Court decisions point in that direction of validating Congressional power.[170] For example, Congress can control the jurisdiction of the federal courts, and can create legislative courts to help carry out legislative functions. In the wake of the Teapot Dome scandal, Congress by Joint Resolution directed the President to bring suit to cancel certain oil leases allegedly obtained by fraud.[171] Furthermore, if the War Powers Resolution of 1973 is valid[172] it must be based either on an implication from the power to declare war or the horizontal application of the elastic clause, or both.

Whether that bit of judicial and legislative history would be sufficient to uphold a statute is problematical. Professor Charles Black of the Yale Law School apparently thinks it does: "The powers of Congress," he said in 1974, "are adequate to the control of every national interest of any importance, including all of those which the President might, by piling inference on inference, be thought to be entrusted."[173] Would, however, the language in

Nixon-I about a quantum of presidential confidentiality override the plain language of the elastic clause? That answer will likely come, not from the courts but from the play of political processes.

j. Finally, executive privilege protects the communication, not the communicator. It is thus akin to the common-law privileges of doctor-patient and lawyer-client, and to the constitutional privilege against self-incrimination. It differs from the "informer's" privilege and the possible "newsman's" privilege to protect his sources (the communicator). (Reporters can go—have gone—to jail for contempt of court for doing that. The Supreme Court has upheld those incarcerations.)

A final question remains: Is the use of executive privilege functional in a nation that calls itself a democracy? Does it serve a desirable *public* purpose? However useful it may be for Presidents, it must be shown to have a larger function—the protection of that nebulous concept called "the public (or national) interest." Answers to those questions will require much more study and analysis than have been forthcoming. Legal and other scholars have thus far contented themselves with parsing judicial opinions. They have not inquired into the sociology and psychology of decisionmaking. Chief Justice Burger's confident ipse dixit about "human experience" is of the same stripe as his assertion in the *Pentagon Papers Case* about an inherent power in courts to enforce secrecy. (He now has, with publication of *The Brethren*, a perfect opportunity to test that observation.)

How open should government be? The question applies to all three branches, not merely the executive. Ideally, perhaps there should be no disagreement with the Supreme Court's statement in *Watkins v. United States*: "The public is, of course, entitled to be informed about the workings of its government."[174] The contrary argument came from Nixon's lawyers in 1973: "The right of presidential confidentiality is not a mystical prerogative. It is, rather, the raw essence of the presidential process, the institutionalized recognition of the crucial role played by human personality in the negotiation, manipulation, and disposition of human affairs."[175]

One can believe that governmental openness is desirable (functional) and still assert that some secrecy is needed. If that be so, then the problem is one of drawing lines through the application of appropriate criteria. Suggested above is that Congress could take the initiative for the employment of executive privilege. We should not expect that to be done. Perhaps because of a tacit recognition that this is the age of executive government (throughout the world) or perhaps because of innate pusillanimity, neither Congress nor the courts have displayed any willingness to challenge the executive's secrecy syndrome. Executive privilege is now, and will remain, a political maneuver, an instrument of policy, and a means by which those with knowledge will remain in control of the levers of powers in government. In sum, the executive is privileged when he can get away with it politically.

In *Halkin* v. *Helms*[176] opponents of the Vietnam "war" filed suit against several officials of the intelligence community, alleging that the National Security Agency (NSA) conducted warrantless interceptions of their international wire, cable, and telephone communications. Judge Roger Robb, speaking for the U.S. Court of Appeals, framed the issue in these terms: "Should the NSA be ordered to disclose whether international communications of the plaintiffs have been acquired by the NSA and disseminated to other federal agencies?" NSA services the intelligence community by electronically monitoring overseas communications. "Watch-lists"—words and phrases identifying communications of intelligence interest—are employed to isolate communications of specific intelligence interest from the enormous numbers of foreign communication. Thus, in actuality, everyone's overseas wire, cable, and telephone messages are monitored by the NSA. Copies of all cables are sent to NSA by Western Union, RCA, and ITT.

One would think that message interceptions of all "communications having at least one foreign terminal" and watchlists of "approximately 1200 Americans" would present an obvious instance of police-state tactics wholly inimical to the American system of government. After all, the Supreme Court has never authorized warrantless wiretaps, even for foreign intelligence purposes, and lower federal courts that have dealt with the question are split. The panel of judges in *Halkin* saw it otherwise. In the words of Judge Robb: "A ranking of the various privileges in our courts would be a delicate undertaking at best, but it is quite clear that the privilege to protect state secrets must head the list. The state secrets privilege is absolute. However helpful to the court the informed advocacy of the plaintiffs' counsel may be, we must be especially careful not to order any dissemination of information *asserted* to be privileged state secrets."

The court accepted the untested assertion of the Secretary of Defense that "civil discovery or a responsive pleading. . . . would severely jeopardize the intelligence collection mission of NSA by identifying present communications collection and analysis capabilities." Not even in camera proceedings are to be permitted. Paying "utmost deference" to the executive, the court found that the interests of the State overrode any interest of the individual. Even though "the" United States, as such, was not a party to the lawsuit, it nonetheless was able to prevail. When *Halkin* is added to President Carter's (1978) executive order authorizing sweeping presidential use of warrantless wiretaps in foreign intelligence matters, it becomes clear that the State prevails in such matters. And that is so even though the Carter administration retreated, by sponsoring a bill that Congress passed in late 1978 that requires a prior judicial warrant for foreign intelligence wiretaps. Those warrants do not have to meet the exacting standards of ordinary criminal warrants. The statute has not yet been tested in the courts, but it seems clear that national security, as determined by the executive, is the overriding goal of policy.

This conclusion is buttressed by Judge Warren's prior restraint injunction in *United States* v. *The Progressive, Inc.*[177] There, for the first time in American history, a judge enjoined the publication of an article for reasons of national security. Judge Warren swept aside prior law in order to reach the decision. In addition, he did not require the government to produce evidence sufficient to fulfill the very heavy burden that any attempt at prior restraint bears. And to cap it off in Kafkaesque style, Judge Warren's opinion was kept secret.[178]

Two lessons may be drawn from the *Progressive* case: First, the mere assertion of "national security" is enough to make some judges scurry for cover; and second, Judge Warren saw the State's asserted interests as pre-eminent and simply refused to enforce the plain language of the First Amendment and First Amendment case law that has existed since *Near* v. *Minnesota* (1931). Judge Warren apparently did not even attempt to balance the interests involved; or if he did, he incorrectly identified the interests of the defendants. In the *Progressive* case, the publishers, editors, and writers posed an issue beyond that of a tiny (40,000 circulation) magazine; what was involved is not merely their interests, as important as they are, but the interests of the entire nation—all of the people, natural and artificial, who fall within the ambit of the First Amendment. The magazine was a surrogate for all Americans. The government speaks for the State, not for the disparate congeries of individuals and groups that make up "society." Once that fact is understood, even a federal district judge should be able to discern that censorship of a magazine article, the contents of which were taken from the public record, cannot comport with the Constitution.

These illustrations are merely present-day instances of what has long been true, but has seldom been asserted: the State wins in constitutional litigation in all cases in which it—the State, speaking through government—considers its interests to be in jeopardy. Secrecy is indeed central to government under the Constitution of Control.

9. *Crisis as the constitutional norm.* Crisis is both a cause and a charac-teristic of the Constitution of Control. The causes have been discussed previously. The socioeconomic crises there outlined—those called the "climacteric"—have in turn created a situation of permanent constitutional crisis. The climacteric is a cause of the fourth Constitution because of the increasingly obvious inability of political institutions created under the second and third constitutions to fulfill demonstrable needs. And the Constitution of Control is emerging for the precise reason of dealing with those several deepset and abiding problems facing humankind.

Anyone who believes that the present constitutional order is sufficient to the need is either a madman or a political scientist (or perhaps a lawyer). Major deficiencies are fast becoming apparent, so much so that it is at least an open question whether the step-by-step adaptations of the past are adequate to the growing needs. The ecology of scarcity places enormous demands upon political systems—upon the constitutional order itself. That it will change cannot be gainsaid, but whether it will do so in ways to preserve humane values associated with the concept of constitutionalism is by no means a foregone conclusion. Were one to guess, as guess one must, about the future—the next fifty years, say—the unavoidable conclusion is the probable contrary. The Constitution of Control means that an era of repression is hard upon Americans.

Constitutional changes that came with the second Constitution were sufficient to the comparatively minor needs of the 1935-1970 period: the growth of bureaucracy, the dominance of the President, the decline of the states, the first beginnings toward multinational resolution of problems common to this nation and its satellites. (That those satellites, or "client States," are not as pliable as American policy-makers wish has become all too obvious since 1970.) The requirements of the ecology of scarcity are of a different type; they present the need for a complete reexamination of the constitutional order.

What *should* evolve is one thing, what *will* quite another. It is easy enough to suggest utopian schemes; many have done it, to little or no avail. The "should" ought to be a reflection of the possible, which in turn means that constitutionalism should be analyzed in the context in which the document operates. That context, as has been seen, is one of the growing climacteric of humankind. That is the challenge of this era. What will be the response?

The choice comes down to this: between "democracy" (however defined) and "dictatorship." My suggestion is that the two concepts, outwardly completely inconsistent, are meeting and merging in the Constitution of Control. Hence, the title of this book: Dictatorship will come—is coming—but with the acquiescence of the people, who subconsciously probably want it. The Grand Inquisitor likely was correct: People want material plenty and mysticism, not perfect freedom. Freedom is an intolerable burden. "Feed men first, then ask of them virtue. That is the message of temptation which Christ rejected and which would come back to haunt Him throughout the pages of history."[179] If we substitute "the State" for Dostoevsky's "the Church," we then can see the leaders of the State are offering "to endure the freedom which people have found so dreadful and have traded for security."[180]

Who says scarcity says authoritarianism. The survival of the political order —the nation itself—is the consistent goal of American policy-makers (in all three branches) as the United States moves from an economy of abundance to an ecology of scarcity. The transition is from a growth-dominated society to a "steady-state" society, one in which some type (not necessarily good) of social equilibrium surely will be attained. That frugality will characterize the emergent society has become obvious. The future beckons: the transition will be rough. Turmoil, staved off for a time by tyranny, may well be the result. The problem, as some see it, is to return to the alleged simplicities of the past. That, however, is a bootless quest; we cannot return to a golden age, simply because no such age ever existed. The real problem is to move forward, trying to avoid the worst aspects of Toynbee's ruthless regimented society.[181] Can it be done? Will it be done? On those questions, the jury, as lawyers say, is still out.

Others perceive a second Protestant Reformation, one in which an ethic of conservation will replace the age-old ethic of domination of nature.[182] That, however, surely is a dream; it is based upon a faith that human nature not only can change but is changing. We can hope, as hope we should, that such a transformation will occur. And we can work, as work we should, toward its fulfillment. But it would be folly to think that it will come without effort—or, indeed, will come at all. Man is a predator, not only against nature itself, but against himself. If change comes, it must be with utmost rapidity. A species that has existed for untold millenia is not at all likely to do that. Mere technological fixes will not permit escape from the ecological trap. We are in for it, deeply and irretrievably, and the sooner we realize it the better; for that realization—and proper action based upon it—provides the only way out.

Epilogue

The social ice age cometh. "The dogmas of the quiet past are inadequate to the stormy present. The occasion is piled high with difficulty, and we must rise with the occasion."[1] When Abraham Lincoln spoke those words, the nation was in the midst of the most sanguinary war in its history. People then rose "with the occasion." Can they do so now?

Today, the problems are immeasurably more difficult than those Lincoln faced. Americans, furthermore, have enjoyed two centuries of unparalleled prosperity. They have become accustomed to thinking that all things are possible to men of good will. They have Aeschylean "blind hopes," hopes that lead them to demand of anyone who foresees doom recommendations for solutions of the problems.

Said Aeschylus three millennia ago:

> *Chorus:* Did you perhaps go further
>   than you have told us?
>
> *Prometheus:* I caused mortals to
>   cease foreseeing doom.
>
> *Chorus:* What cure did you provide them
>   with against that sickness?
>
> *Prometheus:* I placed in them blind hopes.[2]

Americans believe in the "aspirin" theory of social affairs: problems are called headaches, to be cured by the quick fix of an aspirin tablet. But the climacteric of mankind is not a headache; rather, it is a cancer eating away in the bowels of humankind. An aspirin tablet, or even a bucket of them, will not help.

Is the cancer curable? Will there at least be a period of remission? Can the manifold problems that are coming with accelerating speed be dealt with in ways commensurate with traditional constitutional values? The answer, I believe, is still in doubt. There may be a way out of the morass so that human- istic values of freedom and human dignity can somehow not only be preserved but spread, but we do not really know. The mass of people in the world live lives of quiet—at times, not so quiet—misery. At the very peak of the produc- tive capacity of the Technological Age, only a relative few can sup at the laden tables of opulence. And those who can are not likely to share with those who cannot. There is no evidence in human history that leads to the conclu- sion that, in final analysis, selfishness and greed will not prevail.[3]

Man has come a long way since first he crawled out of the primeval slime, took an erect posture, and went forth and multiplied—and thus not only dominated all other beings and subdued the planet but overpopulated it. Civilizations have risen and perished in the past, as Toynbee has shown, and there is no valid reason to believe that the present worldwide civilization—the "global city"—will not suffer the same fate. Dr. Harrison Brown, a perceptive observer of the human scene, asserted in 1978: "Today we are children, but finally after a million or so years our childhood is about to end. With the end of childhood three things can happen: we can exterminate ourselves; we can go back to the ways of our ancestors; we can make a quantum jump upward to a new level of civilization, undreamed of by the philosophers of the past."[4] Anyone who believes that such a quantum jump will occur is either a madman or a Herman Kahn. There is no evidence that civilization has improved in known human history. Since the time of ancient Greece, the only things new under the sun are the proliferation of the species to create the antheap civilization and the scientific-technological revolution. Passions that motivated people 3000 years ago still dominate. Three millennia should be a reasonable time to adapt the species to life on the planet. That adaptation has yet to take place in ways adequate to the manifest needs.

Which of Dr. Brown's alternative futures will occur is, at best, a guess. We can, however, quickly rule out the "quantum jump" that he wants. Of the other alternatives, the likelihood of thermonuclear war gets more probable every year—and with it the end of civilization as we know it. If by some means as yet unknown, man is able to prevent the vaporization of the human race, then "the ways of our ancestors" is not a very palatable avenue. Those ways were Hobbesian—harsh and brutal—for the great majority of people.

Now that technology is available to provide more sophisticated means of repression, there is a high probability (again, absent nuclear war) that people will be forced to learn to love their servitude. No revolution will occur, both because people will not want to revolt and because those who rule will have a near monopoly on the technology of control. Aldous Huxley likely was correct on his views of the future.[5] Niccolò Machiavelli did not foresee the scientific-technological revolution, but he would have approved of the extraordinary measures that future "princes" will bring to bear. The onrushing climacteric of humankind means that Machiavellianism, always present in American history, will be openly and outwardly triumphant in the future.

Given that set of circumstances (and beliefs), it would be the height of intellectual irresponsibility to toss off nostrums, at greater or lesser length, and act as if they could fill the need. Even so, and even at the risk of being simplistic, some general observations can be made. The first deals with the basic idea of constitutionalism.

Constitutionalism to many is the glory of the American experience. With ups and downs and some unacknowledged changes, the original Constitution of 1787 has survived—but only because of extraconstitutional adjustments that were made to meet the various exigencies of successive generations. To many, constitutionalism in America has meant limited government and the rule of law; or, as Professor Daniel Bell has defined it, "the common respect for the framework of law, and the acceptance of outcomes under due process."[6] (As such, constitutionalism was pronounced alive and well in 1979.)[7] Its core may be found in a well-known statement of James Madison: "But what is government itself but the greatest of all reflections on human nature? If men were angels, no government would be necessary. If angels were to govern men, neither external nor internal controls on government would be necessary. In framing a government which is to be administered by men over men, the great difficulty lies in this: you must first enable the government to control the governed; and in the next place oblige it to control itself. A dependence on the people is, no doubt, the primary control on the government; but experience has taught mankind the necessity of auxiliary precautions."[8] Madison believed that political powers ought to be limited and that government should not be omnicompetent.

That is a nice sentiment. But it is just that—a sentiment, an ideal toward which the American people may aspire. That they have never reached it under the living Constitution has been amply demonstrated in previous discussion. Only under the formal Constitution—the Constitution of the books— does one see limited government. The theory of American constitutionalism has, therefore, long been askew with the facts of American life. Unless major changes are made, that gap will be even more pronounced in the future. Constitutionalism, as Madison and others have defined it, is dying, gasping out its life as the waves of repeated crises roll over and inundate the traditional political and legal order. Government, always as strong as circumstances required, will in the future become even stronger. The idea of limited government is giving way to one of burgeoning powers. The facade remains as a legal Potemkin Village; but lurking behind the false front will be the reality of authoritarianism.

Madison suggested the need for "auxiliary precautions" to buttress "dependence on the people" as a means to control government. In the United States, the principal such precaution has been judicial review.[9] The Supreme Court has at times sat as a modern version of Plato's philosopher-kings, ruling on the propriety and wisdom of actions of other segments of government. It has had some success in this, but not nearly as much as many assume. The Court's power is more hortatory than real; it issues admonitions rather than commands. Whether those suggestions are followed depends on the good will of the political officers of government, federal and state. They are followed far less than many believe. The future will mean even less judicial power. No nation can or will allow itself to be ruled by a group of lawyer-judges who happen at any particular time to sit upon the Supreme Court. And without the Court, there are no "auxiliary precautions" available. To repeat: Constitutionalism, as it has been known in America, is dying.

Its demise will mean that limited government has gone, never to return. Of course, the shift will not be so abrupt that all features of constitutionalism, of "the common respect for the framework of law, and the acceptance of outcomes under due process," have vanished. Some still linger, and verbal obeisance is duly paid to them by politicians and other spokesmen. Judges still act as if the idealized ways of the past have not vanished, but deep down inside they know—as many of their decisions reveal—that it is not so. The rule of law is the rule of men; not only that, the rule of *some* men—an elite structure.

A case, however, can be made for change in the formal Constitution. That the institutions established by the Constitution of 1787 are not sufficient to the need has been true throughout American history. That they are fast becoming more insufficient, even obsolescent, should be obvious to all. Those institutions do not have the capacity to cope quickly and effectively with the manifold problems of the modern age. The obvious inability of governmental organs to deal effectively with inflation and unemployment, with energy shortages and nuclear proliferation, to mention only a few current problems, does not give much basis for hope. Constitutional change must come—and soon, even though there is little reason to expect that alteration in law will by itself change the underlying socioeconomic forces that lie behind laws and constitutions. The second Constitution of 1787 came at a particularly propitious time in human history, a time when there was a coalescence of favorable factors—of geography, of natural resources, of freedom from external pressures from other nations, of a small population, of capital and cheap labor from Europe. Now, Americans are faced with polar opposites—a coalescence of crises—of a shrinking planet, dwindling resources, of immersion in foreign wars, of a burgeoning population, of an industrial machine that finds it increasingly difficult to compete in the world market.

The men of 1787 could not have failed in constructing a new government; the conditions all favored success. Today, there are many ways in which their successors can fail dismally. The formal constitutional changes that have become obviously necessary are those that would streamline the governmental structure and make it more efficient. At the same time, provision should be made for minimizing intrusions on the freedom and dignity of human personality.

That is a very large order indeed. Perhaps it is too large. But the effort is necessary. Political change alone will not bring man out of the morass; much more is needed. The (formal) Constitution is but a memorandum of underlying social forces. "Behind institutions, behind constitutional forms and modifications," wrote the historian Frederick Jackson Turner, "lie the vital forces that call these organs into life and shape them to meet changing conditions."[10] So change must also come in the "vital forces" that shape the Constitution and mold it to meet the exigencies of succeeding generations of Americans. In sum, those vital forces are the environment in which legal, including constitutional, systems operate; it must be conducive to the realization of the humane values of the "first" morality—that of the Judeo-Christian tradition.

Will that happen? If so, no one can validly say that it will not be a long and rocky road. Crisis government is becoming the norm. We must hunker down and try to ride out the storm that is sure to come. The strong are going to continue to do what they can, and the weak will continue to suffer what they must. Lord Ashby believes there is evidence of a coming change that will reconcile man with the environment.[11] But his perception seems to be based on faith. He acknowledges that two other reconciliations are necessary if industrial society as we know it is to survive: moderation of demands on natural resources and the affluent sharing the limited resources with others less fortunate; and harmony between people with different ideologies, so that they can live peaceably together. He is optimistic on neither; he anticipates turmoil and strife. That means social convulsion and a diminution of personal freedoms. Can they be kept to a minimum? Says Ashby: "I don't know. If we fail to make the reconciliations. . . . an Englishman, Thomas Hobbes, warned us over 300 years ago what would happen: Leviathan, the world's superstar dictator will take charge."[12] John Locke is often considered to be the main intellectual force behind the Constitution of 1787. No doubt it is true that his views did have considerable influence. But he was the philosopher of the emerging age of economic abundance, who saw in the new world and its seemingly endless riches, a way for humans to escape the ecology trap. Hobbes, writing a century before Locke, did not perceive that the earth would produce unlimited riches—which it has, at least for some, for at least two centuries.[13]

We are now back in the ecology trap, which Hobbes saw and Locke denied. That means that as the United States counts down to the end of the twentieth century, the cloud on the horizon is Leviathan—slowly, steadily, and seemingly inexorably making its way to "take charge." There can be no doubt that Americans have come, with seeming abruptness, face-to-face with the gravest constitutional challenge in their history. No one should be sanguine about the outcome.

Notes

PROLOGUE

1. W. Wilson, Congressional Government par. 10 (1885).

2. See Select Committee to Study Governmental Operations With Respect to Intelligence Activities, United States Senate, Final Report, Book IV at 157-58 (1976) (Nixon's reply to an interrogatory). See also L. Fisher, The Constitution Between Friends (1978).

3. C. Friedrich, Constitutional Reason of State: Survival of the Constitutional Order 4-5 (1957).

4. F. Meinecke, Machiavellism: The Doctrine of Raison d'État and Its Place in Modern History 1 (D. Scott trans. 1957).

5. See, for example, A. S. Miller, The Modern Corporate State: Private Governments and the Constitution (1976); G. McConnell, Private Power and American Democracy (1966).

6. Webster's New World Dictionary of the American Language 474 (1959).

7. J. Smith & C. Cotter, Powers of the President During Crisis 14 (1960).

8. See, for example, D. Boulton, The Lockheed Papers (1978).

9. L. Brown, The Twenty-Ninth Day 324 (1978).

10. N. Machiavelli, The Discourses, Part I, Sec. 34 (first published in 1531).

11. H. Brown, The Human Future Revisited (1978).

12. Southern Pacific Co. v. Jensen, 244 U.S. 205 (1917).

CHAPTER 1

1. Letter from Jefferson to Samuel Kercheval, 12 July 1816, quoted in H. Arendt, On Revolution 250 (1973) (paperback ed.).

2. H. Arendt, On Revolution 11 (1973).

3. T. Hobbes, Leviathan (first published in 1651).

4. See, for example, J. Rifkin & T. Howard, The Emerging Order: God in the Age of Scarcity (1979).

5. D. Ehrenfeld, The Arrogance of Humanism (1978).

6. See M. Crozier, S. Huntington & J. Watanuki, The Crisis of Democracy (1975); Huntington, *The Democratic Distemper*, No. 41 The Public Interest at 9 (Fall 1975).

7. A. Comte, System of Positive Polity (1851).

8. Quoted in H. Arendt, supra note 1.

9. Ibid.

10. W. Bagehot, The English Constitution (1867) (2d ed. 1872), 267 (pagination to 1963 paperback edition of 2d ed.).

CHAPTER 2

1. Lord Ashby of Brandon, *A Second Look at Doom*, the 21st Fawley Lecture delivered at Southampton University, Dec. 11, 1975 (photocopy of typescript). Lord Ashby expanded his views in E. Ashby, Reconciling Man With the Environment (1978). See also M. Shanks, What's Wrong With the Modern World? Agenda for a New Society (1978); W. Harman, An Incomplete Guide to the Future xi (1976): "The world is headed for a climacteric which may well be one of the most fateful in the history of civilizations. This convulsion is now not far off and most people sense something of it—although interpretations vary widely, like the well-known interpretations of the elephant by blindfolded people who feel different parts of the animal."

2. See E. Ashby, supra note 1; J. Platt, Perception and Change: Projections for Survival (1970); L. Brown, The Twenty-Ninth Day (1978).

3. R. Heilbroner, An Inquiry Into the Human Prospect (1974). For Kahn's views, see, for example, H. Kahn and A. Wiener, The Year 2000: A Framework for Speculation on the Next Thirty-three years (1967); H. Kahn, W. Brown, and L. Martel, The Next Two Hundred Years (1976).

4. W. Warner, The Corporation in the Emergent American Society 18 (1962).

5. H. Rosinski, Power and Human Destiny (1965).

6. See J. Galbraith, The New Industrial State (1967), criticized in A. S. Miller, The Modern Corporate State: Private Governments and the Constitution (1976).

7. D. Landes, the Unbound Prometheus: Technological Change and Industrial Development in Western Europe from 1750 to the Present 21 (1969).

8. W. Webb, The Great Frontier (1952). See also F. Turner, The Frontier in American History (1920).

9. M. Weber, The Protestant Ethic and the Spirit of Capitalism (trans. 1930). See also R. Tawney, Religion and the Rise of Capitalism (1926).

10. F. Turner, supra note 8.

11. A. Koestler, The Ghost in the Machine (1968).

12. White, *The Historic Roots of Our Ecologic Crisis*, 155 Science 1204 (1967). See also J. Passmore, Man's Responsibility for Nature (1974).

13. E. Ashby, Reconciling Man With the Environment 84 (1978).

14. W. Harman, supra note 1.

15. President Ford ordered offensive military action when the vessel, the *Mayaguez*, was seized off the Cambodian island of Koh Tang, stating that the action was taken

"pursuant to the President's constitutional Executive power and his authority as Commander-in-Chief." See *President's Letter to the Speaker of the House and President Pro Tempore of the Senate in Accordance with the War Powers Resolution*, 11 Weekly Compilation of Presidential Documents 515 (May 15, 1975). For discussion, see A. S. Miller, Presidential Power 192 (1977); Paust, *The Seizure and Recovery of the Mayaguez*, 85 Yale Law Journal 774 (1976).

16. H. Brown, The Human Future Revisited (1978).

17. See C. Jenkins & B. Sherman, The Collapse of Work (1979); I. Barron & R. Curnow, The Future With Electronics (1979); P. Abelson & A. Hammon (eds.), Electronics: The Continuing Revolution (1977).

18. J. Dewey, The Public and Its Problems 188 (1927); see also J. Dewey, Human Nature and Conduct: An Introduction to Social Psychology (1922).

19. See H. Arendt, The Human Condition (1958).

20. See A. Huxley, Brave New World (1931); see also A. Huxley, Brave New World Revisited (1958).

21. M. Kammen, People of Paradox (1972).

22. Harrod, *The Possibility of Economic Satiety — Use of Economic Growth for Improving the Quality of Education and Leisure*, in Committee for Economic Development, Problems of United States Economic Development, Vol. I, 207 (1958); F. Hirsch, Social Limits to Growth (1976). See also E. Mishan, The Economic Growth Debate: An Assessment (1977); W. Beckerman, In Defense of Economic Growth (1974).

23. See International Bank for Reconstruction and Development, World Development Report, 1979 (1979). See, however, Marsden, *Widening Gap Warning Called Misleading*, Report (World Bank) (Jan.-Feb. 1980) 1; Marsden, *Global Development Strategies and the Poor: Alternative Scenarios*, 117 International Labour Review No. 6 (1978).

24. R. Lapp, The New Priesthood: The Scientific Elite and the Uses of Power 13 (1965).

25. H. Brown, supra note 16.

26. W. Harman, supra note 1.

27. H. Brown, supra note 16.

CHAPTER 3

1. Quoted in G. Stent, The Coming of the Golden Age: A View of the End of Progress x (1969). See also A. Wheelis, The End of the Modern Age (1971).

2. Quoted in A. S. Miller, The Supreme Court: Myth and Reality 8 (1978).

3. Quoted in L. Henkin, Foreign Affairs and the Constitution 271 (1972).

4. A. Sofaer, War, Foreign Affairs and Constitutional Power: The Origins 1 (1976).

5. R. Berger, Government by Judiciary: The Transformation of the Fourteenth Amendment (1977).

6. J. Furnas, The Americans: A Social History of the United States (1969).

7. Ibid.

8. See, for example, H. Zinn, A. People's History of the United States (1980); B. Howard & J. Logue, American Class Society in Numbers (1978).

9. J. Galbraith, The New Industrial State (1967).

10. F. Neumann, The Democratic and the Authoritarian State 13 (1953).

11. H. Maine, Ancient Law (1861).

12. M. Kammen, People of Paradox (1972).

13. Quoted in ibid.

CHAPTER 4

1. J. Acton, Lectures on Modern History 295 (1906) (paperback ed. 1960).

2. W. Bagehot, The English Constitution (1867). Bagehot said in the introduction to the second edition of that classic volume (1872): "There is a great difficulty in the way of a writer who attempts to sketch a living Constitution—a Constitution that is in actual work and power. The difficulty is that the object is in constant change." (267 of 1963 paperback ed.) See W. Wilson, Constitutional Government in the United States (1908); Miller, *Notes on the Concept of the "Living" Constitution*, 31 George Washington Law Review 881 (1963), reprinted in A. S. Miller, Social Change and Fundamental Law: America's Evolving Constitution (1979).

3. See A. S. Miller, The Modern Corporate State: Private Governments and the American Constitution (1976); W. Samuels (ed.), The Economy As a System of Power (1979).

4. In 1803 the Supreme Court decided Marbury v. Madison, the case which established the principle of judicial review of the actions of Congress. In that decision, Chief Justice John Marshall asserted judicial pre-eminence in giving meaning to the Constitution.

5. Miranda v. Arizona, 384 U.S. 466 (1966).

6. Marshall's statement came in the *Marbury* case, supra note 4; and Burger's came in United States v. Nixon, 418 U.S. 683 (1974) (this was the case involving the infamous "Nixon tapes").

7. For discussion, see Miller, *The Elusive Search for Values in Constitutional Interpretation*, 6 Hastings Constitutional Law Quarterly 487 (1979).

8. For discussion, see G. Gunther, Cases and Materials on Constitutional Law 427-29 (9th ed. 1975); Miller, supra note 7.

9. See, for example, R. Pious, The American Presidency (1979); A. S. Miller, Presidential Power (1977).

10. See the works cited in note 3, supra.

11. W. Wilson, Constitutional Government in the United States 57 (1908).

12. For example, R. Berger, Government by Judiciary: The Transformation of the Fourteenth Amendment (1977); N. Graglia, Disaster by Decree: The Supreme Court's Decisions on Race and the Schools (1977). A much more balanced and insightful analysis is J. Ely, Democracy and Distrust: A Theory of Judicial Review (1980).

13. See A. S. Miller, Social Change and Fundamental Law: America's Evolving Constitution (1979), and works cited therein.

14. See the discussion in chapter 9, below.

15. H. Arendt, On Revolution 153 (1973).

16. Ibid., 154.

17. The popular wisdom often refers to Justice Louis Brandeis's dissenting opinion in Myers v. United States, 272 U.S. 52 (1926). Modern scholarship, the leading exponent of which is Dr. Louis Fisher, has shown that efficiency was as much a goal as prevention of despotism. See, for example, L. Fisher, President and Congress: Power and Policy 1-27 (1972).

18. Jefferson's statement is quoted in W. Douglas, Stare Decisis 31 (1949) and also in Miller, supra note 7.

19. M. Kammen, People of Paradox 56 (1972).

20. F. Dostoyevsky, The Brothers Karamazov.

21. R. Lapp, The New Priesthood: The Scientific Elite and the Uses of Power 13 (1965).

22. M. Cohen, Reason and Law 4 (1950).

23. See M. Horwitz, *The Emergence of an Instrumental Conception of Law*, in M. Horwitz, The Transformation of American Law, 1780-1860 at 1 (1977). Professor Horwitz deals with the "common law"—that is, the law that refers to the disputes of private individuals—but his views are applicable as well to constitutional law. See also A. S. Miller, supra note 13.

24. See J. Griffith, The Politics of the Judiciary (1977); Miller, *The Politics of the American Judiciary*, 49 Political Quarterly 200 (1978).

25. J. Griffith, supra note 24.

26. See, for example, R. Rubenstein, The Cunning of History (1975); H. Hart, The Concept of Law (1961).

CHAPTER 5

1. This is the central message of both The Discourses and The Prince, Machiavelli's principal works.

2. Said the President in his inaugural address, March 4, 1933: "Our Constitution is so simple and practical that it is possible to meet extraordinary needs by changes in emphasis and arrangement without loss of essential form. That is why our constitutional system has proved itself the most superbly enduring political mechanism the modern world has produced. It has met every stress of vast expansion of territory, of foreign wars, of bitter internal strife, of world relations." Quoted in C. Rossiter, Constitutional Dictatorship: Crisis Government in the Modern Democracies 213 (1948) (1963 paperback ed.).

3. 4 Wallace 2, at 120-21 (1866).

4. 290 U.S. 398, at 425 (1934).

5. Jacobellis v. Ohio, 378 U.S. 184 (1964). Justice Stewart was talking about the inability to define "hard-core" pornography; he couldn't define it, but he knew it when he saw it.

6. To my knowledge, there has (until this volume) been no comprehensive discussion of Reason of State in the United States.

7. This is the basic fault with the opinion by Justice Davis in the Milligan case, supra note 3.

8. F. Meinecke, Machiavellism: The Doctrine of Raison d'État and Its Place in Modern History 49 (D. Scott trans. 1957). This version of Meinecke comes from Crick, *Introduction* to N. Machiavelli, The Discourses 67 (1970 paperback ed.); Scott's translation of Meinecke, as published in the United States, reads as follows: "Machiavelli's theory was a sword plunged into the flank of the body politic of Western humanity, causing it to shriek and rear up." Professor Crick states, "The pain [of that sword's thrust] is still with us and if ever we cease to feel it, it will not be because the conditions that gave rise to it have miraculously vanished but because our nerves have gone dead."

9. Crick, supra note 8.

10. The term comes from O. Gierke, Natural Law and the Theory of Society 1500 to 1800 (E. Barker trans. 1958); and is discussed in subsequent chapters of this volume.

11. The Discourses, Vol. I, Sec. 9.

12. The Federalist Papers were a series of essays written by James Madison, Alexander Hamilton and John Jay to help get the Constitution of 1787 ratified. The principal author was Hamilton, who wrote at least fifty-one of the eighty-five essays. Although they have had lasting influence, the Federalist Papers were essentially a form of propaganda.

13. See A. S. Miller, The Modern Corporate State: Private Governments and the American Constitution (1976).

14. G. Poggi, The Development of the Modern State: A Sociological Introduction c. V (1978).

15. Ibid., at 127-32.

16. Halkin v. Helms, 598 F.2d 1 (District of Columbia Circuit 1978).

17. Compare J. Griffith, The Politics of the Judiciary (1977) with M. Shapiro, Law and Politics in the Supreme Court (1964).

18. J. Keynes, The General Theory of Employment, Interest and Money 383-84 (1936).

19. Abrams v. United States, 250 U.S. 616 (1919).

20. H. Arendt, On Revolution c. 6 (1973).

21. Hamilton, On the Composition of the Corporate Veil, in R. Eells & C. Walton, Conceptual Foundations of Business 132 (1961).

22. E. Cassirer, The Myth of the State (1946).

23. H. Arendt, supra note 20.

24. Hartwell, Introduction to K. Templeton (ed.), The Politicization of Society 7, 24 (1979).

25. R. Michels, Political Parties (1911).

26. H. Arendt, supra note 20. See also Templeton, supra note 24.

27. R. Unger, Knowledge and Politics 64 (1975).

28. R. Miliband, The State in Capitalist Society (1969).

29. O. Gierke, supra note 10.

30. See J. Shklar, Legalism (1964).

31. A. Bickel, The Morality of Consent (1975).

32. Levinson, The Specious Morality of the Law, Harper's Magazine, May 1977, p. 37.

33. M. Weber, The Protestant Ethic and the Spirit of Capitalism (trans. 1930).

34. Zorach v. Clauson, 343 U.S. 346 (1952).

35. Weber, Religious Rejections of the World and Their Directions, in H. Gerth & C. Mills (eds.), From Max Weber: Essays in Sociology 323 (1958).

36. O. Holmes, Collected Legal Papers (1920).

37. See generally H. Zinn, A People's History of The United States (1980); R. Hofstadter, Social Darwinism in American Thought (rev. ed. 1955).

38. See A. Nevins, John Davison Rockefeller: Industrialist and Philanthropist (1940).

39. See C. Mills, The Power Elite (1956); G. Domhoff, The Higher Circles (1972); H. Zinn, supra note 37.

40. See R. Neustadt, Presidential Power (rev. ed. 1976); R. Pious, The American Presidency (1979); T. Cronin, The State of the Presidency (1975).

41. 252 U.S. 416 (1920).

42. See Miller, *The Elusive Search for Values in Constitutional Interpretation*, 6 Hastings Constitutional Law Quarterly 487 (1979).

43. Quoted in Barker, *Introduction*, to O. Gierke, supra note 10.

44. B. Gross, Friendly Fascism (1980).

45. United States v. O'Brien, 391 U.S. 367 (1968).

46. J. Griffith, The Politics of the Judiciary 213 (1977).

47. Wyman v. James, 400 U.S. 309 (1971), discussed in A. S. Miller, The Supreme Court: Myth and Realty c. 10 (1978).

48. M. Kammen, People of Paradox (1972).

49. Ibid.

50. See P. Bachrach, The Theory of Democratic Elitism: A Critique (1967).

51. Further discussed below, Chapter 12. For preliminary discussion, see Miller, *Constitutional Law: Crisis Government Becomes the Norm*, 39 Ohio State Law Journal 736 (1978); J. Weinstein, The Corporate Ideal in the Liberal State (1968).

CHAPTER 6

1. C. Rossiter, Constitutional Dictatorship: Crisis Government in the Modern Democracies (1948).

2. F. Neumann, The Democratic and the Authoritarian State 8 (1957).

3. N. Machiavelli, The Discourses, Book I, Sec. 34.

4. H. Arendt, On Revolution (1973).

5. Youngstown Sheet & Tube Co. v. Sawyer, 358 U.S. 534 (1952).

6. Ex parte Milligan, 71 U.S. 2 (1866).

7. Ex parte Quirin, 317 U.S. 1 (1942).

8. Berlin, *The Originality of Machiavelli*, in M. Gilmore (ed.), Studies on Machiavelli 149 (1972).

9. F. Meinecke, Machiavellism: The Doctrine of Raison d'État and Its Place in Modern History 49 (D. Scott trans. 1957) (first published in Germany in 1925).

10. This is the interpretation of Professor Bernard Crick. See Crick, *Introduction*, to N. Machiavelli, The Discourses 22 (paperback ed. 1970).

11. Professor Alpheus Thomas Mason so characterized the Supreme Court during World War II. See A. Mason, Harlan Fiske Stone: Pillar of the Law (1956).

12. A. Sofaer, War, Foreign Affairs and Constitutional Power: The Origins (1976).

13. In a message to Congress, quoted in C. Rossiter, supra note 1, at 3.

14. N. Small, Some Presidential Interpretations of the Presidency 31 (1932).

15. 6 Messages and Papers of the President 78 (edited by J. Richardson 1897).

16. Nixon's views are stated in Select Committee to Study Governmental Operations with Respect to Intelligence Activities, United States Senate, Final Report, Book IV at 157 (1976) (Nixon's answer to an interrogatory).

17. The language is that of the Militia Act of 1795, the current version of which may be found in 10 United States Code Secs. 331-34 (1976).

18. The list is taken from Professor Rossiter's account, supra note 1, at 225-28.

19. 67 U.S. 635 (1863).

20. W. Stevenson, A Man Called Intrepid (1976).

21. C. Rossiter, supra note 1, at 267-68.

22. M. Walzer, Just and Unjust Wars (1977).

23. *President's Message to Congress on Inflation Control*, 88 Congressional Record 7042 (1944). See E. Corwin, Total War and the Constitution (1946).

24. J. Locke, The Second Treatise of Civil Government par. 160 (J. Gough ed. 1966). See Hurtgen, *The Case for Presidential Prerogative*, 7 University of Toledo Law Review 59 (1975).

25. For discussion, see Miller, *Government Contracts and Social Control: A Preliminary Inquiry*, 41 Virginia Law Review 27 (1955).

26. The Discourses, Book I, Sec. 51.

27. Ibid.

28. See, for example, Korematsu v. United States, 320 U.S. 81 (1943). See F. Biddle, In Brief Authority (1962); A. Mason, Harlan Fiske Stone: Pillar of the Law (1956), for discussion of this unsavory episode.

29. 320 U.S. 81 (1943).

30. In his opinion in the Korematsu case, supra note 29.

31. In re Yamashita, 327 U.S. 1 (1946).

32. N. Machiavelli, The Discourses, Book I, Sec. 9.

33. D. Halberstam, The Best and the Brightest (1972).

34. See T. Taylor, Nuremberg and Vietnam: An American Tragedy (1970).

35. See F. Biddle, supra note 28.

36. Recounted in A. Mason, supra note 28.

37. See Gittings, *The War Before*, The Guardian (Manchester), June 27, 1975, 10; I. Stone, The Hidden History of the Korean War (1969).

38. 23 Department of State Bulletin 173 (1950). The Department of State issued that statement in an opinion entitled *Authority of the President to Repel the Attack in Korea*, and went on to say: There is a "traditional power of the President to use the Armed Forces of the United States without consulting Congress."

39. Acheson's statement may be found in Senate Committee on Foreign Relations, *National Commitments*, Senate Report No. 797, 90th Congress, 1st Session, at p. 17 (1967).

40. Said President Johnson: "We stated [at the time of the Gulf of Tonkin Resolution in 1964], and we repeat now, we did not think the resolution was necessary to do what we did and what we're doing." New York Times, Aug. 19, 1967, at 10. See also Senate Report, supra note 39. President Nixon concurred in that view of presidential authority, as did President Ford and as did President Carter. For discussion of the general problem, see Casper, *Constitutional Constraints on the Conduct of Foreign and Defense Policy: A Nonjudicial Model*, 43 University of Chicago Law Review 463 (1976).

41. The Discourses, Book I, Sec. 9.

42. Longaker, *The Constitution and the Commander in Chief After 1950*, in C. Rossiter & R. Longaker, The Supreme Court and the Commander in Chief (expanded ed. 1976).

43. This is not atypical, as Professor Rossiter has shown, works cited in notes 1 & 42, supra. See also E. Corwin, The President: Office and Powers (4th ed. 1957). The Supreme Court had a number of opportunities to rule on the Vietnam conflict but

chose to avoid the issue each time. That means, of course, that the vaunted Rule of Law had become the Rule of Men (rather, of one man—the President).

44. War Powers Resolution, Public Law No. 93-148, adopted in November 1973 over President Nixon's veto. Nixon asserted the Resolution was unconstitutional. See 119 Congressional Record 34990 (October 24, 1973).

45. J. Locke, supra note 24.

46. See the discussion in P. Carroll & D. Noble, The Free and the Unfree: A New History of the United States (1977).

47. See the discussion in H. Zinn, A People's History of the United States (1980); R. Van Alstyne, The Rising American Empire (1960).

48. See Muskrat v. United States, 219 U.S. 346 (1911). See, for discussion of aspects of treatment of the Indians, L. Tribe, American Constitutional Law Sec. 16-14 (1978); D. Brown, Bury My Heart at Wounded Knee (1972); P. Carroll & D. Noble, supra note 46.

49. See C. Woodham-Smith, The Great Hunger: Ireland 1845-1849 (1962).

50. G. Johnson, Roosevelt: Dictator or Democrat? 214 (1941).

51. C. Rossiter, supra note 1, at 256.

52. Papers and Addresses of Franklin D. Roosevelt, Vol. II, 11-16 (1938).

53. The National Recovery Act (NRA) was so broadly drafted that it allowed the President to prescribe trade practices and labor policies for almost all of American business and industry. In fact, it permitted industry groups through government to set the terms of their existence; and thus was an express commitment to a corporate State. See, for discussion, A. S. Miller, The Modern Corporate State: Private Governments and the American Constitution (1976).

54. For discussion, see McCloskey, Economic Due Process and the Supreme Court: An Exhumation and Reburial, 1962 Supreme Court Review 34; A. S. Miller, The Supreme Court and American Capitalism (1968).

55. See H. Zinn, supra note 47; J. Weinstein, The Corporate Ideal in the Liberal State (1968). Weinstein discusses the earlier period in the early twentieth century, but his views are applicable to the New Deal period as well. See also F. Lundberg, The Rich and the Super-rich (1968).

56. M. Levin, Political Hysteria in America 28 (1971). See Goldstein, An American Gulag? Summary Arrest and Emergency Detention of Political Dissidents in the United States, 10 Columbia Human Rights Law Review 541 (1978).

57. This is the case of the Rev. Chavis and other civil rights advocates.

58. M. Levin, supra note 56, at 9.

59. 360 U.S. 109 (1959). Wittingly or not, Justice John Harlan, writing for the Supreme Court, adopted a Machiavellian principle: "It is not the well-being of individuals that make cities great, but the well-being of the community." The Discourses, Book II, Sec. 2. And further: "the common good can be realized in spite of those few who suffer." Ibid.

60. 249 U.S. 47 (1919); 250 U.S. 616 (1919).

61. 341 U.S. 494 (1952).

62. See L. Post, The Deportations Delirium in Nineteen-twenty (1923).

63. On political trials in general, see O. Kirchheimer, Political Justice (1961); T. Becker (ed.), Political Trials (1971).

64. Cohen v. California, 403 U.S. 15 (1971).

65. See the discussion in Chapter 12, below.

66. United States v. United States District Court, 407 U.S. 297 (1972).

67. United States v. Butenko, 494 F.2d 593 (3d Circuit 1974), certiorari denied, 419 U.S. 881 (1974); Zweibon v. Mitchell, 516 F.2d 594 (District of Columbia Circuit 1975).

68. See New York Times, Apr. 1, 1979 and Oct. 17, 1975.

69. See *Diego Garcia, 1975: The Debate Over the Base and the Island's Former Inhabitants: Hearings before the Special Subcommittee on Investigations of the House Committee on International Relations*, 94th Congress, 1st Session (1975); Walker, *Price on Islanders' Birthright*, The Guardian (Manchester), Nov. 4, 1975.

70. O. Elliott, Men at the Top 40 (1959).

71. For discussion, see C. Walton & F. Cleveland, Corporations on Trial: The Electric Cases (1964).

72. See S. Dash, Chief Counsel (1976).

73. D. Boulton, The Lockheed Papers (1978). See also A. Sampson, The Sovereign State: The Secret History of ITT (1973).

74. Vandivier, *"Why Should My Conscience Bother Me?"*, in R. Heilbroner and others, In the Name of Profit 3 (1972).

75. For one account of a Japanese Corporation (but by no means atypical), see W. & A. Smith, Minimata (1975) (Chisso Corporation poisoned fishing waters for years but did nothing about it).

76. See, for discussion, L. Silk & D. Vogel, Ethics and Profits (1976); Miller, *A Modest Proposal for Helping to Tame the Corporate Beast*, 8 Hofstra Law Review 79 (1979).

77. J. Borkin, The Crime and Punishment of I. G. Farben (1978).

78. H. Arendt, The Banality of Evil (1965).

79. See, for example, Hymer, *The Multinational Corporation and the Law of Uneven Development*, in N. Bhagwati (ed.), Economics and World Order: From the 1970s to the 1990s at 113 (1972); Hacker, *Politics and the Corporation*, in A. Hacker (ed.), The Corporation Take-Over 260 (1964); D. Finn, The Corporate Oligarch (1969); A. Hacker, The End of the American Era 72 (1970).

80. Quoted in S. Lens, The Forging of the American Empire 270-71 (1971).

81. T. McCann, An American Company: The Tragedy of United Fruit (1976).

82. Lester, *Economics of Labor*, in T. Frazier (ed.), The Underside of American History, Vol. 2, 13 (1971).

83. J. Commons, Legal Foundations of Capitalism 7 (1924).

84. For discussion, see A. S. Miller, The Supreme Court and American Capitalism (1968).

85. 198 U.S. 45 (1905).

86. Discussed in M. Levin, supra note 56; H. Zinn, supra note 47.

87. Ibid.

88. Bethell, *The Myth of an Adversary Press*, Harper's Magazine, Jan. 1977.

89. P. Knightley, The First Casualty (1976).

90. See Lazarsfeld & Merton, *Mass Communication, Popular Taste, and Organized Social Action*, in M. Schramm, Mass Communications, cited in N. Chomsky, For Reasons of State 95, 205 (1973).

91. For discussion, see M. Mintz & J. Cohen, Power Inc. (1976).

92. J. Ellul, Propaganda (1968).

93. See W. Thompson, Evil and World Order (1976); E. Becker, The Structure of Evil (1968); C. Frankel, Morality and U.S. Foreign Policy (1975); R. Niebuhr, Moral Man and Immoral Society (1965).

94. J. Acton, Lectures on Modern History 295 (1906) (paperback ed. 1960).

CHAPTER 7

1. Crick, *Introduction*, to N. Machiavelli, The Discourses 27 (paperback ed. 1970).

2. A. Huxley, Brave New World (1931); see A. Huxley, Brave New World Revisited (1958).

3. Huntington, *The United States*, in M. Crozier, S. Huntington & J. Watanuki, The Crisis of Democracy 59 (1975).

4. See Nisbet, *The Rape of Progress*, 2 Public Opinion No. 3, at 2 (1979).

5. "The illiberal and anti-democratic propensity of the common man is an undeniable fact that must be faced." P. Bachrach, The Theory of Democratic Elitism: A Critique 105 (1967). See also J. Ely, Democracy and Distrust: A Theory of Judicial Review (1980).

6. E. Corwin, A Constitution of Powers in a Secular State (1951).

7. W. Wilson, Congressional Government (1885).

8. War Powers Resolution, Public Law No. 93-148, enacted over President Nixon's veto in 1973.

9. For example, Hutchins, *The Case for Constitutional Change*, 3 Center Report No. 5 (Dec. 1970): "The [Supreme] Court has become 'the highest legislative body in the land'." See also A. Berle, Power 342 (1969): "A revolution has taken place and is in progress" and "the revolutionary committee is the Supreme Court of the United States." See A. S. Miller, The Supreme Court: Myth and Reality (1978) for another view.

10. Corwin, *The Passing of Dual Federalism*, 36 Virginia Law Review 1 (1950).

11. See A. de Riencourt, The Coming Caesars (1957).

12. See W. Wilson, Constitutional Government in the United States (1908).

13. F. Neumann, The Democratic and the Authoritarian State (1957).

14. See United States v. Brown, 381 U.S. 487 (1965).

15. See L. Fisher, President and Congress: Power and Policy (1972); L. Fisher, The Constitution Between Friends (1978); A. S. Miller, Presidential Power c. 11 (1977).

16. See A. S. Miller, The Supreme Court and American Capitalism (1968).

17. In No. 51 of The Federalist Papers.

18. D. Wise, The American Police State: The Government Against the People (1976). See also A. Wolfe, The Seamy Side of Democracy: Repression in America (1973).

19. In Dennis v. United States, 341 U.S. 494 (1951).

20. A. Comte, System of Positive Polity (1851).

21. See T. Lowi, The End of Liberalism: The Second Republic of the United States (2d ed. 1979).

22. O. Holmes, Collected Legal Papers 270 (1920).

23. M. Edelman, The Symbolic Uses of Politics (1964).

24. E. Burke, Reflections on the Revolution in France (1790). See F. O'Gorman, Edmund Burke: His Political Philosophy (1973).

25. See P. Steinfels, The Neo-Conservatives (1979).

26. A. de Tocqueville, Democracy in America (1835).

27. J. Benda, The Treason of the Intellectuals (1928).

28. J. Talmon, The Origins of Totalitarian Democracy (1952).

29. M. Rejai, Democracy: The Contemporary Theories (1967). See E. Schattschneider, The Semisovereign People (1960).

30. The term is meaningless, as usually employed; it is a means of organizing the masses, "a misleading piece of propaganda." Crick, Introduction, to N. Machiavelli, The Discourses 27 (1970).

31. J. Talmon, supra note 28.

32. J. Galbraith, The New Industrial State (1967); J. Galbraith, Economics and the Public Purpose (1973).

33. Quoted in T. Cronin, The State of the Presidency (1975).

34. Quoted in ibid.

CHAPTER 8

1. A. Schlesinger, The Imperial Presidency (1974).

2. Seward is quoted in M. Novak, Choosing Our King: Powerful Symbols in Presidential Politics (1974) at 23 and Henry Jones Ford at 19.

3. A. de Riencourt, The Coming Caesars (1957).

4. See T. Cronin, The State of the Presidency (1975) for discussion of the "textbook" presidency.

5. Wilson, The Rise of the Bureaucratic State, 41 The Public Interest 77 (Fall 1975).

6. See C. Rossiter & R. Longaker, The Supreme Court and the Commander in Chief (expanded ed. 1976).

7. W. Wilson, Constitutional Government in the United States (1908).

8. A. de Riencourt, supra note 3.

9. This was in 1957. This episode culminated in one of the most important Supreme Court decisions in American history, Cooper v. Aaron, 358 U.S. 1 (1958; discussion of that and other aspects of the modern Court may be found in A. S. Miller, Oracle in the Marble Palace: Politics and the Supreme Court (forthcoming).

10. J. Breslin, How the Good Guys Finally Won (1975).

11. The statement that panic reigned in the White House, beginning in the spring of 1973, came from Nixon's son-in-law, David Eisenhower, in a personal conversation with the present author.

12. Butterfield's testimony was pure happenstance; he was interviewed by the Senate Watergate Committee staff only because he was an aide to H. R. Haldeman. Cf. S. Dash, Chief Counsel (1976).

13. See, for example, L. Berg, H. Hahn & J. Schmidhauser, Corruption in the American Political System (1976); N. Miller, The Founding Finaglers (1975).

14. Quoted in M. Novak, supra note 2, at xiii.

15. See D. Cater, Power in Washington (1964) for discussion of "subgovernments." The same phenomenon is described (and somewhat discounted) in Heclo, Issue Net-

works and the Executive Establishment, in A. King (ed.), The New American Political System 87 (1978).

16. See J. Ellul, The Political Illusion (1967).

17. United States v. Brown, 381 U.S. 437 (1965).

18. See L. Fisher, President and Congress: Power and Policy 1-27 (1972).

19. Quoted in Miller, *Implications of Watergate: Some Proposals for Cutting the Presidency Down to Size*, 2 Hastings Constitutional Law Quarterly 33 (1975).

20. See the discussion in Chapter 9, below.

21. J. Galbraith, American Capitalism (1952).

22. M. Novak, supra note 2, at *xiv*.

23. M. Novak, supra note 2.

24. P. Anderson, The Presidents' Men 3 (1968).

25. M. Novak, supra note 2.

26. Quoted in ibid., at 105. Norman Mailer, writing about the Republican National Convention in 1972, asserted: "In America, the country was the religion." N. Mailer, St. George and the Godfather (1972).

27. As this is written, the crisis in Iran and the Soviet invasion of Afghanistan have served to make Carter's popularity soar.

28. B. Skinner, Walden Two (1948).

29. L. Rubinoff, The Pornography of Power 124 (1968).

30. E. Fromm, Escape From Freedom (1941). See also B. Gross, Friendly Fascism (1980).

31. For discussion, see M. Voisset, L'Article 16 de la Constitution du 4 Octobre 1958 (1969).

32. The President acted pursuant to authority delegated to him by Congress in the Economic Stabilization Act of 1970.

33. See R. Heilbroner, Beyond Boom and Crash (1978).

34. See R. Neustadt, Presidential Power (updated ed. 1976).

35. R. Heilbroner, supra note 32.

36. A. de Riencourt, supra note 3.

37. See A. Sofaer, War, Foreign Affairs and Constitutional Power: The Origins (1976); A. S. Miller, Presidential Power (1977).

38. Korematsu v. United States, 323 U.S. 214 (1944).

39. Quoted in A. Sofaer, supra note 36.

40. See Wiarda, *The Latin Americanization of the United States*, 7 New Scholar 51 (1979).

41. Robinson, *The Routinization of Crisis Government*, The Yale Review, Winter 1974, 161-74.

CHAPTER 9

1. "Entitlements" is the code word for the demands now increasingly being made by disadvantaged people for larger shares of economic wealth. See, for example, Michelman, *On Protecting the Poor Through the Fourteenth Amendment*, 83 Harvard Law Review 7 (1969).

2. The Federalist Papers No. 10.

3. A. Bentley, The Process of Government (1908). See D. Truman, The Governmental Process (1951).

4. R. Miles, Jr., Awakening from the American Dream: The Social and Political Limits to Growth 224 (1976).

5. G. McConnell, Private Power and American Democracy (1966).

6. G. Orwell, quoted in D. Ehrenfeld, The Arrogance of Humanism (1978).

7. Quoted in L. Fisher, The Constitution Between Friends *viii* (1978).

8. The London Economist, Dec. 23, 1978.

9. In, for example, G. Myrdal, An International Economy (1956); G. Myrdal, Economic Theory and Underdeveloped Regions (1957). See also Miller, *Foreign Trade and the "Security State": A Study in Conflicting National Policies*, 7 Journal of Public Law 37 (1958).

10. The Economist, supra note 8.

11. Ibid.

12. See, for example, C. Jenkins & B. Sherman, The Collapse of Work (1979); I. Barron & R. Curnow, The Future With Microelectronics (1979).

13. Christian Science Monitor, Feb. 10, 1975, 10.

CHAPTER 10

1. J. Keynes, The General Theory of Employment, Interest and Money 383-84 (1936).

2. E. Ashby, Reconciling Man With the Environment 4 (1978), quoting Professor Lynn White, Jr.

3. C. Beard, The American Spirit 580 (1942). See also D. Marcell, Progress and Pragmatism (1974).

4. See J. Passmore, Man's Responsibility for Nature (1974).

5. Quoted in R. Dubos, So Human An Animal 200 (1968).

6. R. Aron, The Industrial Society 15 (1967).

7. See the discussion in A. Wheelis, The End of the Modern Age (1971).

8. R. Descartes, Discourse on Method and Other Writings (trans. 1968).

9. See P. Bridgman, The Way Things Are (1959), reprinting an article in the March 1929 Harper's Magazine.

10. Justice Johnson in his concurring opinion in Fletcher v. Peck, 10 U.S. 87 (1810).

11. R. Miles, Jr., Awakening from the American Dream: The Social and Political Limits to Growth 11 (1976).

12. This is the school of "sociological jurisprudence," led by Pound and others. It has not met with marked success. See, however, Paust, *The Concept of Norm: A Consideration of the Jurisprudential Views of Hart, Kelsen, and McDougal-Lasswell*, 52 Temple Law Quarterly 9 (1979).

13. See, for example, C. Levi-Strauss, Tristes Tropiques (trans. 1961).

14. A. Wheelis, supra note 7, at 64.

15. E. Ashby, supra note 2, at 9, 84.

16. Ibid.

17. Ibid.

18. C. Lindblom, The Policy-Making Process (1968).

19. B. Bechhoefer, Postwar Negotiations for Arms Control (1961).

20. This is a consequence of the dominant "philosophy" of pragmatism.

21. H. Kissinger, The Necessity For Choice (1961).

22. A. Berry, The Next Ten Thousand Years (1974).

23. M. Bookchin, Post-Scarcity Anarchism (1971).

24. Branscomb, *Information: The Ultimate Frontier*, 203 Science 143 (1979).

25. Ibid.

26. W. Johnson, Muddling Toward Frugality (1978).

27. See International Bank for Reconstruction and Development [the World Bank], World Development Report, 1979 (1979). Compare Marsden, *Global Development Strategies and the Poor: Alternative Scenarios*, 117 International Labour Review No. 6 (1978).

CHAPTER 11

1. H. Gerth & C. Mills, From Max Weber: Essays in Sociology (1946).

2. W. Frank, *Chart for Rough Water*, quoted in R. Seidenberg, Posthistoric Man 1 (1950).

3. H. Thoreau, Walden.

4. McDermott, *Technology: The Opiate of the Intellectuals*, in P. Bereano (ed.), Technology as a Social and Political Phenomenon 78 (1976). See J. Ellul, The Technological Society (trans. 1964).

5. Quoted in P. Bereano, supra note 4, at 10.

6. Weinberg, *Book Review*, 60 American Scientist 775 (1972).

7. Weinberg, *Social Institutions and Nuclear Energy*, 177 Science 27 (1972).

8. Weinberg, *Technology and Energy — Is There a Need for Confrontation?*, 23 BioScience 41 (1973). See generally W. Ophuls, Ecology and the Politics of Scarcity (1977).

9. D. Ehrenfeld, The Arrogance of Humanism (1978).

10. D. Boorstin, The Republic of Technology: Reflections on Our Future Community (1978).

11. Weinberg, supra note 8.

12. Brzezinski, *The Technetronic Society*, 30 Encounter 19 (1968).

13. In, for example, L. Mumford, The Myth of the Machine: The Pentagon of Power c. 10 (1970).

14. Ibid.

15. W. Thompson, Evil and World Order c. 2 (1976).

16. D. Chorafas, The Knowledge Revolution (1968).

17. See T. Veblen, The Portable Veblen (M. Lerner ed. 1948).

18. B. Skinner, Beyond Freedom and Dignity (1971).

19. Ibid.

20. B. Skinner, Walden Two (1948).

21. Quoted in W. Thompson, supra note 15.

22. Quoted in L. Andrews & M. Karlins, Requiem for Democracy? An Inquiry Into the Limits of Behavioral Control 1 (1971). See A. Scheflin & E. Opton, The Mind Manipulators (1978).

23. A. Huxley, Brave New World (introduction to the 1946 paperback ed.).

24. A. Huxley, Brave New World Revisited (1958).

25. Ozbekhan, *The Triumph of Technology: 'Can' Implies 'Ought,'* quoted in E. Fromm, The Revolution of Hope: Toward a Humanized Technology (1968).

26. M. Minsky, Computation, at *vii* (1967). See D. Wooldridge, Mechanical Man (1968).

27. Cf. R. Crawshay-Williams, The Comforts of Unreason: A Study of the Motives Behind Irrational Thought (1947).

28. F. Alexander, The Western Mind in Transition (1960).

29. B. Skinner, supra note 18; A. Huxley, supra note 23.

30. B. Skinner, supra note 18.

31. H. Adams, The Degradation of the Democratic Dogma (1919) (reprinting earlier article).

32. Ibid.

33. R. Seidenberg, Posthistoric Man (1950).

34. Butterfield, *Newton and His Universe*, in A Short History of Science 58 (1959).

35. P. Goldstene, The Collapse of Liberal Empire: Science and Revolution in the Twentieth Century 79 (1977).

CHAPTER 12

1. William Butler Yeats, The Second Coming (1924).

2. See Miller, *Constitutional Law: Crisis Government Becomes the Norm*, 39 Ohio State Law Journal 736 (1978).

3. F. Neumann, The Democratic and the Authoritarian State (1957).

4. Through severe limitation of the franchise, mainly to property owners, the mass of people were kept from participation. For generalization, see G. Mosca, The Ruling Class (1939). In Livingston, *Introduction* to Mosca's book, this statement appears: There is "a fact which has always been perfectly apparent to everybody, *viz.*, that in all human groups at all times there are the few who rule and the many who are ruled." (P. x.) Mosca evolved his theory in the period of 1878-1881. See also R. Michels, Political Parties (first published in Germany in 1911).

5. W. Williams, America Confronts a Revolutionary World, 1776-1976 (1976).

6. Ibid.

7. See C. Rossiter, Alexander Hamilton and the Constitution (1964).

8. Ibid.

9. See J. Furnas, The Americans: A Social History of the United States (1969).

10. In Gitlow v. New York, 268 U.S. 562 (1925). It is noteworthy that Gitlow still went to jail. For general discussion, see P. Murphy, World War I and the Origin of Civil Liberties in the United States (1979).

11. In McCulloch v. Maryland, 17 U.S. 316 (1819).

12. See C. Swisher, American Constitutional Development (rev. ed. 1954).

13. See O. Holmes, Collected Legal Papers (1920).

14. Cooley v. Port Wardens, 54 U.S. 290 (1851).

15. See R. McCloskey, The American Supreme Court (1960).

16. See A. S. Miller, The Supreme Court and American Capitalism (1968).

17. Santa Clara County v. Southern Pacific Railway Co., 118 U.S. 394 (1886).

18. J. Galbraith, The New Industrial State (1967).

19. See A. S. Miller, The Modern Corporate State: Private Governments and the American Constitution (1976).

20. For recent discussion, see J. Ely, Democracy and Distrust: A Theory of Judicial Review (1980).

21. See, for example, E. Rostow, Planning for Freedom: The Public Law of American Capitalism (1959).

22. W. Ophuls, Ecology and the Politics of Scarcity: Prologue to a Political Theory of the Steady State (1977).

23. Ibid.

24. Ibid.

25. See Kolakowski, *Permanent and Transitory Aspects of Marxism*, quoted in C. Frankel, The Democratic Prospect 189 (1962). See also V. Lenin, Marx Engels Marxism 385 (4th English ed. 1951): "the incontestable truth that a Marxist must take cognizance of actual events, of the precise facts of reality, and must not cling to a theory of yesterday, which like all theories, at best only outlines the main and general, and only approximates to an inclusive grasp of the complexities of life."

26. Abrams v. United States, 250 U.S. 616 (1919).

27. D. Price, The Scientific Estate (1965).

28. See, for example, Miller, *Privacy in the Modern Corporate State*, 25 Administrative Law Review 231 (1973). See also United States v. O'Brien, 391 U.S. 367 (1968).

29. See Goodman, *Countdown to 1984: Big Brother May Be Right on Schedule*, 12 The Futurist 345 (1978). But see Hamil, Beckwith, Maloney & Pohl, *George Orwell's Vision of the Future: Pro and Con*, 13 The Futurist 110 (1979).

30. See Gross, *Friendly Fascism: A Model for America*, Social Policy (Nov.-Dec. 1970), p. 44.

31. See Phillips, *Status and Freedom in American Constitutional Law*, 29 Emory Law Quarterly (1980).

32. N. Machiavelli, The Prince c. XV (G. Bull trans., paperback ed. 1961).

33. Ibid., c. XVII.

34. Ibid., c. XIX.

35. R. Nisbet, The Twilight of Authority (1973).

36. For modern discussion of the general phenomenon, see P. Schrag, Mind Control (1978); A. Scheflin & E. Opton, The Mind Manipulators (1978); C. Lasch, The Culture of Narcissism (1979); B. Skinner, Beyond Freedom and Dignity (1971).

37. Dennis v. United States, 341 U.S. 494, 509 (1951).

38. See A. S. Miller, The Modern Corporate State: Private Governments and the American Constitution (1976).

39. Cf. T. Lowi, The End of Liberalism: The Second Republic of the United States (2d ed. 1979).

40. See generally A. S. Miller, Social Change and Fundamental Law: America's Evolving Constitution (1979).

41. For one example, see Miller, supra note 28; see also Miller, *Reason of State and the Emergent Constitution of Control*, 64 Minnesota Law Review 585 (1980).

42. See, for example, Frantz, *The First Amendment in the Balance*, 71 Yale Law Journal 1424 (1962); Mendelson, *On the Meaning of the First Amendment: Absolutes in the Balance*, 50 California Law Review 821 (1962).

43. 395 U.S. *viii* (1969).

44. See S. Halpern & C. Lamb (eds.), Supreme Court Activism and Restraint (1981).

45. See Miller, supra note 28.

46. O. Gierke, Natural Law and the Theory of the State (E. Barker trans. 1933).

47. E. Barker, *Introduction*, to O. Gierke, supra note 46. See A. S. Miller, supra note 38.

48. Santa Clara County v. Southern Pacific Railway Co., 118 U.S. 394 (1886).

49. H. Maine, Ancient Law (1861). See also F. Ganshof, Feudalism (3d English ed. 1964).

50. Cf. D. Ewing, Freedom Inside the Organization (1977).

51. See Phillips, supra note 31.

52. See Wilson, *The Rise of the Bureaucratic State*, 41 The Public Interest 77 (Fall 1975); W. Mommsen, The Age of Bureaucracy (1974).

53. See P. Drucker, The Unseen Revolution: How Pension Fund Socialism Came to America (1976).

54. See Phillips, supra note 31.

55. See F. Ganshof, Feudalism (3d English ed. 1964).

56. A. Berle, Power Without Property (1958). See also A. Berle, The 20th-Century Capitalist Revolution (1954).

57. T. Hobbes, Leviathan (1651).

58. For discussion, see A. S. Miller, The Supreme Court and American Capitalism (1968); D. Ewing, supra note 50.

59. Discussed in A. S. Miller, The Modern Corporate State: Private Governments and the American Constitution (1976).

60. Luria v. United States, 231 U.S. 9 (1913).

61. K. Boulding, The Organizational Revolution (1953).

62. J. Coleman, Power and the Structure of Society 14 (1974).

63. R. Michels, Political Parties (1911).

64. S. Lipset *et al*, Union Democracy (1956).

65. Lipset, *Party Systems and the Representation of Social Groups*, 1 European Journal of Sociology 51 (1960).

66. See G. McConnell, Private Power and American Democracy (1966).

67. Sobolewski, *Electors and Representatives: A Contribution to the Theory of Representation*, in J. Pennock & J. Chapman (eds.), NOMOS X: Representation 95 (1968).

68. J. Ellul, The Political Illusion (1967).

69. See the several essays in J. Pennock & J. Chapman (eds.), supra note 67.

70. For discussion, see R. Neustadt, Presidential Power (revised ed. 1976).

71. See G. Domhoff, The Higher Circles (1972).

72. J. Griffith, The Politics of the Judiciary (1977).

73. See J. Ely, Democracy and Distrust: A Theory of Judicial Review (1980).

74. 395 U.S. *viii* (1969).

75. See J. Ely, supra note 73. See also R. Berger, Government by Judiciary (1977); S. Halpern & C. Lamb (eds.), Supreme Court Activism and Restraint (1981).

76. W. Lippmann, The Phantom Public (1924).

77. See A. S. Miller, Presidential Power in a Nutshell (1977); Wilson, supra note 52.

78. See W. Williams, America Confronts a Revolutionary World (1976).

79. For discussion of the two American economies, see Ginzberg and Associates,

The Pluralistic Economy (1965); M. Harrington, Toward a Democratic Left (1968); Holton, *Business and Government*, Daedalus 41 (Winter 1969).

80. *Moving the World Uphill*, The Economist (London), April 29, 1978, at 89.

81. Freund, *Law and the Future: Constitutional Law*, 51 Northwestern University Law Review 187 (1956).

82. The Economist (London), March 22, 1980.

83. See the discussion in Miller, *Crisis Government Becomes the Norm*, 39 Ohio State Law Journal 736 (1978).

84. See R. Barnet & R. Muller, Global Reach: The Power of the Multinational Corporations (1974).

85. Hymer, *The Multinational Corporation and the Law of Uneven Development*, in G. Bhagwati (ed.) Economics and World Order: From the 1970s to the 1990s (1972). See also Polk, *The Rise of World Corporations*, Saturday Review, Nov. 22, 1969.

86. Louis K. Liggett Co. v. Lee, 288 U.S. 517 (1933).

87. R. Dahl, After the Revolution 120 (1970).

88. A. Pekelis, Law and Social Action (M. Konvitz ed. 1950).

89. For example, Miller, *The Corporation as a Private Government in the World Community*, 46 Virginia Law Review 1539 (1960).

90. See First National Bank of Boston v. Bellotti, 435 U.S. 765 (1978).

91. Cf. S. Melman, Pentagon Capitalism: The Political Economy of War (1970); H. Sherman, Radical Political Economy (1972).

92. See Miller, *Toward "Constitutionalizing" the Corporation: A Speculative Essay*, 80 West Virginia Law Review 187 (1976); Miller & Solomon, *Constitutional Chains for the Corporate Beast*, 27 Business & Society Review 15 (Fall 1978).

93. Cf. J. Weinstein, The Corporate Ideal in the Liberal State (1968).

94. Lasswell, The Analysis of Political Behaviour 146 (1941).

95. See Raskin, *Democracy Versus the National Security State*, 40 Law & Contemporary Problems 189 (1976).

96. The statute may be found in 50 United States Code Sec. 402 (1970).

97. See Raskin, supra note 95; see also A. Cox, The Myths of the National Security State (1975).

98. See Raskin, supra note 95; D. Wise, The American Police State (1977).

99. For early discussion, see C. Rossiter, The Supreme Court and the Commander in Chief (1951).

100. See P. Drucker, supra note 53.

101. H. Lasswell, National Security and Individual Freedom (1950).

102. See Phillips, *Thomas Hill Green, Positive Freedom and the United States Supreme Court*, 25 Emory Law Journal 63 (1976). See also B. Skinner, Beyond Freedom and Dignity (1971).

103. For early, insightful discussion, see O. Kirchheimer, Political Justice: The Use of Legal Procedure for Political Ends (1961).

104. See Goldstein, *An American Gulag? Summary Arrest and Emergency Detention of Political Dissidents in the United States*, 10 Columbia Human Rights Law Review 541 (1978).

105. See D. Wise, supra note 98.

106. P. Schrag, Mind Control xi (1978).

107. B. Skinner, Beyond Freedom and Dignity (1971).

108. P. Schrag, supra note 106.

109. R. Heilbroner, Beyond Boom and Crash (1978).

110. Ibid.

111. See G. Soule, Planning USA (1967).

112. J. Galbraith, The New Industrial State (1967).

113. See A. S. Miller, supra note 19.

114. N. Chamberlain, Private and Public Planning (1965).

115. See Michelman, *On Protecting the Poor Through the Fourteenth Amendment*, 83 Harvard Law Review 7 (1969).

116. Matthew 13:12.

117. Bay, *Access to Human Knowledge as a Human Right*, in I. Galnoor (ed.), Government Secrecy in Democracies 22 (1977).

118. Rourke, *The United States*, in I. Galnoor (ed.), supra note 117, at 113.

119. Ibid.

120. This part of chapter 12 is based on an article of mine published in *Presidential Studies Quarterly*.

121. W. Wilson, Congressional Government (1885).

122. United States v. Burr, 8 U.S. 469 (1807).

123. 345 U.S. 1 (1953).

124. Nixon-I may be found at 483 U.S. 63 (1974).

125. Nixon-II is Nixon v. Administrator of General Services, 97 Sup. Ct. 2777 (1977).

126. See A. Sofaer, War, Foreign Affairs and Constitutional Power: The Origins (1976).

127. See A. S. Miller, Presidential Power (1977); R. Pious, The American Presidency (1979).

128. H. Gerth & C. Mills, From Max Weber: Essays in Sociology (1946).

129. See R. Berger, Executive Privilege: A Constitutional Myth (1974).

130. See the discussion in Fisher, *Raoul Berger on Public Law*, 8 Political Science Reviewer 173 (1978).

131. B. Woodward & S. Armstrong, The Brethren (1979). See also A. Mason, Harlan Fiske Stone: Pillar of the Law (1956).

132. Whether the "facts" set out in The Brethren are indeed facts has been doubted. See, for example, A. Lewis, *Supreme Court Confidential*, New York Review, Feb. 7, 1980, 3.

133. Osborn v. Bank of the United States, 22 U.S. 738 (1824). See A. S. Miller, The Supreme Court: Myth and Reality (1978).

134. This is Professor W. R. Forrester's label for the Supreme Court. See Forrester, *Are We Ready for Truth in Judging?*, 63 American Bar Association Journal 1212 (1977).

135. Recounted in R. Berger, supra note 129.

136. Marbury v. Madison, 5 U.S. 133 (1803).

137. 67 U.S. 635 (1863).

138. See the discussion of these cases, all involving the exercise of presidential authority, in A. S. Miller, supra note 127; and in E. Corwin, The President: Office and Powers (4th ed. 1957).

139. See the discussion in L. Tribe, American Constitutional Law (1978).

140. See the discussion of the important case of Halkin v. Helms in Miller, *Reason of State and the Emergent Constitution of Control*, supra note 41.

141. C. Friedrich, The Pathology of Politics (1973).

142. W. Wilson, Congressional Government (1885).

143. W. Wilson, Constitutional Government in the United States (1908). Although this book was published before Wilson became president, it sets forth his changed ideas about the nature of government.

144. I. Janis, Victims of Groupthink (1972).

145. Suggested in Miller, *Separation of Powers: An Ancient Doctrine Under Modern Challenge*, 26 Administrative Law Review 299 (1976).

146. See N. Chomsky & E. Herman, The Washington Connection and Third World Fascism (1979).

147. The Grand Inquisitor may be found in F. Dostoyevsky, The Brothers Karamazov; De Gaulle was quoted by James Reston in the New York Times, Aug. 21, 1964.

148. A. Mason, supra note 131.

149. See E. Carr, What is History? (1961).

150. 492 F.2d 587 (D.C. Circuit 1974).

151. 71 U.S. 475 (1867).

152. Cox, *Executive Privilege*, 122 University of Pennsylvania Law Review 1383 (1974).

153. 17 Federal Cases 144 (no. 9487) (1861).

154. Senator Goldwater did not prevail. The court said that he did not have a "justiciable" question.

155. See Miller, *The Elusive Search for Values in Constitutional Interpretation*, 6 Hastings Constitutional Law Quarterly 487 (1979).

156. Supra note 124.

157. 498 F.2d 725 (D. C. Circuit 1974).

158. 19 U.S. 204 (1821).

159. 273 U.S. 135 (1927).

160. 243 U.S. 521 (1917).

161. 294 U.S. 125 (1935).

162. 408 U.S. 606 (1972).

163. 421 U.S. 491 (1975).

164. 511 F.2d 430 (D.C. Circuit 1974).

165. 366 F.Supp. 104 (D.C. District Court 1973).

166. *Government Secrecy*, Hearings Before the Subcommittee on Intergovernmental Relations of the Senate Committee on Government Operations, May 1974, part of which contains Relyea, *The Evolution of Government Information Security Classification Policy: A Brief Overview (1775-1973)*, at 843.

167. See Van Alstyne, *The Role of Congress in Determining the Incidental Powers of the President and of the Federal Courts*, 36 Ohio State Law Journal 788 (1975).

168. See the discussion in Miller & Bowman, *Presidential Attacks on the Constitutionality of Federal Statutes: A New Separation of Powers Problem*, 40 Ohio State Law Journal 51 (1979).

169. McCulloch v. Maryland, 17 U.S. 316 (1819).

170. See Van Alstyne, supra note 167; Miller & Knapp, *The Congressional Veto: Preserving the Constitutional Framework*, 52 Indiana Law Journal 367 (1977).

171. See Van Alstyne, supra note 167.

172. 87 Stat. 555 (1973). This was passed over President Nixon's veto. For discussion, see Eagleton, War and Presidentaial Power (1974).

173. Black, *The Working Balance of the American Political Departments*, 1 Hastings Constitutional Law Quarterly 13 (1974).

174. 354 U.S. 178 (1957).

175. Quoted in Cox, supra note 152.

176. 598 F.2d 1 (D.C. Circuit 1978).

177. 467 F.Supp. 990 (District Court, Wisconsin, 1979).

178. It is not published (as of May 1980).

179. F. Dostoyevsky, *The Legend of the Grand Inquisitor*, in The Brothers Karamazov.

180. See L. Rubinoff, The Pornography of Power (1967).

181. Toynbee made the prediction in 1975 that industrial societies, because of external circumstances, would become regimented. See Oka, *A Crowded World: Can Mankind Survive in Freedom?*, Christian Science Monitor, Feb. 10, 1975.

182. See J. Rifkin & T. Howard, The Emerging Order (1979).

EPILOGUE

1. Quoted in C. Rossiter, Constitutional Dictatorship (1948).

2. Quoted in D. Ehrenfeld, The Arrogance of Humanism (1978).

3. See A. Lovejoy, Reflections on Human Nature (1961).

4. H. Brown, The Human Future Revisited (1978).

5. A. Huxley, Brave New World Revisited (1958). See also W. Ophuls, Ecology and the Politics of Scarcity: Prologue to a Political Theory of the Steady State (1977).

6. Bell, *The End of American Exceptionalism*, 41 The Public Interest 193 (1975). See also J. Pennock & J. Chapman (eds.), NOMOS XX: Constitutionalism (1979).

7. Ibid.

8. The Federalist No. 51.

9. See L. Tribe, American Constitutional Law (1978); R. McCloskey, The American Supreme Court (1960).

10. F. Turner, The Frontier in American History (1920).

11. E. Ashby, Reconciling Man With the Environment (1979).

12. Ibid.

13. See J. Rifkin & T. Howard, The Emerging Order (1979).

Selected
Bibliography

An enormous literature exists on the several topics touched upon or discussed in the text of this book. The listing that follows in this bibliography is quite selective; its purpose is to call attention to other relevant books that the reader may wish to consult. For essential background reading, the classics in political philosophy should be consulted; none is cited below because they are available in multiple editions (often paperbound). They include Plato's *Republic*, Machiavelli's *The Discourses* and *The Prince*, Hobbes' *Leviathan*, Locke's *Two Treatises on Government*, Burke's *Reflections on the Revolution in France*, Hamilton and Madison and Jay's *The Federalist*, Aristotle's *Politics*, and Rousseau's *Social Contract*. Those who wish to continue the study of the possible political (constitutional) structures of the immediate and distant future in the United States should begin with the following: Clinton Rossiter, *Constitutional Dictatorship: Crisis Government in the Modern Democracies* (Princeton: Princeton University Press, 1948); Rufus E. Miles, Jr., *Awakening from the American Dream: The Social and Political Limits to Growth* (New York: Universe Books, 1976); and William Ophuls, *Ecology and the Politics of Scarcity: Prologue to a Political Theory of the Steady State* (San Francisco: W. H. Freeman & Co., 1977).

Only books are cited in this bibliography. Numerous articles in both scholarly and popular periodicals touch upon the various themes of this volume. Some are cited in the notes to each of the chapters. Others may be found in the *Index to Legal Periodicals*, the *Social Sciences Index*, the *Reader's Guide to Periodical Literature*, and the *New York Times Index*.

Arendt, Hannah. *The Origins of Totalitarianism*. Cleveland: World Publishing Co., 1958.
_____. *The Human Condition*. Chicago: University of Chicago Press, 1958.
_____. *Between Past and Future*. New York: Viking Press, 1961.
_____. *On Revolution*. New York: Viking Press, 1965.

_____. *Crises of the Republic*. New York: Harcourt Brace Jovanovich, 1972.

Ashby, Eric. *Reconciling Man With the Environment*. Stanford: Stanford University Press, 1978.

Bachrach, Peter. *The Theory of Democratic Elitism*. Boston: Little, Brown & Co., 1967.

Baier, Kurt (with Rescher, Nicholas), eds., *Values and the Future*. New York: Free Press, 1969.

Barnet, Richard. *The Lean Years*. New York: Simon & Schuster, 1980.

Barron, Iann (with Curnow, Ray). *The Future With Microelectronics*. New York: Nichols Publishing Co., 1979.

Barbour, Ian G., ed., *Finite Resources and the Human Future*. Minneapolis: Augsburg Publishing House, 1976.

Beckwith, Burnham P. *The Next 500 Years: Scientific Predictions of Major Social Trends*. New York: Exposition Press, 1967.

Bell, Daniel. *The Coming of Post-Industrial Society*. New York: Basic Books, 1973.

_____. *The Cultural Contradictions of Capitalism*. New York: Basic Books, 1976.

_____., ed., *Toward the Year 2000: Work in Progress*. Boston: Houghton Mifflin, 1968.

Berry, Adrian. *The Next Ten Thousand Years: A Vision of Man's Future in the Universe*. New York: E. P. Dutton, 1974.

Bookchin, Murray. *Post-Scarcity Anarchism*. Berkeley: Ramparts Press, 1971.

Boulding, Kenneth. *The Meaning of the Twentieth Century*. New York: Harper & Row, 1964.

Bronwell, Arthur B., ed., *Science and Technology in the World of the Future*. New York: John Wiley, 1970.

Brandt, Willy. *North-South: A Program for Survival*. Cambridge: The MIT Press, 1980.

Brown, Harrison. *The Challenge of Man's Future*. New York: Viking Press, 1954.

_____. *The Human Future Revisited*. New York: W. W. Norton & Co., 1978.

Brown, Lester R. *World Without Borders*. New York: Random House, 1972.

_____. *The Twenty-Ninth Day*. New York: W. W. Norton & Co., 1978.

Buchanan, James. *The Limits of Liberty*. Chicago: University of Chicago Press, 1975.

Bury, J. B. *The Idea of Progress*. New York: Macmillan, 1932.

Cassirer, Ernst. *The Myth of the State*. New Haven: Yale University Press, 1946.

Chomsky, Noam. *For Reasons of State*. London: Fontana, 1973.

_____. (with Herman, Edward S.). *The Washington Connection and Third World Fascism*. Boston: South End Press, 1979.

Church, William F. *Richelieu and Reason of State*. Princeton: Princeton University Press, 1972.

Clarke, Arthur C. *Profiles of the Future*, rev. ed. New York: Harper & Row, 1973.

Cole, H. S. D. (and others), eds., *Models of Doom: A Critique of The Limits to Growth*. New York: Universe Books, 1973.

Commoner, Barry. *The Poverty of Power*. New York: Alfred A. Knopf, 1976.

_____. *The Politics of Energy*. New York: Alfred A. Knopf, 1979.

Cornish, Edward. *The Study of the Future*. Washington: World Future Society, 1977.

Corwin, Edward S. *A Constitution of Powers in a Secular State*. Charlottesville: Michie, 1951.

_____. *American Constitutional History*. New York: Harper & Row, 1964.

Crozier, Michel J. (with Huntington, Samuel P., and Watanuki, Joji). *The Crisis of Democracy*. New York: New York University Press, 1975.

Daly, Herman E., ed. *Toward a Steady-State Economy*. San Francisco: W. H. Freeman & Co., 1973.

Dahl, Robert A. *Democracy in the United States*. 3d ed. Chicago: Rand McNally, 1976.

De Jouvenel, Bertrand. *The Art of Conjecture*. New York: Basic Books, 1967.

De Riencourt, Amaury. *The Coming Caesars*. New York: Capricorn Books, 1964.

Donelan, Michael, ed., *The Reason of States*. London: George Allen & Unwin, 1978.

Donner, Frank J. *The Age of Surveillance*. New York: Alfred A. Knopf, 1980.

Doob, Leonard W. *Panorama of Evil*. Westport: Greenwood Press, 1978.

Douglas, Jack D. *The Technological Threat*. Englewood Cliffs: Prentice-Hall, 1971.

Drucker, Peter F. *The Age of Discontinuity*. New York: Harper & Row, 1969.

Duignan, Peter (with Rabushka, Alvin), eds., *The United States in the 1980s*. Stanford: Hoover Institution, 1980.

Ehrenfeld, David. *The Arrogance of Humanism*. New York: Oxford University Press, 1978.

Ellul, Jacques. *The Technological Society*. New York: Vintage Books, 1964.

_____. *Propaganda*. New York: Alfred A. Knopf, 1965.

Eyre, S. R. *The Real Wealth of Nations*. London: Edward Arnold, 1978.

Falk, Richard A. *This Endangered Planet*. New York: Random House, 1972.

_____. *A Study of Future Worlds*. New York: Free Press, 1975.

Ferkiss, Victor. *The Future of Technological Civilization*. New York: George Braziller, 1971.

_____. *Technological Man: The Myth and the Reality*. New York: George Braziller, 1969.

Forrester, Jay W. *World Dynamics*. Cambridge: Wright-Allen Press, 1971.

Frazier, Thomas R., ed., *The Underside of American History*. 2 vols. 3d ed. New York: Harcourt Brace Jovanovich, 1978.

Friedrich, Carl J. *Constitutional Reason of State*. Providence: Brown University Press, 1957.

Fromm, Erich. *The Revolution of Hope*. New York: Harper & Row, 1968.

_____. *The Anatomy of Human Destructiveness*. New York: Holt, Rinehart, and Winston, 1973.

Gabel, Medard. *Energy, Earth and Everyone: A Global Energy Strategy for Spaceship Earth*. San Francisco: Straight Arrow Books, 1975.

Gabor, Dennis. *Inventing the Future*. New York: Alfred A. Knopf, 1964.

Gilmore, Myron P., ed., *Studies on Machiavelli*. Florence: G. C. Sansoni, 1972.

Harman, Willis W. *An Incomplete Guide to the Future*. San Francisco: San Francisco Book Co., 1976.

Harrington, Michael. *The Twilight of Capitalism*. New York: Simon & Schuster, 1976.

Heilbroner, Robert L. (with Singer, Aaron). *The Economic Transformation of America*. New York: Harcourt Brace Jovanovich, 1977.

_____. *An Inquiry Into the Human Prospect*. New York: W. W. Norton & Co., 1974.

Helmer, Olaf. *Social Technology*. New York: Basic Books, 1966.

Henderson, Hazel. *Creating Alternative Futures*. New York: Berkley Winhover, 1978.

Hirsch, Fred. *Social Limits to Growth*. Cambridge: Harvard University Press, 1978.

Hofstadter, Richard. *The Paranoid Style in American Politics*. New York: Alfred A. Knopf, 1965.

Janowitz, Morris. *Social Control of the Welfare State*. New York: Elsevier, 1976.

Jaspers, Karl. *The Future of Mankind*. Chicago: University of Chicago Press, 1961.

Jenkins, Clive (with Sherman, Barrie). *The Collapse of Work*. London: Eyre Methuen, 1979.

Johnson, Warren. *Muddling Toward Frugality*. San Francisco: Sierra Club Books, 1978.

Jungk, Robert. *The Everyman Project: A World Report on the Resources for a Humane Society*. New York: Liveright, 1977.

Kahn, Herman (with Wiener, Anthony J.). *The Year 2000: A Framework for Speculation on the Next Thirty-Three Years*. New York: MacMillan, 1967.

_____. (with Bruce-Briggs, B.). *Things to Come: Thinking About the Seventies and Eighties*. New York: MacMillan, 1972.

_____ (with Brown, William, and Martel, Leon). *The Next Two Hundred Years: A Scenario for America and the World*. New York: William Morrow & Co., 1976.

Kariel, Henry S. *The Decline of American Pluralism*. Stanford: Stanford University Press, 1961.

_____. *Beyond Liberalism: Where Relations Grow*. New York: Harper & Row, 1978.

King, Anthony, ed., *The New American Political System*. Washington: American Enterprise Institute, 1978.

Kirchheimer, Otto. *Political Justice: The Use of Legal Procedure for Political Ends*. Princeton: Princeton University Press, 1961.

Knight, Frank H. *Freedom and Reform*. New York: Harper & Bros., 1947.

Kolko, Joyce (with Kolko, Gabriel). *The Limits of Power*. New York: Harper & Row, 1972.

Landsberg, Hans, ed., *Energy: The Next Twenty Years*. Cambridge: Ballinger, 1979.

Levin, Murray B. *Political Hysteria in America*. New York: Basic Books, 1971.

Lewis, Sinclair. *It Can't Happen Here*. New York: New American Library, 1970.

Lindblom, Charles E. *The Intelligence of Democracy*. New York: Free Press, 1965.

_____. *The Policy-Making Process*. Englewood Cliffs: Prentice-Hall, 1967.

_____. *Politics and Markets*. New York: Basic Books, 1977.

Lowi, Theodore. *The End of Liberalism*. 2d ed. New York: W. W. Norton & Co., 1979.

Lukacs, John. *The Passing of the Modern Age*. New York: Harper Torchbooks, 1970.

McConnell, Grant. *Private Power and American Democracy*. New York: Alfred A. Knopf, 1967.

McDougal, Myres S. (with Lasswell, Harold D., and Chen, Lung-Chu). *Human Rights and World Public Order*. New Haven: Yale University Press, 1980.

McHale, John. *The Future of the Future*. New York: George Braziller, 1969.

_____. *World Facts and Trends*. New York: Collier Books, 1972.

Macpherson, C. B. *The Political Theory of Possessive Individualism*. Oxford: Clarendon Press, 1968.

Marien, Michael. *Societal Directions and Alternatives: A Critical Guide to the Literature*. New York: Information for Policy Design, 1976.

Martino, Joseph P. *Technological Forecasting for Decision-making*. New York: American Elsevier, 1972.

Meadows, Dennis L., ed., *Alternatives to Growth*. Cambridge: Ballinger, 1977.

Meadows, Dennis L. (and others). *Dynamics of Growth in a Finite World*. Cambridge: Wright-Allen, 1973.

Meadows, Donella H. (and others). *The Limits to Growth*. New York: Universe Books, 1972.

Meinecke, Friedrich. *Machiavellism: The Doctrine of Raison d'État and Its Place in Modern History*. New Haven: Yale University Press, 1957.

Mendlovitz, Saul H., ed., *On the Creation of a Just World Order: Preferred Worlds for the 1990s*. New York: Free Press, 1975.

Melman, Seymour. *Pentagon Capitalism*. New York: McGraw-Hill, 1970.

———. *The Permanent War Economy*. New York: Simon & Schuster, 1974.

Mesarovic, Mihajlo (with Pestel, Eduard). *Mankind at the Turning Point: The Second Report to the Club of Rome*. New York: E. P. Dutton/Reader's Digest Press, 1974.

Michael, Donald N. *The Unprepared Society: Planning for a Precarious Future*. New York: Basic Books, 1968.

Miliband, Ralph. *The State in Capitalist Society*. New York: Basic Books, 1969.

Miller, Arthur Selwyn. *The Modern Corporate State: Private Governments and the American Constitution*. Westport: Greenwood Press, 1976.

———. *Presidential Power*. St. Paul: West Publishing Co., 1977.

———. *Social Change and Fundamental Law: America's Evolving Constitution*. Westport: Greenwood Press, 1979.

Mishan, E. J. *The Economic Growth Debate*. London: Allen & Unwin, 1977.

Moss, Robert, *The Collapse of Democracy*. London: Sphere Books Ltd., 1977.

Mumford, Lewis. *Technics and Civilization*. New York: Harcourt, Brace and World, 1934.

Murphy, Paul L. *The Constitution in Crisis Times*. New York: Harper & Row, 1972.

———. *World War I and the Origin of Civil Liberties in the United States*. New York: W. W. Norton & Co., 1979.

Neumann, Franz. *The Democratic and the Authoritarian State*. Glencoe: Free Press, 1957.

Niebuhr, Reinhold. *Moral Man and Immoral Society*. New York: Charles Scribner's Sons, 1932.

———. *The Nature and Destiny of Man*. New York: Charles Scribner's Sons, 1941.

———. *The Irony of American History*. New York: Charles Scribner's Sons, 1952.

Nozick, Robert. *Anarchy, State and Utopia*. New York: Basic Books, 1974.

Olson, Mancur. *The No-Growth Society*. New York: W. W. Norton & Co., 1973.

Orman, John. *Presidential Secrecy*. Westport, Conn.: Greenwood Press, 1980.

Peccei, Aurelio. *The Human Quality*. New York: Pergamon Press, 1977.

Pechman, Joseph, ed., *Setting National Priorities: Agenda for the 1980s*. Washington: Brookings Institution, 1980.

Pennock, J. Roland (with Chapman, John), eds., *Constitutionalism*, New York: New York University Press, 1979.

Perloff, Harvey, ed., *The Future of the U.S. Government*, New York: George Braziller, 1971.

Pious, Richard M. *The American Presidency*. New York: Basic Books, 1979.

Platt, John. *The Step to Man*. New York: John Wiley, 1966.

Poggi, Gianfranco. *The Development of the Modern State: A Sociological Introduction*. Stanford: Stanford University Press, 1978.

Polak, Fred L. *The Image of the Future*. 2 vols. New York: Oceana Publications, 1961.

_____. *Prognostics: A Science in the Making Surveys and Creates the Future*. Amsterdam: Elsevier, 1971.

Prehoda, Robert W. *Designing the Future: The Role of Technological Forecasting*. Philadelphia: Chilton Books, 1967.

Raab, Felix. *The English Face of Machiavelli*. London: Routledge & Kegan Paul, 1965.

Rawls, John. *A Theory of Justice*. Cambridge: Harvard University Press, 1971.

Rifkin, Jeremy (with Howard, Ted). *The Emerging Order: God in the Age of Scarcity*. New York: G. P. Putnam's Sons, 1979.

Rosen, Stephen. *Future Facts*. New York: Simon & Schuster, 1976.

Schattschneider, E. E. *The Semisovereign People*. New York: Holt, Rinehart and Winston, 1960.

Schrag, Peter. *The End of the American Future*. New York: Simon & Schuster, 1973.

Schumacher, E. F. *Small Is Beautiful*. New York: Harper & Row, 1973.

Seaborg, Glenn T. (with Corliss, W. R.). *Man and Atom*. New York: E. P. Dutton, 1971.

Shonfield, Andrew. *Modern Capitalism*. London: Oxford University Press, 1965.

Skinner, B. F. *Beyond Freedom and Dignity*. New York: Alfred A. Knopf, 1971.

Somit, Albert, Ed., *Political Science and the Study of the Future*. Hinsdale: Dryden Press, 1974.

Stover, Carl F., ed., *The Technological Order*. Detroit: Wayne University Press, 1963.

Talmon, J. L. *The Origins of Totalitarian Democracy*. London: Secker & Warburg, 1955.

Taylor, Gordon Rattray. *How to Avoid the Future*. London: Secker & Warburg, 1975.

Theobald, Robert. *An Alternative Future for America's Third Century*. Chicago: Swallow Press, 1976.

Tawney, R. H. *Religion and the Rise of Capitalism*. New York: Harcourt, Brace & Co., 1926.

Thompson, William Irwin. *Evil and World Order*. New York: Harper & Row, 1976.

_____. *Darkness and Scattered Light*. Garden City: Anchor, 1978.

Thomson, Sir George. *The Foreseeable Future*. Rev. ed. Cambridge: Cambridge University Press, 1960.

Thurow, Lester C. *The Zero-Sum Society*. New York: Basic Books, 1980.

Tugwell, Franklin, ed., *Search for Alternatives: Public Policy and the Study of the Future*. Cambridge: Winthrop Publishers, 1973.

Tyler, Gus. *Scarcity*. New York: Quadrangle Books, 1976.

Watt, Kenneth E. F. *The Titanic Effect: Planning for the Unthinkable*. New York: E. P. Dutton, 1974.

Winner, Langdon. *Autonomous Technology: Technics-out-of-Control as a Theme in Political Thought*. Cambridge: The MIT Press, 1977.

Wise, David. *The American Police State*. New York: Random House, 1976.

Wolfe, Alan. *The Seamy Side of Democracy: Repression in America*. New York: David McKay Co., 1973.

Zinn, Howard, *A People's History of the United States*. New York: Harper & Row, 1979.

Of special interest is the work of the World Future Society, 4916 St. Elmo Avenue, Washington, D.C. 20014. It publishes several periodicals, holds meetings on questions of the future, and has published a 603-page directory, *The Future: A Guide to Information Sources*, 1977, which is a valuable source-book listing information on individuals, research projects, books and reports, films, periodicals, video cassettes, and other data concerning study of the future (including the political and economic forecasts of some of the world's leading scholars).

Index

ARTHUR SELWYN MILLER is Professor Emeritus of Law at George Washington University. He is the author of many books, including *The Modern Corporate State* (Greenwood Press, 1976), *The Supreme Court: Myth and Reality* (Greenwood Press, 1978), and *Social Change and Fundamental Law* (Greenwood Press, 1979).